About the Author

Dr Brian Bates is Director of the Shaman Research Programme and teaches courses in Shamanic Consciousness at the University of Sussex, where he has also been chairperson of Psychology. His bestselling book *The Way of Wyrd*, explores the shamanic mysticism of ancient England, while *The Way of the Actor* examines shamanic performance, and is based on his directing work at the Royal Academy of Dramatic Art in London. He is the author of numerous scientific papers and articles, and is frequently a guest lecturer at other universities, and on radio and television. He leads seminars and workshops about his work in Europe and America, at institutions including the C.G. Jung Institute, Zurich; the Open Centre, New York; and Esalen, California.

Reviews for *The Way of Wyrd* include:
'A brilliant, vivid, entertaining and precise distillation of the scholarship on Anglo-Saxon sorcery, magic and shamanism . . . a refreshing reminder that the source of our heritage is both historical and perennial.'
R.D. Laing

'A compelling read. Brian Bates has brought vividly and sympathetically to life and light the innermost thoughts and spiritual feelings of 'Dark Age' Anglo-Saxon England. Profound human understanding and meticulous research have joined with a real writer's talent to produce the kind of book that I could not put down.'
Magnus Magnusson

'As a way of psychological and spiritual exploration it offers not just uncanny similarities with some of our present thinking, but notions which we seem only now to be rediscovering.'
The Guardian

'. . . a fast-paced tale about an Anglo-Saxon sorcerer and shaman which reads like a fusion of Carlos Castaneda's *Teachings of Don Juan* and Tolkien's *Lord of the Rings*.'
Time Out

'A gripping and informative work of psychological archaeology . . . provides a unique insight into the authentic world and cosmology of the Anglo-Saxon shaman.'
East West Journal

'. . . a thoroughly engrossing story of a way of spiritual liberation that is all the more powerful because it echoes much of what is happening in the human psyche today . . .'
One Earth

THE Wisdom of the Wyrd

Brian Bates

By the same author

The Way of Wyrd
The Way of the Actor

THE
Wisdom
of the Wyrd

Brian Bates

RIDER

LONDON · SYDNEY · AUCKLAND · JOHANNESBURG

First published in 1996

3 5 7 9 10 8 6 4 2

Copyright © Brian Bates 1996

Brian Bates has asserted his right to be identified as Author of this Work in accordance with the Copyright, Designs and Patents Act, 1988.

All rights reserved. No part of this publication may be reproduced, stored in a retrieval system, or transmitted in any form or by any means, electronic, mechanical, photocopying, recording or otherwise, without the prior permission of the copyright owners.

Published in 1996 by Rider,
an imprint of Ebury Press, Random House,
20 Vauxhall Bridge Road, London SW1V 2SA

Random House Australia (Pty) Limited
20 Alfred Street, Milsons Point, Sydney,
New South Wales 2061, Australia

Random House New Zealand Limited
18 Poland Road, Glenfield,
Auckland 10, New Zealand

Random House UK Limited Reg. No. 954009

Papers used by Rider Books are natural, recyclable products made from wood grown in sustainable forests.

Typeset by SX Composing DTP, Rayleigh, Essex
Printed by Mackays of Chatham plc

A CIP catalogue record for this book
is available from the British Library
ISBN 0-7126-7277-X

To the people of our ancient past,
for their wisdom and
inspiration down through the centuries

And to the memory of Violet Wood

Contents

Acknowledgements — xi

Introduction: *The Ancient Wisdom of Our Ancestors* — 1

1. How Our Ancestors Lived — 19
2. Incantations: *Attuning to the Healing Spirits* — 26
3. Guardians: *Learning From the Power Animals* — 54
4. Mother Earth: *Freeing the Flow of Life Force* — 72
5. Deep Waters: *Consulting the Wells of Wisdom* — 89
6. Weavers of Destiny: *Changing Our Life Patterns* — 107
7. Dwarfs: *Transforming With the Web of Wyrd* — 121
8. Seeress: *Divining Through Deep Intuition* — 149
9. Heart of the Wolf: *Transcending Warriorhood* — 168
10. Vision Journey: *Riding the Tree of Knowledge* — 192
11. Giants: *Trusting Death and Rebirth* — 212
12. Love Magic: *Creating the Elixir of Life* — 234
13. Reflections — 250

Notes — 271
Bibliography — 291
Index — 301

Acknowledgements

Among the many people to whom I owe especial debts of gratitude are two who have now passed into the Otherworld. The late Alan Watts gave me the encouragement I needed when I began my quest for a western parallel to the great Eastern traditions about which he wrote so lucidly. His transcendent laughter and practical suggestions helped to launch the project that led to my first book *The Way of Wyrd*, and now to this one. And after I had drafted the first book, I was fortunate to have the advice, Glaswegian wit and remarkable scholarship of the late R. D. Laing; I am grateful for his shamanic inspiration, his shapeshifting, and for our many discussions into the wee hours.

Peter Lattin has sustained, encouraged and advised me over the many years of this and other projects. I have benefitted enormously from his remarkable, wide ranging knowledge, his empathic understanding of my work and his warm sense of humour – he is so often the catalyst for some of the best ideas.

John Cleese has inspired me, both by his example and through our various discussions, to try to ask the hard questions which help to make accessible work which otherwise would become lost in the abstract. His integrity and discipline have helped me in whatever progress I have made in this direction, and I thank him for all his encouragement and support.

I thank also Spenny and Pamela Northampton for our many exhilarating adventures and discussions about mythology, spirituality, alchemical mysteries and the nature of dragons; my friends Ulrico and Beatrice Obrecht for our stimulating 'round table discussions' and for the archetypal pleasures of writing amongst the wood carvings in their mountain house at Klosters; the German artist Fion for her deep understanding of my work and for her Wyrd images; and Roger and Joan Evans of the Institute of Psychosynthesis for their encouragement and support for my work.

In developing the implications of the Wisdom of the Wyrd for life today I have, over the past decade in particular, taught courses, led workshops, written and directed plays, participated in seminars, supervised and examined theses, practised psychotherapy and so on. So much comes back to me from these activities in the way of insights, ideas, criticisms, materials and invaluable references and sources, that I am sure the work could not have moved forward without it. I thank the many people who have participated in these activities, especially those who ventured with me on the path into Wyrd Shamanism in my experiential workshops at various venues in England, Switzerland and America.

My friend and colleague Michael Tucker, who has joined me from time to time in teaching my course on Shamanic Consciousness at the University of Sussex, has given invaluable help, advice and wonderfully humorous companionship on the shamanic path.

Friends and colleagues, with whom I have discussed various aspects of the research that led to this book and who gave me valuable feedback, include Alan Bleakley, Paul Devereux, Norman Dixon, Simon Drake, Richard Dufton, John Goodman, Joan Halifax, Chris Hall, Katherine Hunt, Francis Huxley, Ruth-Inge Heinze, Theodore Itten, Tim Jasper, Stephen and Robin Larsen, Mimi Lattin, Jane Mayers, Lisbet Meyer, Penny Morse, Susanne Nessensohn, Philip Nadin, Richard and Shelley Olivier, Nigel Pennick and Gabrielle Roth. I thank them for their knowledge, insights and encouragement.

Of my many colleagues at the University of Sussex who have supported my work I am especially grateful to John Simmonds, Stuart Laing and Brian Short who, in their capacities as Deans, made available periods of study leave and helped me in various other ways.

I thank Anthony Sheil for the patient support he has provided over the many years that this project has been evolving. The late Oliver Caldecott was the first editor of this book when it was just a beginning project; I much appreciated his enthusiasm and encouragement. More recently Judith Kendra has served as editor with the sensitivity and determination which helped me to bring it to fruition.

Finally, but above all, I thank my family. My late mother, Vicky Bates, read me 'Bengazi the Magic Cat' when I was four and thereby started my interest in magic and shamanism! She unfailingly encouraged me ever since. My father Clifford Bates is a wonderful and warm source of support and sound advice. My wife Beth understands the Wyrd and my efforts to bring it to life with great insight and understanding – many of her suggestions and ideas clarified the work for me. My daughter Pearl embodies the wisdom of the Wyrd in her life and her work as an artist/designer, and teaches me how to live it practically. And my son Robin offers encouragement and cogent advice which stems from his deep understanding of both myself and my work. I thank them for all their love and support.

Introduction

The Ancient Wisdom of Our Ancestors

— Acknowledging Our Tribal Heritage —

Today many of us hunger for guidance on how best to live our lives. We feel that our personal and social experiences could be richer and more rewarding. This book offers a new path to sustenance; a journey into a way of wisdom which once was ours a thousand years ago, when we lived as indigenous peoples in ancient Europe. I believe that we need to rediscover the wisdom of our 'native' heritage, knowledge from our ancestors which can help to infuse our lives with new meaning.

Over the centuries our early tribal culture was overtaken by the forces of 'progress'. But today we are questioning the quality of our lives, even in the midst of the relative material comfort afforded us by this very progress. In the contemporary Western hemisphere we have all the advantages of modern science, engineering and medicine. But sophistication comes in many forms. Recently we have realised that the surviving indigenous peoples of the world, while less developed technologically than ourselves, nevertheless have knowledge about how to live which seems to be in tune with the deep harmonies of our souls, and to be in touch with important truths we have lost. Some may consider this to be romantic, but it does not take a deep analysis to acknowledge that we need urgently to re-vision our outlook in the face of the social, ecological, political and, most fundamentally, the deep psychological and spiritual crises facing us today.

Accordingly, in seeking ways to enrich our experience of life, an ever-increasing number of Westerners are turning to the insights of the shamans of indigenous cultures and the mystics of the ancient East, in the belief that enduring truths about life and death may have survived with them. Today this search is central to the lives of millions of Westerners, people in Europe and North America, and other technologically developed societies such as Australia. It is no longer merely the passion of a small minority 'counter culture'. Many of us read books, watch television programmes, see feature films, and attend seminars and workshops about the wisdom of ancient cultures and indigenous peoples: the Buddhists of Tibet, the Native Americans, the Kogi of South America, the African Bushmen, the 'Dreamtime' practitioners of Australian Aboriginal culture, in search of inspiration in dealing with our personal lives and the great issues of our times.[1]

But now the indigenous cultures are beginning to put a stop to our enquiries into their sacred worlds. Some of the Native Americans, for example, pleased at first that their beliefs and practices were at last being treated with respect rather than vilification, are now changing their minds, feeling that 'white culture', which first stole their land, and then undermined their social structure, is now trying to steal their religion. Medicine peoples of many tribes have recently been forbidden by the tribal elders to teach their wisdom to the modern cultures of the West.[2] I find this backlash completely understandable.

It is also timely, for it may serve as the catalyst we need in order to embark on a journey long overdue; the rediscovery of our own sacred heritage, for we were all indigenous peoples once. So rather than travelling in miles to learn of the wisdom of other cultures, this book chronicles a different kind of journey. A journey in years. Our destination, the ancestors of many of today's Europeans and North Americans, is the largely forgotten civilisation of the forest peoples of Europe, the Anglo-Saxon and Celtic tribal cultures, the 'native Europeans' of one thousand years ago and more, and their ways of deep understanding which I have called the wisdom of the Wyrd.

Today the word 'weird' means 'strange'. Unexplainable. Odd. Something that is weird is beyond the scope of normal understanding. But in the ancient cultures of Europe, the word had a very different status. The original, archaic form meant in Anglo-Saxon 'destiny', but also 'power', or 'magic' or 'prophetic knowledge'.[3] 'Wyrd' still meant the 'unexplainable', but the unexplainable was the sacred, the very grounding of existence, the force which underlay all life; it is a tradition from our own cultural heritage which parallels the great Tao of the East, the perennial wisdom of Buddhism, and the Great Spirit of the Native Americans.

— Rescuing Ancient Wisdom —

A thousand years sounds a long time when expressed in years, but it is only forty or fifty generations, and is a sufficient span to take us back to the historical period, when our ancestors lived in largely forested landscapes in small tribal communities of local chieftains, shamans, warriors, hunters and farmers. In some ways, of course, it is recent. Evidence of human habitation of western Europe goes back at least half a million years, to the time when elephants, rhinos and other large animals we associate with Africa today roamed the now tamed European countryside. But in the few centuries BC, the hundreds of tribal communities spread across mainland Europe and in Britain were living in ways that are beginning to be discernible to archaeologists and to scholars of early written records. While we need to build carefully from the evidence, an ancient world is undoubtedly beginning to emerge from the former shadows of our historical ignorance.

Tribal cultures all over the world, whether surviving today amidst the intervention of modern societies (precious few remain in anything like their former lifeways), or the thousands which once formed the characteristic way in which human communities formed, are specific in their complexity. Each small community has its pattern of custom and ritual, iconography and art, social organisation and deep spiritual identity. But having acknowledged the uniqueness of each tribal community, it is also the case that, when contrasted with contemporary Western society, the variation between tribal communities immediately pales into relative insignificance compared to their similarities. There is a commonality of experience, a core way of being in the world, which marks out their traditional ways of life as being radically different from contemporary culture as we experience it. And it is this level of analysis with which I am concerned in this book. While the tribal life of ancient Europe was rich and varied, it was sufficiently homogeneous, in comparison with life today, to serve as a single destination for our journey back in time, especially in its pathways to the deep psychological and the sacred.

The 'tribal nature' of the settlements of ancient Europe was characterised by the presence of a chieftain (in Anglo-Saxon the term translates as 'head kinsman') who was considered sacred, full of mana or life force, with the tribe being perceived as his extended family, though symbolically rather than biologically. The identities of these small communities were consolidated by rituals and customs particular to each, and by totems or icons which symbolised that identity.[4] With few exceptions, I believe that these tribal peoples of ancient Europe experienced and practised in varying degrees the way of knowledge which I have characterised as the wisdom of the Wyrd.

In this book I detail material from tribal cultures which were located all over north-west Europe and into Scandinavia. A primary focus for my account of the wisdom of the Wyrd is England, partly because this is where I have done most of my research, but also because the culture of England throughout the first millennium (AD 0–1000) was representative of much of the lifeways of people all over Europe: migrants from these tribal groups came to England in large numbers early in the millennium to join the tribes already here, especially from those lands known now as Germany, Holland and Denmark, and there were more migrants (some would say invaders) later from Scandinavia (the Vikings) towards the end of the millennium. Also, England proved to be a volatile meeting ground for the two umbrella terms by which the tribal peoples of ancient Europe were often distinguished by scholars: the Germanic peoples (including Scandinavia), and the family of peoples known (to the Romans) as Celts. At the root of the distinction between the two designations of peoples were linguistic differences, but in a shifting kaleidoscope of migrating tribal groups this distinction can be overstated. In the last decade or two, modern historical scholarship has revised our view, and the two peoples are now seen as sharing spiritual, ritual and various other beliefs. Certainly warfare took place between tribes of the two peoples, but the process of migration, invasion and settlement of the later Germanic groups on an island formerly occupied by mainly Celtic peoples is now understood as a much more complex array of relationships, from cooperation all the way to open antagonism.[5]

I concentrate mainly on the Anglo-Saxon, Germanic and Scandinavian tribal peoples, but also with some reference to those usually designated as Celtic. Partly this is because the Celtic tradition has been subject to considerably more investigation, focusing especially on the medieval legends of Merlin and Arthur, whereas very little attention has been paid at any level to the tribal wisdom of the Anglo-Saxon and Scandinavian peoples. The distinctions between the two groups of peoples are small compared with the commonality of experience consequent upon living as tribal peoples in landscapes relatively unformed by human intervention, and occasionally I have referred to Celtic tradition in those aspects of this study in which I believe the differences between the beliefs and practices of the people is negligible.[6]

The history of this period, while increasingly documented by archaeologists and historians, has been generally ignored in favour of the earlier cultures of Greece and Rome, although schoolchildren in north-west Europe are now beginning to be introduced to the history of their ancestors. Denigrated as the 'Dark Ages', it was considered, until recently, a regrettably primitive period which dominated Europe between the fall of the enlightened age of Roman occupation, at about AD 400, until the full advent of Christianity across Europe and into Scandinavia by around AD 1000. But research in a wide range of disciplines is revolutionising our view of the peoples of ancient Europe, and enables me to develop a very different perspective. I emphasise those aspects of our ancestors' culture from which I believe we can learn today, and while this analysis inevitably is not a comprehensive evaluation of every element of first-millennium living, and while I do not claim that the indigenous peoples of ancient Europe represent some sort of utopian society, they are far from being peoples of the 'dark ages'. Indeed, seen from the viewpoint of what they offer us today, the best of their ancient civilisation represents a millennium of glittering and glorious tribal culture which is rich in knowledge and insight in areas of life in which we are relative paupers.

— The Nature of Wyrd —

A main theme of this book concerns the rediscovery of the spiritual life of our ancestors. I illustrate how, most fundamentally, our tribal ancestors and the mystics of ancient Europe lived out a view of life called Wyrd: a way of being which transcends our conventional notions of free will and determinism. All aspects of the world were seen as being in constant flux and motion between the psychological and spiritual polarities of fire and ice: a creative, organic vision paralleling the classical Eastern concepts of yin and yang, and echoed by recent developments in theoretical physics in which the world is conceived of as relationships and patterns.

Following from the concept of Wyrd was a vision of the cosmos, from the gods to the Lowerworld, as being connected by an enormous, all-reaching system of fibres rather like a three-dimensional spider's web. Everything was connected by strands of fibre to the all-encompassing web. Any event, anywhere, resulted in reverberations and repercussions throughout the web. This image far surpasses in ambition our present views of ecology, in which we have extended our notions of cause and effect to include longer and more lateral chains of influence in the natural world. The web of fibres of the Anglo-Saxon shaman offers an ecological model which encompasses individual life events as well as general physical and biological phenomena, non-material as well as material events, and challenges the very cause and effect chains on which our ecological theories depend.

The Anglo-Saxon shamans, people who were believed to be able to mediate between the everyday world and the realm of the sacred, dealt directly with life force, a vital energy which permeated everything but which in humans was generated in the head, flowed down the spinal column and from there throughout the body. This system of energy, which has intriguing similarities to Eastern concepts of prana and chi, encapsulated physical, psychological and spiritual domains within a single, unified system. The manipulation of life force was central to the shamans' healing work, and has implications for much of the contemporary debate in holistic medicine concerning mind/body interaction, healing energies, and complementary approaches to health. Life force connected individual human functioning with the pulses of Earth rhythm, a psychological and spiritual dimension of life which has been excluded by our technological cocoon.

A dynamic and pervasive world of spirits coexisted with the material world in Anglo-Saxon culture. The spirits, manifestations of forces pertaining to Wyrd, were invisible to most humans, although they played a prominent and superstitious role in the everyday lives of Anglo-Saxons. But the spirits were visible to the shamans, because shamans were people believed to be naturally endowed with perceptual abilities beyond the normal, abilities to see, hear and experience things which we would probably consign to the realms of the paranormal or madness. These abilities were recognised, cultivated and nurtured as evidence of a person's fitness for admission to the status of the shaman.

The spirits of our tribal ancestors seemed to give identity and form to many phenomena in life which contemporary psychology recognises but often fails to deal with directly: coincidence, deep-seated fears, psychic experiences, prophetic dreams and nightmares and other aspects of ourselves that remain unconscious. Recent developments in existential psychiatry and the new psychotherapies have begun to look for ways of working directly with these forces.

This, then, is a summary glimpse of a remarkable world view, a way of life.

Rediscovering Wyrd for Today

As a psychologist, I believe that the task which faces us in rediscovering the wisdom of our ancestors and evaluating its relevance for our lives today is not so much a reaching for something 'Other', something we do not possess, but instead a removal of the layers of ignorance and repression which prevent us from knowing what it is we already know, deep in our tribal cultural memory. The past is always within us, in our hearts and minds, just beneath the surface of life, encoded and embedded in a multitude of cultural forms and linguistic patterns which reach back to our tribal times, but which we no longer recognise as having especial significance. This knowledge is in each of us, but confined to the deep unconscious, locked away, banished from everyday life. Sometimes it surfaces unbidden, in amusing and surprising ways.

For example, in the colloquial language of the 1960s, something approaching the ancient meaning of Wyrd re-emerged, even though we were unaware of the origins of the concept; 'Weird, man!' became a much-used phrase of 'hippy' streetwise society. The phrase was usually a response to an event, statement, thought or feeling which seemed to touch the 'beyond', the synchronous, the 'out of bounds'. In that decade, when mystical and spiritual concerns were being rediscovered, 'weird' coloured the strange or unexplainable qualities of life with a positive, approving, even reverential hue. It acquired a special significance. Now, 'Weird, man!' has become a cause for nostalgia, amusement, or embarrassment, depending upon one's opinion of 1960s culture.

It may be simply a bizarre coincidence that the word came back into some sort of special use. But since I believe that the original potency of the concept is embedded deep within our cultural heritage, it is quite possible that it re-emerged amidst the seeking-the-sacred culture of the 1960s, even if some aspects of that seeking may have been less deep than people would have wished.

Wyrd, along with many elements of ancient cultural psychology, has been encoded within the collective memory of the peoples of contemporary western Europe and North America since the original shamanic cultures of ancient Europe. The concept and energy of the principle has lain just beneath the surface of our consciousness in a shadow world, awaiting the time when it may again be needed in the light. Now is that time.

— Buddhist Beginnings —

More than twenty years ago, in California during the summer of 1971, I was on my way to visit one of the heroes of my young adulthood: the philosopher and writer Alan Watts. He was, and is still, two decades after his death, one of the most influential exponents of the great Eastern ways of liberation, especially the ageless wisdom of Buddhism and Taoism.[7]

In the early 1970s a questioning of cultural assumptions, and a seeking for clearer insights, new perspectives, better ways of understanding psychological, social and spiritual issues was gathering momentum. Like many others interested in such things, I had been enchanted, inspired, and stimulated by the writings of Alan Watts. His lucid introductions to the wisdom of the East had opened up undreamed-of psychological and spiritual vistas for us: notions that while material comfort is not to be scorned, it means nothing without the deeper dimensions to life; that many of the bases on which we were living our daily lives rested on assumptions which were culture-specific and were not the only ways to see things, indeed were not, in his view, the best way to see things. The way we defined and understood ourselves as individuals, our notions of love, energy, freedom, our models of health and healing, the role of fantasy and imagination in life, techniques of meditation, deep connections between people and the environment: these and other ideas were called into question through his lucid books.

Like many other young people who had come to value his work, I had gone to university to study the traditions of the Western scientific paradigm; in my case in the psychology laboratories of the University of California, Berkeley, and the University of Oregon. In these institutions I trained as a scientific psychologist. Today, a quarter of a century later, I run research studies at the University of Sussex, investigating altered states of consciousness. But this is not the path that led me to the wisdom of Wyrd. For try as we might to live our lives rationally, to make 'sense-ible' decisions, most of us realise that choices about life paths are rarely intellectual ones. No matter how hard we try to identify and articulate our options, in reality we are attuning to an inner pattern which is already unfolding.

Most of us had vivid inner lives as children. But as we grow up we all learn to subjugate the imaginal, to deny that realm of experience in favour of the consensually validated 'real world'. But it has often struck me that the ways that enable us to move forward in life involve going back to the realm of inner experience, re-entering the image world we knew as children and returning to that source of wisdom which, as adults, we have forgotten. The experiences are not new, they are renewed.

In retrospect, I can see that my path into the culture of Wyrd actually started in my childhood. During the period from four to nine years of age, I had many recurring dreams involving wolves and eagles, and also experienced compelling visions during the fevers of illnesses. These propelled me inwards to the imagery of the unconscious. And so years later as a doctoral student in California and Oregon I knew, even as I calculated the statistics and carried out the scientific analyses necessary for my objective, outerworld-directed research, that empirical psychology could not encompass some of the deeper issues which fascinated me. I began to suspect that the clues to our self-understanding lay not in the mere detailed amassing of facts about observable behaviour in empirical psychology, but rather were waiting to be discovered in the wisdom traditions of the world; the great storehouse of knowledge about the human spirit which has been built up over the centuries in every culture and encoded in the organic computers of religion, ritual and artistic expression.

This is when I had discovered the work of Alan Watts, and along with my scientific work I began reading about, and practising, the meditative disciplines of the great Eastern traditions of Zen and Tao. The dream was to balance the applied power of Western science and technology with the wisdom of the East, a wisdom which might help us to know how to apply such science as a benefit to the Earth and not a curse. This dream has not been accomplished, of course; we have the knowledge, technology and wealth to feed the world, but still people starve in famines as wretched as we have ever known.

My excitement mounted as I turned into the long, hidden driveway of Watts's mountain retreat on Mount Tamalpais, just north of San Francisco, edging the car along the rough track which snaked towards his house through the groves of tall, silvery eucalyptus trees, their leaves whispering in the wind like the breakers on a seashore. I had a particular reason for wishing to visit him, to ask his advice. Like Watts, I had been born and raised in England, and had moved as a young adult to the United States. I had lived there for ten years, during which time I had become involved in the beliefs and practices of Buddhism. But now, having just returned to England, thousands of miles further from the East than I had been in California, something else was stirring in my mind. Something connected with the landscape of England, with the heritage of the West. Inspired as I was by the Eastern wisdoms, I wondered nevertheless whether the West might, at one time, have had a parallel way, a tradition for entering the world of the sacred, of the intuitive, of the deep psyche.

Alan Watts was warm and friendly, and took me to the small building he used as his library and study. This was quite remarkable. It was constructed from a very large redwood water barrel, which had been placed on a wooden deck clinging to the edge of the mountain slope. A tall, conical roof extended over the sides of the barrel, screening the wooden walkway. Inside, the study was round, with a white-carpeted floor, and a large single-paned window looking down over the side of the mountain. Bookshelves encircled the room, with beautifully handwritten labels dividing his collection into subjects; psychology, Buddhism, Taoism, philosophy and so on. And his desktop was made of maple wood, with the outside edge still in its original form, rather than being sawn off straight. Above the desk was an opaque stained-glass panel which admitted a soft light. On cushions, in this magical room, we sat and discussed the issue I had come to ask him.

We talked of early mystical Christianity, its wonders and strengths, failings and disappointments as part of the heritage of the West. But I was seeking something other than this, perhaps an earlier tradition, less a religion and more in tune with the sacred paths of spiritual liberation of the Buddhists and Taoists. I put to him whether England could ever have had such a way of liberation.

He liked this question. It made him laugh. He thought about it for a while. After each question I put to him, there followed a brief pause while he contemplated it, and then a cogent, sometimes witty reply; an answer delivered with erudition but no trace of smugness. This time he thought longer. When he responded, it was to encourage me in the view that every culture has at some time in its history evolved teachings and techniques which enable individuals to transcend conventional reality in search of a separate vision; a dimension in which our notions of time, space and causality are integrated in a way which helps us, in ordinary consciousness, to live more fully, more wholly. We discussed sources, books, traditions, including the Druids and alchemy. He was enormously well read, and his mentoring at the start of my project was invaluable.

Perhaps most of all, I remember his laugh. When Alan Watts laughed, he made the most wonderful, warm, knowing, chuckling sound, like a bubbling spring emanating from the deepest waters of life. He believed that scholarship, contemplation and practical work should all be undertaken with sincerity and integrity, but not with seriousness. For the very grip on the mind and emotions which seriousness imposes strangles the flow of originality, spontaneity and flair which such work requires. I like to think that wisdom, whenever and wherever we encounter it, brings forth a laugh like Alan's, and that a deep chuckle lies at the heart of the cosmos.

When I finally left, I felt that I had been given the best start imaginable: a sense of personal destiny, a quest which would occupy much of my adult life, although I was not to know that then. A few weeks later I returned to England and eagerly began my search for a Western tradition which might parallel some of the perspectives of the East.

— The Anglo-Saxon Spellbook —

In the vaults of the British Museum Library is stored a small book of spells, written in England about one thousand years ago, but reckoned by historians to reflect oral traditions stemming from many centuries earlier. It is a handbook of magical and medical remedies, initiation procedures, incantations and rituals for an indigenous shaman of ancient Europe. This ancient book changed my life.[8]

Discovering it took about three years. I had begun my quest for a Western path by studying the Druids. Contemporary British Druids (famous for their summer solstice rituals at Stonehenge) have an approach to spirituality which reflects a deep reverence for the landscape and the sacred forces of nature. They look to the ancient Druids of two thousand years ago as a source of inspiration, although they do not claim direct descendance from them. Because my goal was to find a path from the ancient Western tradition, I set out to find documentation on the original Druidic beliefs and practices, but became frustrated by the paucity of material. I wanted a Western way which could be grounded on a more substantial foundation of historical authenticity. The contemporary Druidic path is rich with insight, but was not the one that I was seeking.[9]

I then studied alchemy, a tradition which conjures up images of ancient, secret laboratories in which eccentric seekers heated and distilled substances in crucibles in a vain attempt to create gold from base metals. This is a caricature, of course, for the alchemical practices included sophisticated meditations focused on inner and outer transformation. These practices taught me how to be sensitive to inner change, how to observe the workings of the psyche in response to archetypal imagery, and how to use external objects and interactions as metaphors for internal work. I am still fascinated by alchemy, but as a system alchemy was largely a private, inner discipline.[10] After a time, I realised that I was looked more for a folk-way, a path which might entail some esoteric knowledge, but which had been, and could be again, more widely accessible.

But then I came to witchcraft, or Wicca. This is a very rich vein of wisdom. I was fortunate to be able to study with some remarkable women, who taught me things that would be important for my later understanding of Wyrd. But while I became convinced of the spiritual depths of the craft of Wicca, the necessary details were not to be found in the witch-hunting documents of the Middle Ages, in which women were required, often under torture, to confess to acts defined by the Church as devilish. But as I continued to read further and further back in history, looking for the origins of the beliefs which were so distorted in the trials, the tomes referred to material increasingly ancient, the language ever more archaic.[11]

Finally, I found what I was looking for, although I had not been sure in what form it would appear. As I delved deeper into the historical roots of Wicca, I came upon a reference to the existence of an obscure document which is essentially the healing manual, or 'spellbook', of an indigenous, pre-Christian healer or shaman from the Anglo-Saxon tribal culture of ancient England. The historical sources

I was consulting described the book as a collection of 'charms': magical healing remedies, rituals and incantations which, historians reckon, were written down by Christians in the tenth or eleventh century, although the material had probably been passed down orally for several hundred years, from the pre-Christian era. I refer to this text as the *Anglo-Saxon Spellbook*, or just the *Spellbook*.

— Scribes: *Secret Incantations* —

Dotted around the forested landscape of early Europe were monasteries housing Christian missionaries. Their task was to convert the natives to Christianity. Many of the Church officials openly condemned indigenous beliefs and practices, and set out to eradicate them. However, despite the public proclamations of the Christian officials, nothing is ever quite so black and white as it first seems. While 'official' Christianity had a mission to convert the indigenous tribespeople of western Europe to the path of Christ, the individuals who served as monks were not clones stamped out of an evangelical machine; some of them understood and respected the ways of the indigenous peoples. At least, that is one interpretation of the motives behind the monastic recording of the healing spells of native healers, shamanic practitioners of the way of Wyrd, in the *Anglo-Saxon Spellbook*.

The *Anglo-Saxon Spellbook* was written in the AD 900s or 1000s, certainly in a monastery and probably, in the view of several historians of Anglo-Saxon England, by scribes or initiates rather than monks. For although the entries of healing remedies, with plant concoctions, rituals and incantations, were usually 'Christianised', by for example replacing the names of 'pagan' gods and goddesses with those of Christian saints, nevertheless the material is strongly pre-Christian, and some of it is so intimately connected with initiation rites into Wyrd mysticism that it is surprising that the material was collected at all. Certainly, historians reckon, the material was probably too controversial to have been written by the monks.[12]

It is wonderful that it *was* recorded, of course, for the monasteries were one of few settings for narrative writing; the indigenous cultures of north-west Europe were based on oral transmission of knowledge, and without the documents prepared by the Christians (including their condemnatory diktats!) we would have far less information about the native traditions than we have. Usually writing in the monasteries was confined to the preparation of copies of classical medical texts, and the language employed was Latin, the international language of the Church. But the *Spellbook* was written in Anglo-Saxon, the spoken language of the tribespeople.

We do not know precisely why the *Spellbook* was written. Perhaps the healing spells were collected from an indigenous 'informant', a knowledgeable native healer, in case they actually worked! The monks were active in arranging medical clinics (mainly for their own use, although they sometimes made available their medical expertise to the local inhabitants, as missionaries do to this very day), and may have wished to incorporate native knowledge into their practice.

Another possibility is that the spells were required to be recorded by the scribes as an exercise in writing in the vernacular Anglo-Saxon, although this seems unlikely, for there must have been many less controversial subjects for such practice in penmanship.

Much more likely was that the *Spellbook* was prepared from field research by a scribe who had been sent to travel in the pagan lands of the area to gather information on how the indigenous practitioners carried out their healing; this would have been useful 'intelligence' for the monks in their bid to counter the native healers and replace them with their own approach to medicine. The *Spellbook* would have been, from this perspective, a 'research document', prepared for political purposes.

— The Manuscript —

The *Spellbook* is a small manuscript of thick vellum leaves, with straight margins scratched down the left-hand side of each soft page with a sharp instrument. The magical and medical remedies are written in continuous text, although with several different handwriting styles, suggesting that it had been transcribed by more than one person. And to indicate the point in the narrative where a new medical or magical entry begins, there is drawn in the margin a little cartoon-like diagram of a hand with a finger pointing to the first line, and to mark the end is sketched a cartoon foot.

Seeing these small marginal notes using hands and feet as paragraph markers made me laugh, and I felt a thrill of empathy, a warm sense of connection with the person who had drawn them. It may be that they were not meant by the artist to be humorous, simply indicative of paragraph breaks. Nevertheless, the images were so informal and appealing, and such a contrast to the careful calligraphy of the Anglo-Saxon text, that they reminded me vividly of the fact that the *Spellbook* was a living piece of documentation put together by our ancestors.

The entries in the book make fascinating reading; I shall detail some of them later, but essentially they each comprise a description of symptoms of an illness, a herbal or plant remedy, and a ritual indicating how and when the remedies should be applied, as for example over 'running water' or 'at full moon'. Sometimes incantations are transcribed to be sung along with the remedies. While most of the entries were healing remedies and herbal treatments, I also discovered among them rituals, guidelines and texts for shamanic initiation and training. The manuscript was an entry into the world view of the people of ancient Europe.

— Sources of Knowledge —

The source material is substantial for reconstructing the way of Wyrd, the world view behind the manuscript, but is widely scattered in sometimes obscure manuscripts, books, journals, and museums throughout the academic world. One of my main tasks over the years has been to pull together this information and integrate it, a process rather like weaving a tapestry. I have consulted sources in disciplines as diverse as the history of medicine, Anglo-Saxon, Celtic and Germanic social history, Icelandic sagas, comparative mythology, folklore studies, archaeology, anthropology and, of course, psychology. While I feel fully expert only in this last discipline, I have sought to incorporate the expertise of leading scholars in all the other disciplines in putting together my research programme. I have indicated generally accessible sources in the notes and bibliography at the end of the book, so that readers who wish to explore for themselves may follow up particular aspects of the wisdom of the Wyrd.

The evidence shows that in early western Europe a thousand years ago, shamans, whom we now recognise as the inspired mystics and healers of traditional societies, served our tribal ancestors by communicating with a world beyond everyday life, an 'Otherworld' regarded as sacred. Using techniques for altering their states of consciousness, these shamans of Wyrd were able to 'vision' beyond ordinary sight, travel to and communicate with the spirit world, and bring back to the rest of the tribal communities stories and healing insights which formed the elements of the wisdom of the Wyrd.[13]

— The Way of Wyrd —

After the first ten years of my research into the ways of our ancestors, I published a book, *The Way of Wyrd*,[14] which detailed the process of initiation into the mystical and shamanic secrets of the practitioners of Wyrd. I constructed that book as a documentary novel (with bibliography), trying to bring to life the atmosphere and flavour of such a way of being. It attracted the interest of hundreds of thousands of readers in Europe and America, and in translation into German and French. This enormous level of interest has encouraged me now, ten years further on in my research, to write this book, this time non-fiction, in which I detail wider aspects of Wyrd, reflecting the mass of documentation I have collected since then.

Also since the publication of *The Way of Wyrd*, I have sought to bring the insights I was reconstructing from the wisdom of Wyrd not only into my own life, but also into the lives of a wide variety of people through my therapeutic work with individual clients, in lectures and tutorials in universities and other settings, and in the many seminars and workshops I have had the opportunity to lead around the world in which I have attempted to introduce people to the teachings of Wyrd in a more directly experiential way. Along with my recounting of the ancient ways of Wyrd, I have included examples of these attempts to bring the teachings to life for our practical benefit today.

— So What Happened to Wyrd? —

So what happened to Wyrd? Religious suppression. Early Christianity, as an evangelical religion with political power behind it from Rome, drove Wyrd underground. The sacred traditions of the indigenous peoples who were our ancestors were lost as surely as are those of the disappearing tribes around the world today. It seems to have been yet another example of our age-old curse: the human inability to come to terms with sacred realms free of political tyranny. The way of Wyrd disappeared beneath the waves of 'progress', slipping ever deeper into the obscurity our historians denigrated as the Dark Ages.

But a thousand years and more have passed. While today, sadly, in some regions of the Earth there are wars still being fought on religious grounds, on the whole Christianity is no longer such an evangelising, missionary movement. In an age of ecumenical sympathies, coexistence of spiritual paths is once more becoming possible. We are also now much more aware than we used to be of the fact that we live, and need to coexist, in a multi-faith world.

In considering here the wisdom of our ancestors, I do not present it as an exclusive path. I take the view that there are many paths to God. But I believe that in that multi-faith world, it is imperative that the ancient wisdom of the Wyrd reasserts its rightful position alongside the other great spiritual traditions. This book is about how we can rekindle Wyrd wisdom in the intimacy of our own lives, and allow its light to illuminate our personal search for knowledge and the sacred.

CHAPTER ONE

How Our Ancestors Lived

— The Forest People —

From an aeroplane on a clear day, the lush green landscape of England looks like a patchwork of farm fields, with scattered settlements connected with ribbon roads, and punctuated by great towns and cities. But two thousand years ago, if we could have made the same airborne survey, the land would have appeared radically different. At this time, before the centuries of forest clearing for agriculture and building, great woodlands covered the island, broken only by tracts of open heath and moorland and hilltops ridged with scrub cover.[1] Scattered within this forest landscape, a few hundred thousand of our 'native' ancestors lived in small tribal societies. The same scene was repeated all over western and northern Europe.

The shadows of the old world still fall across today's landscape, for many of the names of these early forests survive. In the middle of Britain, for example, forests called Dean, Morfe and Kinver each covered scores of square miles, and dense stands of oak and ash formed the forest called Sherwood, later famed as the hiding place of the legendary outlaw Robin Hood. Hornbeam, thorn, oak and ash covered much of south-east Britain, where the great forest of Andred was described by an annalist writing in the year 892 as '30 miles wide and stretching 120 miles from east to west'. On the small island of Britain, forests of this extent dominated the landscape.

Small groups of hunter-gathering people had inhabited the island for thousands of years, but the population had begun to increase during the last few centuries BC when tribal groups, subsumed for convenience now under the umbrella title of 'Celtic peoples', came across to Britain from the European mainland. They formed a rich and thriving culture. Later they were colonised by Rome, and became the wild outer fringe of that great empire. The Romans built roads, manor houses and towns, and the ruling aristocracy was modelled on Roman lines, but many of the Celtic peoples continued to live in the ways of old, in tribal groups with local chieftains.

In the mid-400s AD, the Romans withdrew their occupying military forces and their administrative aristocracy because Rome itself was coming under attack from other kingdoms, and needed to retrench. With the Roman military gone, many more tribal groups from the north-west European mainland rowed and sailed across the Channel to raid, invade and settle.

They came mainly from the area of what is now Denmark, northern Germany and Holland, people from the tribes known as the Angles (after whom the country of England was eventually named: Angle-Land), Saxons, Jutes, and Friesians, among others. One of the earliest sources records for 514 that 'In this year the West Saxons came into Britain with three ships.'[2] These and many similar entries reveal the repeated spectacle of a few score men at a time rowing across the choppy, grey waves of the English Channel in their low boats, stilling their oars in sheltered coves, and scrambling ashore on to deserted beaches. Their boats, constructed from planks joined by rivets, were narrow and easy to handle, and on occasion they were able to sneak along the rivers past Celtic settlements deep into the countryside, before docking inland and carrying the boats to protected sites.

Each boatload, or small flotilla of boats, formed their own little settlement, and created territories in which members were linked by tribal loyalties and blood ties, and which were ruled over by local chieftains. They formed defensible stockades, often surrounded by a deep pit to make the walls more difficult to scale, then sent for their extended families in subsequent boat journeys.

It used to be thought that the Celts were all driven out to the west, or enslaved, by the new invaders from the continent, but now historians realise that there were all manner of accommodations between the various tribes. In some cases the newer arrivals and existing Celtic settlements traded, cooperated, lived together and intermarried; on other occasions skirmishes and raiding persisted, and some of the

Celtic tribes moved west and south to live in what is now Wales and the county of Cornwall.

If we could row up the rivers or trek through the countryside of that time we would pass through the territories of tribes whose names survive even today, immortalised in the local place names. In the seventh century an area of one of the large forests was called Iinderauuda, meaning 'in the wood of the Deirans', and today Wychwood in north-west Oxfordshire is the modern name of Hwicce Wood, the forest home of the Hwicce tribe. In the west of England low-lying ground was covered with water for much of the year, with a few islands of higher ground offering sites for early settlement; rowing to Glastingii, the oldest name for the town of Glastonbury, would bring us to the island of the Glast tribe.

— Tribal Villages —

Approaching the villages, we would see first the grey firesmoke drifting in the wind above the trees; fires were needed all year round for cooking and blacksmithing, and in the winter for heating. Built in areas cleared of trees, most settlements had at their centre a large timber hall surrounded by a stockade for defence, with smaller houses and huts spilling neatly around the perimeter of the stockade wall.

Around and amongst the houses the sights and sounds would include tethered goats and clucking chickens; perhaps the shrill cries of an ox-herd taking oxen to plough the nearby fields. The land was broken up for sowing seeds with ploughs pulled by oxen. Few peasants owned more than a couple of oxen, and so where large ploughs were available, they shared animals to form a full team of eight oxen to pull it. More distant sounds would include the forge hammers ringing on metal in the blacksmith's hut, placed, for symbolic reasons, as we shall see later, on the edge of the settlement.

The houses were framed in wood, with walls often formed of long, pliable sticks called wattles. They were woven together and then daubed with mud to keep out draughts. Others would look larger, like 'A-frames' with plank floors and an excavated pit under the floor for a cool food store. Some of the outer walls were covered with turf, which provided insulation and weather protection, and the roofs thatched. In the summer months these small buildings were humming with activity, for most of them were used as summer workshops, and in the larger ones people slept, with clay hearths in the centre of the floor holding a wood fire.

The interior of such a one-room house was cool and dark, save for chinks of light filtering through the smoke hole in the roof and gaps around the door. Down either side of the room, against the two longest walls, ran raised benches topped with linen-covered mattresses stuffed with straw or horse hair, and the centre of the room was taken up by a raised fire-pit, raked clean and laid with fresh kindling. The planked floor was strewn with dried rushes and aromatic, creamy-flowered meadowsweet. Clothes and domestic implements hung from pegs driven into the beams of the wooden frame.

— Halls of the Chieftains —

The main hall or longhouse was sometimes an impressive building, constructed for the local chieftain and elite warriors, but often also inhabited by many of the peasants in the winter. An example of these longhouses is the farmhouse-like wooden structure excavated in the manor of Cheddar in Somerset, almost eighty feet long and twenty feet wide in the middle, and dating from the eighth or ninth century. Even earlier, in the seventh century, a massive timber hall was built at Yeavering in Northumbria, with lesser halls set about it, probably dwellings for the kings' companions-in-arms. One structure of a more primitive type may have housed servants. There was also a grandstand for open-air assemblies. In later years, the excavations show, the grandstand was enlarged, additional small dwellings were built, and a hall of more ambitious design took the place of the original great hall.[3]

— Food and Drink —

Around the edges of the settlements, in fields cleared of timber which had been used for building and firewood, stretched farmland, crop fields divided into strips by grassy baulks and bounded by headland bumpy from turning ploughs. By the fifth and sixth centuries AD the tribal farmers had an effective and organised system of land management.

Land was shared among the people who had cleared it for agriculture, and the fields were laid out in strips, each strip fenced and farmed by one extended family. They were expected to take full responsibility for it, and to respect their neighbour's patch. In the late seventh century King Ine declared that: 'If free peasants have a common meadow or other land divided into shares to fence, and some have fenced their portion and some have not, and if cattle eat up their common crops or grass, those who are responsible for the gap are to go and pay to the others, who have fenced their part, compensation for the damage that has been done there.'[4]

Each year, in rotation, some of the arable land was left to lie fallow from crop production to replenish its energies and become fully fertile again. Such practices were developed through close observation, through feeling the power of the land, through intimate experience of its moods and capacities.

Along with oats, rye and wheat, barley was the main crop, ground into meal for bread-making or converted into malt for brewing. Beer and alcoholic apple cider were the usual drink, with mead, made from honey, a more expensive drink for the aristocracy.

Baking and cooking were carried on much as they were on the American frontier a century ago. The Anglo-Saxons knew and used yeast and so the opportunities for varied means of preparation were considerably enhanced. Fruit and vegetables, generally smaller and perhaps less sweet than those of today, included cabbage, onions, leeks and turnips, plus lettuce, peas, and parsley. Apples (which could be stored through the winter) and berries were the main fruits, being available in wild and domestic varieties. Cherries, pears, plums and nuts were available too.

The villagers kept cattle, sheep, pigs and poultry, but fresh domestic meat was an occasional luxury for the peasant. Pigs were popular and practical because they could root a living out of the woods and because their meat lent itself to smoking or salting for winter use. Sheep were raised for wool.

There were also chicken, geese, mutton, rabbit, deer, eggs, eels, fish and shoreline shellfish, cheese, other dairy products and, on occasion, game. Salt was a necessity for meat preservation, and was obtained mostly from sea water by means of salt pans. Garlic was considered to be more a vegetable, eaten for its bulk, than a spice, although there was extensive use of herbs. The people did without sugar, which was introduced into Europe by Norman Crusaders returning from the East. Honey was produced in bulk and highly prized.

So this, in practical terms, is how they lived. I have focused on England to provide a specific context for the study of Wyrd, but this was the primary pattern of tribal settlements extending right across Europe, the basis for essentially the same way of living, similar beliefs and practices, common insights and knowledge.

— Living in Nature —

Of course, like surviving indigenous peoples today, the everyday environment of our ancestors was comprehensively different from ours in form, structure, sight, sounds, smells, tastes. To our senses it would feel alien. They lived not what we call 'close to nature' but actually involved in nature: they had to be on intimate terms with nature in order to survive.[5]

It sounds idyllic in some ways, but it was not, of course, a utopian environment. As with all traditional societies where agriculture is subsistence, life was extremely dependent upon the cycles of crop success or failure. The *Anglo-Saxon Chronicle*, a history of England compiled in the ninth century from earlier sources, contains repeated references to great famines and epidemics of disease, and the monk Bede records that in 664 'a sudden pestilence depopulated the southern coast of Britain and afterwards extending into the province of Northumbria, ravaged the country far and near, and destroyed a great multitude of men.'[6]

The indigenous Europeans had to respect the imperatives of the forces of nature. Such an intimate interweaving of fates, in which the state of the environment had such a direct impact on human wellbeing, meant the tribespeople observed, attuned to and grew to know their landscape in all its nuances, intimacies and moods. From this necessarily acute and deep awareness of the living connection between humans and the environment our ancestors created many of the cosmologies, myths, wisdom stories and shamanic practices of Wyrd.

— Lessons for the Concrete Jungle —

But what has this to do with us today? Most of us in the Western world live in urban or suburban environments, and even those who live rurally usually do so with the support of modern technology: our houses and transportation shield us from the rigours of the environment. And even if we wanted to, it would be impossible to redistribute ourselves wholesale out of the cities and back into the countryside.

The issues that face us are far more subtle and complex than a simple romanticising of the charms of nature, although we all know that as a species we are at crisis point in our balance with the wild environment. But the answers to this need to be sought within our inner worlds as much as in the external world. What I believe we can learn from the wisdom of Wyrd is the *essence* of the deeper aspects of the relationship between people and nature which our forebears experienced. It is in these deeper aspects that the implications of their world view, developed in their environment of forests and glades, has relevance for our lives in the concrete jungles of our cities.

Let us therefore enter as fully as we can into their cosmology, their understanding of life and death, Earth and sky.

CHAPTER TWO

Incantations:
Attuning to the Healing Spirits

— The Missionaries Arrive —

Ironically, the Christian missionaries, who brought the 'new religion from the East' to the wooded landscapes of western Europe, are among the most important of our sources of information about the indigenous peoples and how they lived. For the purposes of the rediscovery of the wisdom of Wyrd, the early missionaries and monks were like ancient anthropologists, observing, reporting, and writing about the tribal cultures within which they lived (and of course many of the missionaries were themselves from those tribes, though sometimes going abroad for religious training).

Unlike anthropologists the monks made no claim to 'academic objectivity', for they had an objective of their own: to convert the natives of western and northern Europe to Christianity. But balancing the natural and predictable bias of their observations is the fact that they had a practical need to understand the beliefs and practices around them, so that they could set about converting the people. This gives a pragmatic edge to their writings; I believe that their observations accurately report the things they saw, even if they were intent on condemning them as evil, and therefore reported their findings in language which reflected their task.

The response of the indigenous peoples to the first arrival of the missionaries is revealing; it tells us a lot about the nature of the existing beliefs. Aethelbert, chieftain of the native population of south-east England, insisted that his first meeting with the missionaries should be in the open air; if they were black magicians they would have less chance of harming him than if they were inside a building, where they 'might deceive him by surprise, prevailing against him'.[1]

Pope Gregory of Rome had sent the missionaries, led by a monk called Augustine with a party of about forty monks and assistants, early in the year 597. They were rowed across the English Channel, and the natives allowed them to land on the island of Thanet, just off the coast of Kent. The monks asked to speak to Aethelbert, a powerful chieftain.

King Aethelbert was not Christian, and neither were his subjects, but he was a sophisticated and worldly man, and knew what he was facing, for he was married to a Christian, the daughter of the King of Paris. Aethelbert allowed his wife to worship at a little church which had been built near Canterbury centuries earlier by the Romans when they occupied the island. Early Celtic Christianity had survived in isolated monasteries, and they had been allowed to continue as practising monasteries, although the monks seemed to carry out little or no missionary activity. But the arrival of Augustine and his band signalled the beginning of a renewed assault from Rome, a fresh attempt to 'convert the natives'.

Bede tells us that King Aethelbert, on hearing of the arrival of the missionaries, ordered that they be treated with courtesy, and be provided with shelter and hospitality. Nevertheless he played it safe, just in case the priests of this new religion had powers they might use against him; he may well have been advised by his own shamans to exercise caution by insisting that the missionaries remain on the island, where he would go to meet them. It seems certain that Aethelbert must have taken with him one or more indigenous shamans to inspect these interlopers.

Bede tells us that: 'the monks . . . approached the king carrying a silver cross as their standard, and the likeness of our Lord and Saviour painted on a board. First of all they offered prayer to God, singing a litany for the eternal salvation both of themselves and of those for whose sake they had come.'[2]

Having regaled Aethelbert with their litany, they called upon him to forsake his ways of error and be baptised into the Christian faith; it is recorded that Aethelbert declined their invitation. However, he was very generous to them, allowing them to come off the island and to enter the mainland of Kent, providing them with a house in Canterbury, and making available to them the little church as a base for their worship. He also, remarkably, gave the monks licence to engage in missionary activity, telling them that they may seek to 'win unto the faith of your religion with your preaching as many as you may'.

This is a tolerant welcome, especially when we consider what happened: Christianity, with the backing of Rome, accomplished a takeover of the spiritual life of England, at least in law if not in popular practice. It has been suggested that perhaps the extant ways of sacred practice were weak, or fading, and that the missionaries found a ready audience for their proselytising. I think that the truth is likely to be very different, and it is worth considering what happened a little more closely for the illuminating light it casts on to the indigenous attitudes towards the sacred.

— The Response of the Indigenous Peoples —

Aethelbert, as the chieftain responsible for first allowing the missionaries on to the island, clearly saw them for what they were. Although his wife was Christian, and through her he had dealings with the Christian King of Paris, he nevertheless did not welcome the missionaries as envoys from friends. He kept them first on the Isle of Thanet, where he met them in the open air. It may have been merely a checking of 'passports', letters of introduction from Rome and so on, to be sure that they had indeed come with the blessing of the Pope. There may also have been some diplomatic, trade or military considerations: connections with Pope Gregory would have been extremely useful and influential for a regional, tribal chieftain of part of England.

But in understanding the open attitude to the preaching and politicking of the missionaries, it is important to realise that the awareness of the sacred which characterised the indigenous practices was integrated with all elements of life, and did not constitute what we now think of as an official religion. There were mystics who mediated with the spirits, conducted the celebrations and calendar customs in honour of gods and goddesses, carried out shamanic healing, and so on. But it was not a centrally organised institution, with dogma to impart and souls to convert. When initially encountered, a religion like that of the Christians must have seemed to many of the indigenous tribespeople, used to a multitude of gods, goddesses and spirits, like an optional extra, another god to add to the pantheon of sacred beings.

Beyond this, I also believe that the deep underlying nature of the way of Wyrd matches closely what has been identified as the attitude of early Native American tribes to the incoming of Christianity. Historian of religion Joseph Epes Brown suggests that Native American ways of the spirit meant that 'all forces of the experienced natural environment can communicate to man the totality of what is to be known of the sacred mysteries of creation, and thus of the sacred essence of being and beings.'[3] Beliefs and practices were closely identified with direct experience; the sacred was not an ideology, or debating point. Each person's experience of the spiritual was respected, and so, in Epes Brown's words, when the Christian message came to the people through 'dedicated missionaries who led exemplary and sacrificial lives, the people easily understood the message and example because of the profundity of their own beliefs'.

Epes Brown proposes that the historical phenomenon represented by the adoption of Christianity by indigenous peoples is not one of 'conversion' as understood exclusively by bearers of Christianity; it is simply a continuation of the people's ancient and traditional practice of open sacred attunement. Study of the process of conversion in early Europe gives the same impression, although this open integration of spiritual views was not to last, for as the organised Christian Church grew in power, it began to outlaw the ancient practice of Wyrd.

The so-called conversion of the kings, advocated by Rome in the belief that the populace would follow their leaders into the fold, was a tenuous and fragile arrangement. Frustrations abounded for the missionaries. For one thing there was the annoying propensity of 'converts' to relapse to their indigenous practices. For example, King Redwald of East Anglia, who had agreed to be baptised into Christianity, relapsed, reportedly owing to the influence of his heathen wife. The result was that 'in the same temple he had an altar to sacrifice to Christ, and another small one to offer victims to the devils',[4] the devils being, of course, indigenous deities!

Eventually, over time, more warrior kings converted to Christianity, sometimes out of genuine faith, more often for the links it provided with the power of Rome. But the populace did not follow the example of their kings, unless 'officially' baptised by royal order. At first, the kings of the late Dark Ages who had become Christian tolerated the continuing presence of Wyrd; or rather, they had to. The attitude of the indigenous populace to the imperatives of baptism hardly came from the heart.

One wonderful example of the purely pragmatic approach to conversion is the response of a Saxon seaman to the Christian missionary practice of, having captured pirates at sea, offering them the choice of accepting baptism into the faith or being put to death. The historical annals record that this pirate, when confronted by the proposition, opted for baptism, saying 'that he had no objection; he had been baptised nineteen times before, and supposed that the twentieth would not hurt him.'[5]

Missionaries tried to accommodate some of the indigenous views, and sometimes were minded to do so because they themselves still had a sneaking belief in many of the elements of the pre-Christian sacred ways. There are stories of missionaries having to deal with the indigenous 'heathen' spirits, and taking it seriously. Even as recently as the thirteenth century, the Icelandic Bishop Gudmund Arason was reckoned to have had great power among trolls:

> He was once, it is said, going over the steep little holm of Drangey, blessing it and casting out the trolls, when, after they had done their worst, there came a petition from them in reasonable terms. In his purification of the island, which was carried out very thoroughly, he was let down by a rope over the cliffs to bless them. At one place a shaggy grey arm in a red sleeve came out of the rock with a knife, and cut two strands of his rope: the third strand was hallowed and would not give and the bishop hung there.
>
> Then a voice from the rock said: 'Do no more hallowing, bishop; the Bad folk must live somewhere.' The bishop had himself hauled up, and left that corner as a reservation for trolls, so it is said.[6]

— The Missionaries Appropriate Indigenous Customs —

In general, the deliberate policy of the Church to effect conversion with the least possible disturbance was to tolerate and absorb as much of the indigenous practice as they could bear, to make it more likely that the natives would accept the new religion. Thus Pope Gregory, writing in AD 601 from Rome to Mellitus, assistant to Augustine, one of the missionaries sent under the protection of Rome to convert the English tribespeople, says: 'Tell Augustine what I have determined upon after mature deliberation on the affairs of the English: namely that the temples . . . ought not to be destroyed, but let the idols that are in them be destroyed; let holy water be . . . sprinkled in the said temples, let altars be erected and relics placed.' Thus 'the nation . . . may the more familiarly resort to the places to which they have been accustomed . . . For there is no doubt that it is impossible to efface everything at once.'[7]

Because the Christian churches were usually built of stone, in contrast to the pagan sacred enclosures which were, if constructed rather than being a naturally occurring sacred site, made of wood, some accommodation had to be made by the Christians. To this end the common folk were allowed by Gregory 'to build themselves huts of the boughs of trees about those churches which had been turned to that use from temples, and celebrate the solemnity with religious fasting, and no more offer beasts to the Devil'.

The times of the pagan ceremonies and those of the Church festivals were made to coincide: the heathen feast at the winter solstice became identified with Christmas, and so on. The churches themselves were used in ways that symbolised the transference of sacred practices from Wyrd to Christ. Because the north was regarded as the abode of the heathen gods, the north side of the churchyard was not used for burials until the south side was full – except that the north side could be used from the start for burying suicides and murderers.

Also the north door, to be found in most Anglo-Saxon and early Norman churches, is said to be the one built so that a person could be brought into the church through it for baptism, signifying the change from pagan to Christian influence about to be effected.

And this in essence is what happened to the shamans of the indigenous Wyrd peoples. For the Rome-backed missions to England targeted the tribal chiefs and warrior kings for conversion. Over the next centuries, some royal courts were converted, some affected a conversion by adding the Christian God to their pantheon of 'pagan' deities, while others became nominally Christian and later reverted to their pre-Christian Wyrd. But the long-term effect was to replace the male shamans, or to drive them underground, and supplant them as advisers to the kings and leaders of sacred ceremony with Christian priests. However, the evidence suggests that the general populace remained, for the most part, committed to their traditional beliefs and practices.

So later, when its continuing vitality among the peasantry could not be usurped by stealth, Wyrd was marginalised, suppressed and finally outlawed. The practice of certain rituals, celebrations, sacred acts of Wyrd were punishable by death. Those elements of it that could be appropriated were recast as aspects of Christian practice; those that could not be accommodated were suppressed with a brutality which reached its culmination in the witch-burning of the Middle Ages.

The hostility of official Christianity towards the indigenous Wyrd practices, and its attempts to replace and suppress native customs, is important here principally because it is largely through the Christian recording in writing of their condemnation of folk beliefs and customs that we have discovered so much about them. Let us explore, a thousand years on, some of the things that the Christian functionaries wrote about the sacred ways of our ancestors.

— Dominion —

Wulfstan was Archbishop of York from AD 1002 to 1023, a tough time for a Christian. Many English warlords and aristocracy had converted to Christianity, but the great mass of people living on the land and even in the villages and towns were still practising the sacred rituals of Wyrd; indeed these had been given a shot in the arm by the invasions of the Vikings and their reintroduction of 'pagan' ways.

Wulfstan composed a large body of directives which railed against the Wyrd, saying deprecatingly of the indigenous shamans: 'they took it as wisdom to worship the sun and moon as gods on account of their shining brightness ... Some men also said that the shining stars were gods and began to worship them earnestly; and some believed in fire on account of its sudden heat, some also in water, and some believed in the earth because it nourished all things.' He contrasted these caricatures of indigenous beliefs with the truth according to the gospels: 'But they might have readily discerned, if they had the power of reason, that he is the true God who created all things for the enjoyment and use of us men, which he granted mankind because of his great goodness.'[8]

Today these words have an ominous ring. In a time of ecological reawakening, Wulfstan's early Christian view as man in all his goodness being granted dominion over the Earth is one from which many of us recoil. In modern Christianity some argue for a more aware, and sensitive dominion. Others counter that the assumption of dominion is the root problem: we are *of* the world, not 'in charge' of it. Either way, we are seeking urgently to build new models of human-environment relations, and to transcend the alienating dogma which can be seen already in Wulfstan's sermons a thousand years ago.

In contrast, and in tune with some of the work today to revision our understanding of the environment, the indigenous pre-Christian tribes of Europe saw the natural world as breathing a special kind of life force, a spiritual power. The historian Burckhardt says that: 'The Germanic races, which founded their states on the ruins of the Roman Empire, were thoroughly and specially fitted to understand the spirit of natural scenery.'[9] For them, features of the environment were suffused with life force and sacred power: trees, rocks, natural springs and wells were expressions of the spiritual realm, and proffered healing powers to those who needed it. The shamans of Wyrd saw spirit energies in the natural features of the landscape, rather than seeing in them the workings of an overall God. And so the Christian missionaries set out to destroy the sacred significance of the landscape in the minds and hearts of the people.

But, Burckhardt explains: 'though Christianity compelled them for a while to see in the springs and mountains, in the lakes and woods, which they had till then revered, the working of evil demons, yet this transitional conception was soon outgrown.'[10] Revivals of Wyrd in 'converted' ancient Europe were rife, when the populace rebelled against the outlawing of indigenous shamanic practices by newly baptised kings and warrior chiefs.

— Forbidden Wyrd —

Written records of the laws and sermons forbidding Wyrd practices form timeless documentation of the comprehensive activities of our ancestors in engaging with the landscape of which they were a part, including the conducting of spiritual and healing ceremonies at trees, wells and springs, stones, and sacred enclosures, divination, incantations, enchantments with herbs, and the making of vows by fires.

Some of the prohibitions denied religious freedom in the most repressive manner possible. The laws of Alfred, the most prominent and active Christian king of the ninth century, threatened: 'Let him who sacrifices to gods, save God alone, perish by death.'[11] Clearly it is not the act of sacrifice which is here being called into question, but the identity of the god to whom the offering is made. And if it were a god of the Wyrd pantheon, the punishment was death.

— Attunements to the Sacred —

But more usually it was the indigenous tribespeople's attunement to the sacred in nature that was attacked by the Church, sometimes through secular law. The laws of King Cnut, for example, 'earnestly forbid every heathenism: heathenism is, that men worship idols, that is that they worship heathen gods, and the sun or the moon, fire or rivers, water-wells or stones, or forest trees of any kind; or love witchcraft, or . . . perform anything pertaining to such illusions'.[12]

Admittedly, 'love witchcraft' adds an intriguing extra dimension to the array of natural phenomena covered by Cnut's condemnation, but the main target of his 'earnestly forbidding' diktat is the attunement to, celebration of, and sacred connection with elements of the landscape of which people are a part. In Wulfstan's terms, the true path is to seek to dominate nature, to bend it to our will, since it is provided for our convenience. To acknowledge the importance and special qualities of nature was anti-Christian.

Church penitentials, laying down a raft of actions required in 'penance' from those who were judged to have strayed from the true Christian path, were repressive: anyone who 'sacrifices to demons in little things shall do penance for one year, but if in big things, for ten years. If he shall eat or drink in the vicinity of a heathen shrine or if he shall partake of food which has been used in a heathen sacrifice he shall likewise do penance.'

Being caught participating in a major sacred feast could therefore require ten years of penance, a kind of community-based sentence restricting freedoms as if in a 'penitentiary'. Here it is not so much the act of eating itself which is condemned, for the wine and wafer of communion is to take drink and food as part of a sacred ritual; the problem is that people were doing this act in honour of the spirits of nature, rather than exclusively in honour of the Christian God.

Communicating with the life force of the natural landscape, divining the pattern of future events, and performing healing incantations were forbidden: Edgar, one of the first churchmen to hold high political office in England, urged the priesthood to even greater efforts to stamp out the indigenous spiritual practices: 'we enjoin that every priest zealously promote Christianity and totally extinguish every heathenism, and forbid well-worshipping and necromancies, and divinations and incantations and with sacred circles – and with elders and also with other trees, and with stones.'

Today, a thousand years after Edgar's missive to 'zealously extinguish' every act of indigenous practice, his writings provide a clear idea of the specific ways in which our ancestors related to the features of the landscape, and by implication the general principles which underlay those practices. They believed that waters be regarded as sacred, that areas of wildland be set aside as sanctuaries for ceremony, that trees and stones are containers of sacred power.

Further details are revealed by the proclamations of St Eligius who, in about AD 640, ordered that: 'No Christian place lights at the temples or at the stones, or at fountains and springs, or at trees, or at places where three ways meet . . . Let no one presume to purify by sacrifice, or to enchant herbs, or to make flocks pass through a hollow tree or an aperture in the earth; for by so doing he seems to consecrate them to the devil.' And we know that sacred bonds and vows were carried out at such places, for an early Christian penitential says: 'No one shall go to trees, or wells, or stones, or enclosures, or anywhere else except to God's church, and there make vows or release himself from them.' The 'enclosures' were circles of trees, or stones, in which a natural shrine was kept.

Clearly the sum total of activities denied, derogated, and made punishable by penance at best, death at worst, provides a remarkable, vivid picture of a highly active indigenous spiritual practice.

— Plants of Enchantment —

Today, tucked into the verges of country roads and spread across the wild fields of lowland England, Wales and Ireland, thrives a herb which stands one or two feet tall, has toothed leaves and bears lilac, five-petalled flowers from July to September. Nectar is secreted below the ovary, and white hairs at the mouth of the corolla tube form a barrier to the explorations of insects. It is called vervain, or verbena, and it features often in the one-thousand-year-old healing concoctions and salves of ancient England. The Christian authorities objected to 'enchantments with herbs' such as vervain. Some of the entries in the Anglo-Saxon *Spellbook*, and other ancient sources, are revealing.

In the Old English version of the *Herbarium* of Apuleius Platonicus (one of the texts from ancient, classical sources), it is recorded that the Anglo-Saxons believed that vervain drove away all poisons and was 'said to be used by sorcerers'. In other words, the herb was part of the mystical practice of indigenous shamans who did in ancient England what shamans all around the world have done since time immemorial: healed. And in the Anglo-Saxon *Spellbook*, with rue, dill, periwinkle, mugwort, betony and other powerful herbs, vervain was an ingredient in a healing salve against the 'demons of disease'.

The medicinal qualities of herbs such as vervain were well known;

ancient European herbal practice used many plants which have, within today's scientific medicine, achieved recognition as having therapeutic qualities, and from which some modern medicines are prepared. We can even recognise the healing qualities of some of the preparations from today's everyday knowledge of medicines: for example, to cure a cough, the Anglo-Saxon *Spellbook* calls for: 'honey droppings and marche seed and dill seed. Pound the seeds small, mix into the droppings to thickness, and pepper well. Take three spoonfuls after the night's fast.' Clearly today we would recognise this as an effective intervention for breaking up congestion.

But although the application of herbal medicines aimed to heal physical ailments directly, it is clear that more was being done. Herbs were being 'enchanted' with incantations and rituals before they were prepared for use as medicines, or as they were administered to the patient. Vervain has retained some of its identity even to the present day as a herb of enchantment: one of its popular names in Wales is 'enchantment herb', or 'wizard's herb'!

— Elves' Arrows —

So vervain was being used by 'sorcerers', and it was thought to be effective against the 'demons' of disease. These demons had a specific identity, for indigenous conceptions of the causes of disease included the idea of 'elf-shot', in which the illness had been caused by the victim having been pierced by the arrows of malevolent elves, the arrows and elves being invisible to the naked eye, though believed visible to the shamans, people with special abilities and training. These theories of illness seem to refer to the 'spirit world' rather than to the material causes of organic illness as we would understand them. And the remedies to be applied by the shamans were aimed at driving the elves' arrows out of the body.

For example, the Saxon *Spellbook* has a concoction which is called, 'for a salve against the race of elves'. It is a preparation which includes a large variety of plants: 'the female hop plant, wormwood, bishop's wort, lupine, vervain, henbane, harewort, viper's bugloss, sprouts of heathberry, leek, garlic, seeds of cleavers, cockle and fennel'. The

Spellbook then instructs the shaman to 'put the herbs in a vessel', enchant them by singing incantations over them, then the mixture is boiled in butter, strained through a cloth, and the resulting salve smeared on the face and painful areas of the body to release the patient from the pain of illness caused by elves.

In England vervain garlands were worn on St John's Eve (a religious occasion established to displace a formerly important pre-Christian Midsummer festival). Another 'St John's plant' was mugwort. Common throughout lowlands in the British Isles, mugwort has divided leaves with tiny red-brown flowers which appear in July and August. Clumps of mugwort three to four feet high grow by roadsides and in hedge bottoms. It was picked, purified and strengthened in the smoke of the bonfires on St John's Eve, and then made into garlands and hung over doors to keep off, we are told, 'all the powers of evil, including the spells of sorcerers'.

But the plant also had special significance in ancient Europe not as a superstitious protection for the general populace against sorcerers, but as a plant used on behalf of the populace by sorcerers and shamans in order to counteract malevolent spells made by other spellcasters. In the Anglo-Saxon *Spellbook* a magical medical incantation called the Lay of the Nine Herbs begins with an incantation to the powers of mugwort:

> Have in mind, Mugwort, what you made known,
> What you laid down, at the great denouncing.
> Una your name is, oldest of herbs, of might
> against thirty, and against three,
> Of might against venom and the onflying,
> Of might against the vile She who fares through the land.

In the lore of incantations, the number three and its multiples was traditionally employed to construct word magic, to weave a spell, and mugwort was believed to be able to counter such attempts to send malevolent magic. Venom and the onflying, the 'She', refer to the forces of the elves, who were sometimes depicted as agents of the Wyrd Sisters, the forces of the 'She' who determined fate, as I shall explain in a later chapter.

When I first read about these concepts of flying elves and elves' arrows, I thought they were fascinating, but quaint and frankly ignorant. They appeared to superstitiously ascribe spurious causal connections between events based on fantasy; concepts that had been completely supplanted by modern scientific understanding of illness.

But as I pondered the nature of these beliefs, it began to dawn on me that they bore a strange resemblance, after all, to our contemporary lay concepts of illness. For example, it is commonly assumed that illnesses are caused by bacteria or viruses which 'invade' our bodies. These micro-organisms are invisible to the naked eye, but are indeed visible to trained specialists who, in place of the 'spirit vision' of ancestral shamans, have microscopes to enhance their perceptual capacities. There is a strangely compelling parallel between the micro-organisms and the arrows.

And when we are ill from these 'invasions', we go to a doctor, one of these people who during training has indeed seen these invisible invaders, who prescribes for us a medicine concocted out of our sight, and containing substances which for the most part we, as lay people, do not know, indicated by an unreadable Latin name.

Even the rituals of taking medicine have some faint resemblance between the cultures. For example, in the Anglo-Saxon *Spellbook*, to cure a neck tumour, the manuscript instructs the healer to take neckwort, wood-marche, wood-chervil, strawberry runners, boar-throat, cockle, ironhard gathered without iron, farthingwort, butcher's broom, broad-bishopwort and brown-wort. 'Let him collect all these plants, an equal amount of each, three nights before summer sets in, and make them with Welsh ale into a drink. And then, on the eve of the first day of summer, the man who intends to drink that drink must wake all night. And at first cock-crow let him take a drink once, at first dawn a second drink, at sunrise a third drink. And let him rest thereafter.'

The admonition to begin the healing on 'the eve of the first day of summer' must apply to the spiritual forces of the plants rather than to their material qualities. But the form of the instructions sound familiar, for when we receive the medicine, we are instructed to take it according to a detailed ritual: e.g. in a five ml spoon, three times a day, immediately after meals. Not so colourful as 'on the eve of the first day of summer' and 'at first cock crow', but nevertheless perhaps possessing some ritual potency in its very specificity.

No matter how tenuous some of them are, these parallels of form, even when the content seems radically at variance, have encouraged me to believe that in our basic ways of seeing the world we are not so far away from that of our ancestors as we normally assume. And that makes it all the more likely that we are able to learn from some of those aspects of our ancestors' belief system which do differ from our own, for their system is not entirely alien to us.

However, although there is a way in which we can see a parallel between the conception of illness of our ancestors and our own ideas today, this is only at the biologically based realm of understanding. We can see from the way in which the herbs were addressed by 'incantations' that they had a sacred nature, as well as a practical status as medicinal plants.

Certainly the sacred nature and spirit power of these enchantments were recognised by the early Christian authorities, and they developed invocations for disarming the plants of their powers. For example, St Hildegard, a twelfth-century nun, feared the indigenous sacred plants; talking of the mandrake: 'When it is dug out of the earth, at once let it be put into running water for a day and a night, and thus all ill and evil humour which is in it is expelled, so that it is thus no longer of value for magical purposes. But when it is uprooted from the ground, if then it is laid down with the earth adhering to it which has not been removed . . . then it is an evil agent for much hurtful magic.'[13]

So from this negative Christian view we can see that the mandrake plant, used for healing purposes by Wyrd shamans, was believed to retain its healing power only while still in contact with the earth. But since it was the indigenous healers who employed this power, rather than Christian monks, it was depicted as 'hurtful magic' by Hildegard. Despite their derogation of indigenous shamanic practices, as for example St Eligius's exhortation in AD 640 that 'no-one enchant herbs', we know that the practice continued.

Celandine is a commonly growing perennial, one to two and a half feet high, with yellow, four-petalled flowers and much-divided hairless leaves. It is a member of the poppy family and is easily identified by the drop of poisonous, deep orange latex which is exuded if a stem is broken. This was once used as a cure for warts, and was also believed to be a cure for sore eyes. In the Anglo-Saxon *Spellbook*, the plant gatherer is instructed to: 'Dig round a clump of celandine root, and take with thy two hands turned upwards, and sing thereover nine Paternosters; at the ninth, at "Deliver us from evil", wrench it up; and take from that shoot and from others to make a little cup full, and then saturate them, and let him be fomented by a warm fire; he will soon be better.'[14]

The spell seems to indicate that the stems be broken and the juice milked until a small cupful is obtained, and then the stems saturated, or covered with water. The patient takes the concoction and sits by the warmth of a fire. This incantation, obviously Christianised, almost certainly involved the enchantment of the plants by singing the incantations nine times (sacred to the pagans) over the plant before digging it up.

And so vervain was Christianised (confirming its continued use among the populace as a sacred herb), as in a prayer which made it a plant of Calvary: 'Hallowed be thou, Vervain, as thou growest in the ground, For in the mount of Calvary there thou was first found. Thou healedst our Saviour Jesus Christ, and stanchedst his bleeding wound; In the name of the Father, the Son, and the holy Ghost, I take thee from the ground.'

Clearly this is meant as a Christian prayer to be used by the indigenous people as they picked the plant for 'magical medicine', hopefully as a step in their conversion to Christianity, to replace the Wyrd incantations. Further, the recorder of this charm wrote that the vervain was picked, crossed with the hand, and blessed with the charm, and then worn against 'blasts', a general category of illnesses caused by 'ill winds'. From the praising lines, the indication of the herb's power in staunching bleeding wounds, and in the making the sign of the cross over the herb and blessing it with 'the charm', we get some idea of the detailed process of 'enchantment'.

— Plant-Collecting Rituals —

The indigenous peoples of Wyrd collected their herbs and plants with great care, sometimes observing strictures concerning the location for collecting, the phase of the moon, and the particular individuals who were allowed to cut the plants from the ground.

This picture is further coloured by the evidence of the Roman writer Pliny, reporting on the Celtic tribes in Britain.[15] Pliny explains that the Celts gathered vervain at sunrise after a sacrifice to the Earth 'as an expiation'. And the maladies for which vervain was used by the Celtic tribes were similarly not always of an organic nature, but more to do with psyche or spirit: Pliny says that they believed that 'When it was rubbed on the body all wishes were gratified; it dispelled fevers and other maladies; it was an antidote against serpents; and it conciliated hearts.'

There were various other procedures and taboos in collecting sacred plants, common to most ancient tribal groups. For example, Pliny also describes a herb which the Celts collected called selago (which they believed 'preserved one from accident, and its smoke when burned healed maladies of the eye') and explains that they culled it without the use of iron, and after a sacrifice of bread and wine. The person gathering it wore a white robe and went with unshod, freshly washed feet.

And yet another plant, samolus, which was placed in drinking troughs as a remedy against disease in cattle, was culled by a person fasting, and with the left hand only; it must be wholly uprooted, and the gatherer must not look behind him.

Clearly, beyond any possible, but unlikely, basis of chemical contamination of the plant chemicals by using iron to dig it up, the rituals of plant gathering and preparation for the tribal peoples had to do with the 'spirit' of the plant rather than any material aspects that we would recognise today.

The rituals used in gathering these plants were extensive including, in the above list, fasting, washing and keeping the feet bare, wearing white, not using iron, using the left hand only, uprooting the whole plant, collecting at sunrise, not looking over the shoulder, maintaining silence, and sacrificing to the plant in 'expiation'.

Expiation to whom? Or what? The plant? Many of these practices were, as I have said, later incorporated into Christian worship in order to render a new and alien religion familiar, user-friendly. The Wyrd shamanic practice of giving thanks to the plant being picked or harvested was incorporated into the Christian fold by prayer, in which thanks and praise were accorded to the plants and to the powers of the Earth: 'Ye [herbs] whom earth, parent of all, hath produced . . . this I pray, and beseech from you, be present here with your virtues, for she who created you hath herself promised that I may gather you with the goodwill of him on whom the art of medicine was bestowed, and grant for health's sake good medicine by grace of your powers.'[16]

It is remarkable that in this prayer, the source of creation of the herb was credited to the Earth in her feminine aspect apparently, for it refers to the 'she who created you' rather than to the masculine God of Christianity. Further, the plant is addressed directly, as an indigenous shamanic tradition, rather than addressing God about the plant and asking Him for His strength and blessing to be applied to the plant (as in another incantation turned into a prayer directed to God: 'Whatsoever herb thy power do[th] produce, give, I pray, with goodwill to all peoples to save them and grant me this my medicine'). The 'him on whom the art of medicine was bestowed' was in this case the shaman about to collect the herb. His direction of his thought, and heart, is to the herb he is addressing; the sacred presence he is 'expiating' is the feminine aspect of Earth: Mother Earth.

— Meditation on Plants —

Our ancestors regarded plants as special entities unto themselves, rather than as merely the 'plant materials' of today. They knew the plants to have direct organic effects, as a medical herbalism, but they were also believed to work on other levels, in other ways, to do with the spirit and the gods. No distinction seems to have been made between these two realms: plant medicines, and the sicknesses they addressed, were seen as existing simultaneously on a physical and a spiritual level. In this regard, the collecting and preparation of plants, the respecting of the plant and the offer of some 'sacrifice' in return for its benefaction, was a kind of active meditation, an attuning to the language of spirit as expressed through plants.

Today most of us do have a sense of the wonder of nature, although it is often mediated so that we encounter nature as spectators. We see, for example, the mysteries of nature being teased apart, revealed, in science documentaries on television, in which the processes of plant life are illustrated by time-release photography so that we can view the movement of the plants through their daily cycle, or even life cycle, at the speed of animal movement. Such images help us acknowledge that the plant world has movement, a rhythm of its own, but on a time scale that puts it outside our direct apprehension. When we see this movement speeded up we are able to identify with the plant more immediately, more closely.

For our ancestors, the shamans were expected to be attuned to the plants, to understand their otherworldliness. The altered states of consciousness of the shaman, the spiritual sensitivity of which shamans were possessed, provided for them a vision of the plant realm, and of the sacred presence in that world. The impeccably detailed rituals for collecting plants, and the complexity and specificity of their preparation into salves and other concoctions, are evidence enough that the shamans of old journeyed in their own way into the wonders of nature, its spirit and power.

Today we rely on plants all the time: the oxygenating of the Earth by the Amazon rainforest; the use of plant substances for making medicines; plants as food for us and for the animals that we eat; the restful and uplifting qualities of plants when given to us as bouquets of flowers, as a gift, an expression of love; as a healing presence, even if only in an aesthetically pleasing sense, when flowers are taken to patients in hospital; the use of flowers in sacred rituals as in bouquets and garlands at weddings; and as accompaniment to the Otherworld when they are placed on coffins, and at gravestones. Plants and flowers, in window boxes, gardens, parks, in the wild, accompany us and help us in myriad ways. Even though we appreciate each of these manifestations of plant presence and power, it is in a 'taking it for granted' sort of way; rarely do we ponder the greater significance of their role in our lives.

But in a personal way, perhaps the high level of awareness, respect and care which our ancestors showed to the plants in their lives might help us to realise their greater significance. One way for us today to make a small step in that direction is to work to relate, as an active meditation, with a particular plant. It could be in a park, for example, and be visited often. But even better if the plant can be encountered in a more active way, so that one is doing something to acknowledge the plant: a sacrifice, even if only of time to care for it. Probably, for most of us, there are such plants in our lives already, and many people are well aware of the therapeutic pleasures of gardening. But we do not give the matter deep thought. Selecting one plant is a simple meditation of benefit for us today; a small gift of practical awareness from our ancestors.

— The Wyrd of Sun and Moon —

For the people of Wyrd the position of the moon was another extremely important variable in collecting plants for healing purposes for it was believed to influence the state of the plant and its readiness for healing tasks. The Anglo-Saxon *Spellbook* says that the plant periwinkle must be plucked 'when the moon is nine nights old, and eleven nights, and thirteen nights, and thirty nights, and when it is one night old'. The mulberry plant must be picked 'when to all men the moon is seventeen nights old, after the meeting of the sun, ere the rising of the moon'.

This latter specification of the time of night for picking was also common. A manuscript called the *Anglo-Saxon Herbal* prescribes in the case of sea-holly: 'And when thou shalt take up this wort with its roots, then beware that no sun shine upon it, lest its beauty and its might be spoiled through the brightness of the sun.'[17] On the other hand, in another remedy, the bark from ash and oak trees must be taken from the eastern side in order to be efficacious. The east is the side of the rising sun, and perhaps the presence of the sun's heat on the growth of that portion of the tree was a material factor here.

So the alternation of night and day, darkness and light, had significance for the tribespeople's assessment of the state of a plant for collecting. But this is a detailed instance of something which manifested itself much more widely in the lives of our ancestors. The moon and sun were of symbolic significance in that they represented a fundamental polarity which permeated every sector of life, and which underlay an understanding of the balance of forces in our cosmos which is akin to the Eastern principles of yin and yang.

Although there was undoubtedly an element of worship, with its implications of awe, reverence, even love for the sun and moon, these heavenly bodies were not regarded as gods. But they did have a view, a perspective, which is fascinating for us, for in some ways the influence of the sun and moon has not altered in the fifty or so generations since the time of the Wyrd peoples; what has altered is our awareness of these influences.

In the culture of Wyrd, the passage of time was often measured in nights, and longer time spans in moons, as did the Native American peoples until much more recent times. But this counting by the moon was not simply a unit of time passed, metered out in equal measures of no particular significance, like our minutes, hours, and days. Each stage of the moon had a presence which could be felt, was acting upon the land, and upon people. We know this to be the case today, of course. The moon moves the oceans into tides, and if it can directly affect huge bodies of water, then it can certainly affect us, since we are composed of at least sixty per cent water; at least this would seem to be true in principle. Since we rarely attend to the moon's influence over our lives, there has never been a systematic programme of research on the matter.

Stories were told about the sun and moon in tribal lore. In one account there first was a woman called Night. She married a god called Shining One, and they had a son called Day. Here Night represents the feminine, Shining One (sun) the masculine, and between them they produced Day, who was also masculine. Note that for the people of Wyrd, night came first. Night was primary, the most important phase of our rhythm in which in deep darkness the imagination roams, when external images are no longer visible, and internal images come to the fore. The secondary realm of day was for more prosaic mental functions, the analytical considerations of the material world.

We have today lost the balance in our lives between these two states. Night for us is the time when we use our imaginations for recreation, as in films, theatre, and television, but psychologically it has lost its importance as a symbol of the deep imagination on a par with analytical modes of being. We value much more highly our analytical, daytime states of mind, when we can 'see what is really there' and 'get things done'. And so our lives are relatively uninformed by the intelligence of night, the power of the imaginal, the states of mind that soar when the constraints of a consensually negotiated, objective, material world are lifted.

The duality, balance, polarity was important.[18] And as the day consisted of night and day, so the year consisted of winter and summer. The year began on 31 October, All Hallow's Eve, and this marked the beginning of winter, a position on the calendar celebrated with great festivals. Winter is the dark side of the year, nature is asleep, it is a time for dreams. Then the first day of May brought in the summer, as night brings in day. Summer months were those of outdoor activities, of crop farming and animal husbandry, land clearing and building. These two festivals divided the year into two halves of six months each. Even the months themselves were made up of two parts, in the first of which the days are numbered up to fifteen and in the second up to fourteen or fifteen according to the length of the month. As in Indian and other calendars, one half was the 'bright half' of the lunar month, the other the 'dark half'.

The dividing lines between the contrasting periods of time, whether night and day, first and second halves of months, halves of the year, were charged by a power in which the fundamental principles of life and death were in balance. These liminal moments, spaces of time, were to be entered with care, and often marked with ritual attunement. Certain acts were forbidden at sunrise and at sunset because these were moments of danger; on the other hand, as we saw above, morning dew and morning water had a particular virtue, and cures could be effected by remedies sought at sunset.

This supernatural power is present in its most potent form on

November Eve and May Eve, the joints between the two great seasons of the year. These two eves (together with Midsummer's Eve) were known as 'spirit nights' and were propitious moments for the practice of divination.

In another story, the Allfather, the original sky god from early Wyrd culture, took Night and her son Day, and gave to each of them a horse and chariot and put them in the sky, so that they should ride around the world every twenty-four hours. Night rides first on a horse called Frosty-Mane, and showers of water droplets from the mane create the night dew on the surface of the Earth. Day's horse is called Shining-Mane and the whole earth and sky are illumined by the flow from his mane.[19]

Alternatively, the chariots are driven by Moon and Sun, who are depicted as being chased through the sky by powerful wolves who represent wildness, untamed forces, entropy and chaos. And one day one of the wolves will catch the moon and, in the words of one of the poems, 'he will swallow the moon and bespatter the sky and all the air with blood. Because of this the sun will lose its brightness, and the winds will then become wild and rage on every side.'[20] It is an image of the end, the time when we humans lose our balance, our attunement to both the bright and dark sides of life, and are overwhelmed by the chaos that ensues. The vision is remarkably like our nightmare conception of a nuclear holocaust: deep red sky, then darkness as the sun is blotted out, mighty winds raging on every side. Death. The vision is timeless.

The Wyrd tribespeople ascribed importance to attunement, harmony and balance between the great polarities, the forces that shape our lives. One way in which they did this was in their crop rituals.

— Festivals of the Sun and Moon —

The Earth's fertility, the fecundity with which it had 'babies', be they animal, human, crops, fruit and so on, was of prime importance in the subsistence economy of ancient Europe. This concern was expressed partly through an intimate knowledge of, and involvement in, the cycle of the seasons, the months, the weather, but also an awareness of the sacred dimension. In the spring, through dramatic metaphor,

Incantation: *Attuning to the Healing Spirits*   49

their rituals attuned to the heat of the sun and the cool of the moon in drawing sprouting seedlings from the ground.

Sun and moon festivals took place at high points in the agricultural cycle, and Bonser reports that in ancient times in Europe there were traditions which survived until very recently, especially in Germany, in which the ceremonial to bring fertility and a blessing for the coming year was about the time of the vernal equinox, and not later than 25 March.[21]

We know something of the complex ritual through the inclusion in the Anglo-Saxon *Spellbook* of, among other things, a contemporary detailed account of a shamanic invocation for fertility of the fields. This ceremony affords a remarkable glimpse of the sacred world of our ancestors; a ritual entirely comparable to the religious services around the world today.

The entire ceremony began in the cool dark of night, before dawn, and reached its climax in the rays of the setting sun at the end of the day. The activities have three aims: relating to the sun and its power over the vitality of the grass fields; invocations in honour of Mother Earth to bless the crops; and protection of the crops from damage by hostile magicians.

The *Spellbook* is clear: 'at night before daybreak take four sods from four sides of the land and mark how they stood before'. In the early hours of the morning, by the light of bright moonlight or fire torches, chunks of earth were dug up, and markers placed on them so that they could be restored later to the holes in their original positions. Still in the hours before dawn, the shaman then takes 'oil and honey and yeast and milk of all the cattle that are on the land, and part of every kind of tree growing on the land, except hard trees, and part of every well-known herb, except burdock only, and pour moonglow dew on them, and then let it drip three times on the bottom of the sods'.[22]

This is an incredible recipe. Days of preparation would be needed for collecting 'part of every kind of tree and well-known herb on the land' to enable elements of the vegetation of the land to be joined together in sacralised and ritualised form. Hard trees such as oak and beech are excluded, perhaps because they are slow-growing and are not therefore appropriate for encouraging the fertility spirit of fast-growing crops.

Moonglow dew was a sacred liquid. It sprinkled on to the Earth at night, a result of the overflow from the daily nourishing of the World Tree by the Wyrd Sisters, three sacred beings who symbolised the heart of the cosmos. And since swarming bees are represented in early European literature as the Wyrd Sisters, so the honey may also be an image of their nurturing presence. Milk and honey are offerings to the Earth in many ancient societies, and the Anglo-Saxons here added yeast and oil. 'At the first ploughing the Indians, like the Germans, offered as sacrifice milk and honey into the fields, and the Romans poured mead and honey into the earth when they dug up any herb.'[23] Oil, honey, yeast and milk were all catalysts used in cooking and fermentation; in other words, processes in which the bounty of the land was prepared and transformed for people to eat and drink. This spell itself is like a recipe, with tips for the ways in which the ingredients should be combined for maximum benefit.

The sods of earth and grass were then sprinkled three times (a sacred number) with water and the shaman chanted: 'Grow, and multiply, and fill the Earth.' In the *Spellbook*, written by Christians, the account of the ceremony has the sods being taken to a church and placed with their grassy sides facing towards the altar, while masses were sung. But historians agree that the mass is a later Christian substitution, or even just an interpolation by the Christian author of the manuscript. In the original ceremony it is likely that the sods would be taken to a sacred site, a forest sanctuary or stone circle, where they could be placed so that the first rays of the sun would strike upon the grass, and incantations would be sung rather than a mass.

The shaman then made rune-staves of slivers of 'quickbeam' (aspenwood), small strips of wood on which were engraved sacred symbols. With appropriate rune-messages carved on them he laid the rune-staves on the bottom of each of the four pits formed by cutting away the sods, so surrounding and criss-crossing the field with magical powers. Eventually the pieces of turf were brought back from the sacred site, returned to their original places, and laid on top of the rune-staves. The shaman turned to the east, with his back to the setting sun, bowed nine times, and chanted this incantation:

> To the East I stand, for the gifts of use I pray:
> So I pray the Mighty One, so I pray the Great Lord,
> So I pray the Holy One, Ward of heaven's kingdom.
> Earth I also pray and the heavens above
> And the might of heaven and its high-built Hall,
> that I may this magic spell, open from my teeth,
> through a thought firm-grasped;
>
> Waken up the swelling crops for our worldly need;
> Fill the fielded earth, and make the
> green fields beautiful.[24]

In its modern translation, the rhythm of the lines is lost, but the message is clear. The first three lines describe the kind of action the shaman is to carry out, though they look suspiciously like Christian interpolation, for the second three lines really do the business: he is invoking the powers of Earth and sky, and the 'high-built Hall', that is Woden's stronghold, through the words of a magic spell. This is not a prayer, but a formation 'through a thought firm-grasped', of sacred language to bring together the great powers of Earth and sky. And the aim is simple, to make the fields green and swell the crops for a bountiful harvest.

After chanting the incantation the shaman turned about three times 'sunwise', then stretched full length along the ground, chanting for the fields to be green for the benefit of the owner of the land and all those who were subject to him.

Parallel beliefs can be seen reflected in the more recently surviving rituals of some of the Native American peoples. Among the Pueblo Indians, 'the sun, sky, the earth, and corn play prominent roles . . . The sun is very powerful and is usually spoken of as "father" or "old man".' It is prayed to for longevity, as a hunt deity, and its warmth fertilises the field. It makes its daily journey across the sky, reaching its house in the west at sundown. Among the Hopi, planting dates are established by the 'progress of the sun toward the summer solstice; the progress itself is calibrated by the successive positions of the rising sun relative to the landmarks on the horizon. There may be no further planting after solstice.'[25]

The sun has an equally powerful influence in our contemporary agriculture, of course, but we tend to focus more on the human-generated interventions we have introduced to modify the natural processes: fertilisers, crop sprays, agri-business machinery, and so on. But for indigenous peoples across the Earth, including our own culture a thousand years ago, the task was not one of intervention, but rather one of attunement. A sensitive and sophisticated knowledge of the sun and moon patterns was vital. And anything of great import, of central concern to life, was expressed not only in the material world, but in the spiritual realms too.

One way of heightening this awareness and of taking it beyond the mechanical, the mundane, into the sacred was ceremonies such as the one described above. Of course, spiritual ceremonies of the established religions in today's world are just as heavily symbolic, ritualised and detailed as the field ceremony of the people of Wyrd. But the difference is that, even for people who subscribe to a major religion, the emphasis is more often on personal salvation, not on the external world. For dealing with the machinations of the environment, we depend upon our scientific, head-driven paradigms. We construct cause-and-effect sequences out of the stream of events, a way of apprehending and predicting life processes which lies at the heart of the empirical approach. It has led to scientific farming, with its consequent hugely increased crop yields.

But linear cause-and-effect chains alone are too narrow truly to reflect the unimaginably complex interactions of events and factors in the dynamics of agriculture, nature, life. We try to broaden our understanding, paying attention to events previously thought lateral, tangential and of no consequence. But we simply could not control enough variables, even if we could identify and understand them all, in order to engineer a satisfactorily comprehensive analysis of the processes.

We are surprised and baffled by many of the more complex ecological disasters, and can barely keep up with monitoring them, let alone developing interventions to head off their worst effects. In a world in which the rainforests are being depleted, and the ozone layer disappearing, through our actions, we can hardly have been said to have used our technological knowledge with wisdom.

In approaching a world in which our ancestors experienced layers of meaning, from the physical to the psychological to the sacred, we can do so nowadays in a more open-minded way than we might have some decades ago. For then, we had the arrogance of certainty, of believing that civilisation progresses in historically linear fashion, and that we had solved the problems of the ancients through our technology. We have indeed achieved some wonders, but our technology needs to be embedded in a deeper view of its purpose and its use, a view which might be better informed about the psychological and the sacred, rather than the merely physical, material gain.

We need to rediscover some of our ancestors' sense of an engagement with the environment which goes beyond the mundane, and reach some wisdom of perspective and scale about our ability to intervene in the processes of the natural world in which our technology is rendered puny and dwarfed by the influences of the sun and moon.

— The Monks Do a Rain Dance —

Despite the decrees of Wulfstan, proclaiming the errors of the ways of our indigenous ancestors, not all monks were quite so dismissive, especially when they were desperate. Adomnan, in his *Life of St Columba*, says:

> About fourteen years before the date at which we write, there occurred during the spring a very great and long continued drought in the marshy regions . . . We therefore . . . took counsel together, and resolved that some of the senior members of the community [i.e. Iona] should walk round a newly ploughed and sown field, taking with them the white tunic of St Columba, and some books written in his own hand, that they should raise in the air and shake three times the tunic which the saint wore at the hour of his death . . . When these directions had been executed . . . copious rain fell day and night, and the parched earth . . . yielded the same year a most abundant harvest.[26]

Successful! And if Dark Age monks, locked in battle with indigenous shamans, could profit from borrowing the rituals of Wyrd, then I hope that we can benefit from at least some of their principles.

Chapter Three

Guardians:
Learning From the Power Animals

— Heeding the Crow's Message —

Edwin was a tribal chieftain who came to power in AD 617, ruling over peoples in an area of northern England called Northumbria. The incident I am about to recount introduces the beliefs of our ancestors concerning the spirits of animals, but in order for you to appreciate the story, I have to tell you first a little of the political and religious intrigue surrounding Edwin.[1]

At the time that Edwin became King of Northumbria there had been a period of inter-tribal warfare between rival chieftains. These troubles were ended, temporarily, by Edwin, who became the head of a confederation of English kings which omitted only the south-east corner of the land, a kingdom called Kent. Unfortunately, Edwin was ambitious to control that tribal area also, and so, to extend his power to the entire island, Edwin proposed a marriage of convenience with Aethelburga, the daughter of the King of Kent.

But the leaders of Kent had been converted to Christianity, and they said that it would be improper for their Christian princess to marry a pagan. Edwin pressed his claim. He not only promised that she and her retinue would be allowed to practise their faith in Northumbria, but that he himself would consider converting to Christianity if the marriage were allowed. The King of Kent sent from Canterbury his leading missionary, Paulinus, to Edwin's court in Northumbria to teach the Christian ways to Edwin, and the overlord of England was baptised on Easter Eve 627. His renunciation of Wyrd for the Christian religion proved to be his downfall.

Edwin removed his shaman advisers and appointed in their place a Christian bishop and other functionaries to carry out the establishment of the Christian Church in his kingdom, as he had agreed. And he decreed that the populace of Northumbria should all become Christian; mass baptisms were carried out in the rivers, though it is unlikely that his subjects took the ritual seriously.

The incident I want to narrate happened on a Sunday, when Edwin was on his way to church, accompanied by his bishop and retinue, to carry out the religious instruction of those of his long-suffering people who were still 'heathen'. As Edwin and his companions strode down the street, a crow suddenly perched in a tree nearby and 'sang with an evil intent'. The whole company stopped in the street to listen to it, transfixed. Amongst the tribal peoples of ancient Europe, ravens and crows were regarded as animals with powers of divination, who were able to deliver messages and omens to shamans who could understand their language, especially in the foretelling of matters of life and death.

The European pre-Christian god Woden (Wotan in Germanic lands, Odin in Scandinavia) had two 'spirit animals' in the form of ravens: 'Upon this brooding Odin's shoulders perch the two ravens Huginn and Muninn; they whisper into his ears every scrap of news which they see or hear tell of . . . At crack of dawn he pushes them off to flap all around the world and they return in time for second breakfast. This is the source of much of his information, and the reason why men call him the Raven god.' Odin's ravens were named Thought and Memory. They were symbols of the spirit of the seer or shaman, sent out over vast distances and returning with important messages.

So Edwin and his retinue, recently converted to Christianity but still, of course, indigenous people with all the beliefs that entailed, were scared. Edwin was faced with a singing crow, but no longer had shamans with his party. There was no one to translate the message from the bird, and to decipher for whom the message was intended. Bishop Paulinus, seeing the fear on the faces of the chieftain and his native entourage, realised that drastic action was called for to preserve the veneer of Christianity which Edwin and his followers struggled to maintain. Swiftly he gave the order to a servant: 'Shoot an arrow carefully into the bird.'

Paulinus brought the dead bird and arrows into the hall and, brandishing them to the heathen populace, proclaimed that this 'proved that they should know by so clear a sign that the ancient evil of idolatry was worthless to anybody', since the bird 'did not know that it sang of death for itself' and so could not prophesy anything for those 'baptised in the image of God'. In other words, a bird which could not even foretell its own imminent death probably could not prophesy anything at all, and the heathens should abandon their beliefs in such Wyrd things as they became baptised into the Christian faith.

However, it is unlikely that the populace were impressed by his demonstration of the futility of heathen beliefs. For one thing, to shoot a bird with an arrow is no mean feat unless the bird is motionless at a very short distance; it had obviously perched close to the people, unafraid of Paulinus's warriors. Paulinus assumed that had the crow known it was going to be shot it would have tried to save its life by flying away. But if this was a crow whose presence was as a 'spirit messenger', it would not, in the eyes of the populace, have been afraid of death in the material world. Its task may well have been to give a warning to Edwin, but the crow's message went unheard and unheeded by the king. A shaman present might, the indigenous people believed, have given Edwin an interpretation of what the crow was saying, some inkling of what was in store for him and allowed him to take precautions.

A parallel story, from the preceding century, foreshadowed Edwin's fate; in about AD 500 a singing crow sitting on a tree was interpreted by a shaman as prophesying to Hermigisel, King of the Warni, that the king would die within forty days. The event happened as prophesied.

The crow killed and brandished by Paulinus proved to be equally accurate in its prognostications, had they been interpreted for Edwin, for soon after the above-recorded event, King Edwin was killed by a pagan assassin, Bishop Paulinus and the other Christian missionaries fled the kingdom, and the populace renounced their official baptisms and returned to the way of Wyrd.

To our ears, this story sounds like a catalogue of coincidences and superstition; a connecting of events which, while happening in some temporal proximity, really had no cause-and-effect relation with each other. To understand the way of Wyrd, we need to open our minds to our ancestors' very different way of perceiving, experiencing and encountering the animal world.

— The Animal Spirits —

Evidence for the ubiquitous presence of animals in the psychological and sacred life of the early Europeans comes in the annals of Tacitus, describing for the elite of Rome the ways of life of the indigenous peoples living on the periphery of the Roman Empire. He reports that the tribespeople often wore animal skins as outer garments, including those of sea creatures, and that on whole pelts they also sewed small fragments of other skins.[2] These decorated animal skins probably had a symbolic importance.

In many recently surviving indigenous cultures the concept of animal species which were personal and tribal 'guardians' is widespread and potent. The spirit of the animal accompanied the person, or could be called to help the individual; everyone is believed to have such protective help from the spirit world, although the shaman may have a greater number of guardian animals, and a more articulate relationship with them. The guardian spirit is sometimes called the 'tutelary spirit' in anthropological literature on Siberian shamanism, and the 'nagual' in Mexico and some other South American traditions.

The common term for these guardian animals, or essences, in the tribal peoples of Wyrd was the 'fetch'. It was a kind of shadow self, and cultural historian Hans Peter Duerr reckons the etymology of the worlds relating to it suggest 'fulga', 'skin, cover', i.e. the 'clothing of an animal'.[3] This 'spirit skin' could detach from the body, and travel vast distances. Often shamans, who were believed to be able to journey to the spirit world in the form of their own spirit, were helped in these journeys by their guardian animals, who sometimes 'lent' their animal form. Amongst recently surviving tribes in Siberia, for example, shamans wore symbolic bird costumes.[4]

Tribal peoples wore emblems of their guardian animals, usually their skins, in sacred festivals and shamanic healing rituals. The early Germanic tribespeople may have been wearing the talismanic body parts of their animal guardians, identifying themselves with their animals by fastening small pieces of their pelts to their clothing.

Animals and birds were believed to be able to deliver warnings and messages to people, especially those of spirit-sensitive abilities, such as shamans. But the animals did not always appear in material form, like the crow in Edwin's story. Sometimes they could speak directly to the recipient in visions or dreams.

In the ancient Icelandic saga of Njal, for example, Njal himself often has predictive dreams. However, he also has the ability to receive messages of this kind while in a waking state, as though he can slip in and out of the dreamtime. In the saga, Njal cannot sleep, for he is being visited by visions of menacing shapes, the fetches of Gunnar's enemies, who have massed in a nearby wood on their way to murder the hero. Back in the waking, real world, a shepherd arrives who has seen men lurking in the wood, confirming Njal's premonition. Thus forewarned of the danger, Njal warns Gunnar, whose doom is postponed through this visionary intervention. In another dream, a character called Hoskuld looked into his own visions and recognised Gunnar by seeing his fetch alone, without the corroborating evidence of a 'material world' sighting of him.[5]

— Guardian Animals —

Some animal spirits were especially favoured as guardians because of their particular qualities (although this was not always the main criterion). Sacred animals in Anglo-Saxon tribes included boar, who were admired for their strength and their reproductive prowess; the bear; the stag, who had nature fertility connections; and of course the raven and crow.[6] In other tribal groups guardian spirits appeared as bears, wolves, stags, hares, all kinds of birds (especially the goose, eagle, owl and crow), serpents and snakes, but also as phantoms and other forms.[7] These helping spirits in animal form play an important role in many aspects of shamanic healing and ritual.

The boar was one of the most widely regarded wild creatures among the tribespeople of early Europe. In the famous Anglo-Saxon seventh-century poem *Beowulf* the warrior heroes are pictured as wearing metal headgear for battle, or for ceremonial purposes, which are decorated with images of the boar:

> Boar images shone
> over cheek protectors
> adorned with gold,
> radiant and fire-hardened-spirit guardianship
> the war minded boar held for the resolute warriors.[8]

The Anglo-Saxon scholar Stephen Glosecki analysed the lines of *Beowulf*, and concludes that the words used in Anglo-Saxon in the poem to denote the animal designate living things; they mean 'boar-body' and not 'boar-like'. With these terms goes the connotation that these bodies are animated, no matter what material they happen to be made from. Further, he confirms that the images so represented are suffused with sympathetic properties, in which the boar body brings boar power to the man beneath the helmet. The word usage suggests that the boar helmet is a living thing, with life force of its own. The boar on the helmet is clearly a 'spirit helper'.

Glosecki proposes that, in common with more recently surviving shamanic cultures, the Anglo-Saxon tribespeople regarded their soul as something which needed to be guarded, something which could be lost or stolen. So while the material helmet might help the warrior guard against physical blows to the head, the boar crest would perform the equally important task of warding off assaults upon the warrior's ethereal soul form from unseen but extremely powerful enemies lurking in the spirit realm.

The evidence of Anglo-Saxon poetic references suggests also that they believed there was a separation of body and soul. The soul could be lost (causing illness or death), stolen, or separated from the body and sent out on missions into the spirit world by specially trained shamans who knew the techniques required for achieving spirit flight.

Another way in which the presence of 'spirit' in war apparel was recognised and acted upon lies in the common practice of destroying the weapons of defeated enemies. Historian of religion Hilda Ellis Davidson describes the kind of destruction which took place: 'many articles were deliberately damaged: swords bent and broken, shields and coats of mail cut in pieces, stones forced into metal vessels and also hurled at the objects as they lay on the ground. At Illerup weapons had been burned on a pyre and then smashed and bent before being carried to a pool in the bog.' After battle, war gear was ritualistically 'killed' to get rid of the residual spirits of the slain enemies, placed there by the shamans and magical weapon smiths of the opposing tribes. This explains why otherwise valuable helmets, swords and coats of mail were destroyed rather than being plundered.[9]

Another animal highly prized as a spirit animal was the bear. At first glance the reason for this seems obvious, for the bear was the largest and probably supreme fighting animal roaming in those times in western and northern Europe. But a closer consideration of the qualities of the bear suggests other factors, other ways of regarding the significance and sacred use of the essence of the bear. For one thing, the fact that the bear makes its den in the earth, and seems to live *in* the earth during winter hibernation, suggests a shaman-like passage between Middle Earth and the Lowerworld, or the realm of the living and the realm of the dead. Its subterranean den is an entrance to the Underworld; its 'long hibernation demonstrates knowledge of life and death; its reappearance in the spring with green shoots and summer birds links it closely to the fertility of mother earth, in whose womb it waits out winter'.[10]

Kenneth LaBudde considered the nature of the bear in literature, and his conclusions, in the light of the sacred significance of the animal for the people of Wyrd, prompt a fresh perspective on this animal and the ways in which such creatures were regarded by our ancestors. In northern and western Europe, where there are no ape or monkey populations, no other wild animal is so anthropomorphic. The bear performs a range of human-like actions: it rears up and walks human-like on two legs, and sits down squarely on its haunches with its back resting against a tree. It eats omnivorously, as do humans, and it has quite a wide range of facial expressions of apparently emotional states.[11]

Further, LaBudde points out that the bear, unlike other animals, walks on the sole of its foot with the heel touching the ground and leaves a footprint of a heel, toe and arch like that of a human being. The bear has other human-like traits too. Its head and ears – more rounded than those of most other animals – resemble the features of man. The mewling of cubs sounds remarkably like the crying of human infants; and the grown bear has an unusually wide range of vocalisation, including a human-sounding high-pitched whine. Rhys Carpenter, in a study of the presence of the bear in folk-tales and ancient epics, is another author identifying the bear's anthropomorphic traits: 'because of . . . his erect gait, his swinging arms, his human footprint, the bear seems half human.'[12]

Similarity to humans is not quite the point of these remarks, because the early Europeans used images of many kinds of animals as representative token of their spirit guardians, and clearly some of them (e.g. the snake) bore much less comparison with human life than does the bear. But what is important is the extent to which our rather stereotyped and simple impressions of wild animals today have strayed from the more detailed, more sympathetic, even empathetic relations with the animals which must have characterised the approach of the Wyrd people.

It was not simply the size or ferocity of an animal which appealed and spoke to them but many other subtle features, some of which identified the animal, like the bear, remarkably closely with that of the human. Such parallels render it easy to imagine the kind of comradeship engendered between the person of the Wyrd culture and the essence of the bear.

— The Animal Within —

In the ancient Irish tale of Tuan mac Cairill, the hero describes his transformation into an animal briefly but vividly: 'I fasted my three days as I had always done. I had no strength left. Then I was from hill to hill, and from cliff to cliff, guarding myself from wolves, for twenty-two years . . . and I was hairy, clawed, withered, grey, naked, wretched, miserable. Then, as I was asleep one night, I saw myself passing into the shape of a stag. In that shape I was young and glad of heart.'[13]

The belief that people could be transformed into animals, at least in spirit form, featured in many areas of tribal life, including battle, and in shamanic journeying.

In warfare, the essence of animals was sought to enhance the physical capabilities of the human. In the early cultures of Europe there was a special class of warriors, common to many tribal groups, who were rather like the later Japanese samurai. The outstanding feature of these warriors was the ferocity with which they fought, in a kind of raging trance, and the psychological preparation for battle of these people echoes too the samurai tradition, or the more recent martial arts. But what distinguishes these early European warriors from more recent Oriental traditions is that the people of Wyrd fought as animals.

These warriors were called berserks or berserkers; literally the forerunner of the modern word, which means to go 'out of control'. But the beserkers were controllably out of control. They were 'shapechangers', who took on animal form, and the original meaning of the word berserk was 'bear shirt', indicating that they were 'clothed' with the spirit-skin of the animal they were inspired by: the bear. Certainly they fought without the usual armoury. In the *Ynglinga Saga*: 'Odin had his men fight without a mail shirt in battle and made it that they raged like dogs or wolves. They would bite into their shields, and they were as strong as bears or bulls; they killed the men, but neither fire nor iron could injure them; this is what people called the berserker rage.'[14]

A man who had been a berserker in his youth, called Ulf, and who had been inspired in his fighting rage by the spirit of the wolf, apparently was possessed by the spirit long after his fighting career was over: 'Every day towards evening he would become so surly, not many people could engage him in conversation. As it became dark, drowsiness would overcome him. There were stories that during the night, he often roamed about in a changed shape (*hammrammr*). People called him *Kveldulfr*, meaning evening wolf.' In the morning, they said, 'he lay in bed, totally exhausted.'[15]

For truly shamanic warriors, however, the transformation into animal form went further than merely imitation, no matter how totally convincing and invincible. 'Bothvar Biarki, the celebrated champion of King Hrolf of Denmark, was said to fight in the form of a great bear in the ranks of the king's army, while his human form lay at home and seemed asleep.'[16]

This was the true nature of the shaman's transformation: to shapeshift in order not necessarily to appear elsewhere in the material world, but to adventure into the spirit world. 'Odin could change himself,' writes Snorri Sturluson. 'His body then lay as if sleeping or dead, but he became a bird or wild beast, a fish or a dragon, and he journeyed in the twinkling of an eye to far-off lands, on his own errands or those of other men.' In *Ynglinga Saga* Snorri emphasises Odin's skill in magic lore, and his power of shape-changing.[17] Here he brings out the shamanistic characteristics of Odin, who like the shaman had the power not only to ride upon an animal but to send forth his spirit in animal forms. This is a characteristic shamanic way of entering the Otherworld of animals: becoming their essence, either as biological or mythological animals, and travelling to other realms in their form in order to carry out shamanic healing tasks.

In more recently surviving shamanic cultures, similar processes are seen at work. Shamans can leave their body physically, while another aspect of themselves becomes the animals and roams and travels and performs all sorts of important shamanic tasks. Usually their presence is manifested by the shaman imitating animal cries or behaviour. In north-east Siberia, the Tungus shaman, who has a snake as a helping spirit, attempts to imitate the reptile's motions during the healing ritual; Eskimo shamans turn themselves into wolves; Lapp shamans move as wolves, bears, reindeer, fish.

Often the shaman works in animal skins as, for example, the hide and horns of a stag. The purpose of the shaman is to embody the essence of the animal. Part of this is in accurate mimicking of the movements, gait, sounds of the animal; part is entering a trance state in which the animal is subsumed as part of the shaman, and the spirit of the animal species enters and becomes as one. In appearance, this shamanic imitation of the actions and voices of animals can pass as 'possession'. But it would be more accurate to term it a 'taking possession of his helping spirits by a shaman'. It is the shaman who 'turns himself' into an animal. Another way of articulating the transformation is to speak of the shaman as having a new identity, an animal spirit who speaks, sings, or flies like the animals and birds.[18]

— Animal Images —

All this presents a picture of human-animal relations amongst our ancestors which is very different from that of today. To summarise their viewpoint: many species of animals could serve as 'guardians' or helpers for people, and that in their 'spirit' form they could be summoned in times of need. Shamans, people who specialised in dealings with the spirit worlds, might have a large number of guardian animals.

There were a number of ways in which these relationships with the spirit of animals could be manifested. One was that birds such as crows and ravens could deliver messages and omens which were intelligible to shamans. Also, tribal peoples wore the skins of their special animals to maintain connection with them, especially during sacred rituals. Some warriors were able to take on the spirit of brave-fighting animals, and they carried with them amulets and crests which were believed to be the living essence of the animal spirit, and transferred to the warrior the power of the animal itself.

Shamans were helped to go on their 'journeys into the spirit world' by their guardian animals, and sometimes wore animal-skin costumes, especially of birds, to gain close identification with those helping creatures. In fact, their experiences were akin to their being 'possessed' by the spirit of the animals.

What can we make of all this today? Our relationship with animals has changed enormously over the centuries. Perhaps the closest animal relationships most of us develop are with domesticated animals, such as a pet dog or cat, or when we own a horse. Pet dogs and cats become 'part of the family'. We get to know them as individual personalities: to predict their behaviour, to recognise consistencies, to realise when they are ill or out of sorts. And in modelling in our minds their needs and motivations, we sometimes ascribe to them certain human-like characteristics.

But on a dimension of inter-species communication, relationships with pets are obviously only a dipping of the toe in the water. Our ancestors, as in the examples above, had a much more involved and involving perception of the animals in their environment. Humans depended on animals to enable them to journey to the spirit world. In the culture of our ancestors, animals were our guides, our guardians, our teachers.

In bridging the gap between contemporary views and those of the past, it is sometimes informative to set aside the differences that divide us from our ancestors, and to recognise that in some ways, beneath our level of awareness, we still retain aspects of this ancient view, this intimate connection with the symbolic power of animals. Ancient ways run deeper than we realise.

For example, in contemporary society we live for the most part separated from wild animals. And yet twenty minutes on any busy street demonstrates just how potent still are images of animals in gripping our imagination, stirring our emotions, and changing our behaviour. The power of these images is exploited every day by the advertising industry on posters as well as on television and in magazines to help to sell every conceivable product. For example, car advertisements, especially those targeted at male buyers, come with an image aimed at our deepest inner needs: the cars have animal names, wild personas such as the Chevy Impala. The Ford Mustang. The Cougar. The Jaguar. These are not animal names drawn at random. There is no such car as the Chevrolet Parrot, or the Ford Frog. Automobile companies know that, for European and, especially, North American men, the images of fast and powerful animals help to sell cars. The vehicles themselves are bigger, heavier, faster and more powerful than the animals whose image is appropriated to sell them, but it is the psychological connection with the animals that people are seeking. Cougars, Mustangs and Jaguars roar, buck and kick down the highway, while research confirms that men see their vehicles as expressions of their personal identity. So a man driving a car called a Cougar takes upon himself something of the identity of that impressive animal. We wear our cars like animal skins.

Today, for us to experience the sensation of the spirit of the jaguar, its strength, speed and style, we have to build a machine to ride in and call it a Jaguar. But to sit in a car called Jaguar and drive to work in it is a transient and fairly weak form of identification. In shamanistic cultures, this was all done much more directly, and so had a more profound impact on the way a person lived their life. Our ancestors changed themselves physically, psychologically and spiritually to take on as much as possible of the essence of the animal.

To dress in an animal skin of a jaguar, to imitate its walk, its growl, its threat movements, and to meditate on its inner nature until some form of communication is set up with the cougar spirit would be, in our terms, a remarkable psychological transformation. For a modern executive to go through this will give him much more animal power than driving to work in a machine with the label Jaguar on the front!

The biologist Barry Lopez has characterised our distance from the animal world as a failure, a breakdown of what was once a spirit of reciprocity with our fellow creatures. We once thought of animals as belonging with us in a realm beyond the material, one 'structured by myth and moral obligation, and activated by spiritual power'. He proposes that our departure from this original conception was founded in Cartesian dualism – the animal became a soulless entity with which people could have no moral relationships.

We have lost our relationship with animals in two ways. One is that we are no longer in everyday contact with them; our attitudes towards animals have become those of owners and our knowledge skewed because we no longer meet with them, and rarely enter their landscapes. The second is, in Lopez's terms, a failure of imagination. We have lost our understanding of the place of awe and mystery in adult life. We have banished animals from our minds, as though they were not capable of helping us with our predicaments. He suggests that we will never find a way back to our sacred roots until we 'find a way to look the caribou, the salmon, the lynx, and the white-throated sparrow in the face, without guile, with no plan of betrayal ... our loss of contact with them leaves us mysteriously bereaved.'[19] If we could re-establish a degree of connection, identification, respect and even a sense of the sacred presence of animals, I think we would feel revivified both individually and as a species. But how?

— The Practice of Shapeshifting —

In attempting to understand the indigenous view of animals, and accommodate it within the frame of our contemporary thinking, we can imagine pretending to be an animal. Indeed, in various experiential shamanic workshops people frequently attempt a process of such imagining, although usually in a superficial manner, by 'finding their power animal' in a simple guided imagery exercise, and then 'dancing' it. The principle of this work is sound: a direct attempt to gain a sense understanding of an animal, an emotional bond, and perhaps identify with its spirit, an elementary mimicking of the animal connections of our ancestors. Done with commitment and discipline, this can be a valuable process. But done superficially it simply confirms our casual attitude towards the animal world, and our propensity to use animals like a psychological fast-food dispenser: instant guardian animal.

But believing that this sort of imaginative process is worth a more serious effort, and in the light of the dramatically different view of animals of our ancestors, I worked with a small group of people on a six-month project aimed at establishing a deep degree of rapport with an animal, or animal species. This was a rich meditation, and became a profound experience of self-knowing for the participants, much more so than we had anticipated at the outset. The principles of the work are fairly straightforward, and I shall describe some of it here, for you may like to adapt parts of it for your own explorations into the realm of animal powers.

We began by exploring the 'animal history' of the participants. Each person wrote an autobiographical journal detailing their relations with animals, including family pets; wild animals they had encountered (one participant had helped to rescue a crow with a broken wing when he was ten years old, and after it had been released back into the wild the bird had stayed in the vicinity of their family house, visiting the boy, and perching on his shoulder); fictional animals (the famous novel *Black Beauty* had haunted the younger years of one of the participants); dreams, especially recurring dreams about animals, specific incidents and images, and so on. Each of the participants in this work filled at least one large sketchbook with writing, drawings, diagrams, notes, published information, and photographs.

We then did a series of workshops aimed at tapping personal connections with animals that were beneath the level of conscious memory, including imaginal 'journeys' with the help of drumming, in which the participants imagined themselves travelling in a landscape of their own creation, encountering any animals that came along. The rhythmic drumming, like the monotonous beat of shamanic ritual, drives the imagination along, so that long journeys of thirty minutes or more can be sustained without the mind wandering or concentration flagging (you can help your imagination work by using one of the commercial drumming tapes that are available in shops, and which can be listened to through earphones). Participants wrote detailed accounts of their journeys and the animals they encountered, many of which were surprising and not necessarily directly connected with 'real world' life experiences that the participants could recall.

All the participants devoted time to being with animals of all kinds, observing them, listening to them, feeding them. This involved treks into wilderness areas, visits to wildlife parks and breeding zoos, bird sanctuaries, scuba diving, and also spending time with domestic animals.

Following this preparation period of a month or so, some of the participants began to develop strong ideas about which kind of animal they felt drawn towards, and would like to work with in an attempt to establish a close connection. Sometimes these ideas arose spontaneously as strong feelings, obsessions, even. Other people had powerful dreams, in which the animal vividly presented itself to the person, essentially choosing the human, rather than the other way around. Some of the participants made themselves ready for the animal to choose them during a weekend retreat specifically for this purpose, in which there was concentrated time for reading their journals, preparing themselves through meditation, and then undertaking a final journey with live drums, one in which the task of the participant was to allow an animal to come to him or her.

Once each person had an animal, the process of accompanying the animals began in earnest. Most participants found it easier to concentrate on one individual animal, but sometimes other animals of the same species were useful too. And in weekly workshops we heard descriptions and stories about the animal visits and, especially, began a programme of being the animal. This started as movement mimicry, in which the individual would attempt to show us the gait, sounds, movements of the chosen animal, and as the weeks went by, these sessions began to take on a powerful, transformational, almost eerie air, as the participants progressed beyond stereotypical movement patterns which merely sketched the animal's presence, and began to build the ability to get inside the animal.

Surprisingly, human body limitations did not appear to be an encumbrance, for after a time the presence of the animal in the person's depiction was a psychological essence, in some cases spirit presence. Some of the work was fantastic, and the transformations remarkable. Images are still vivid in my mind of one woman, of only average size, who developed a connection with a bear who lived at Regent's Park Zoo in London. When she walked into the room, on all fours, and then sat back on her haunches, she *was* a bear. The speed, the rhythm, the gait, the balance and sense of size and weight, use of eyes and nose, head angles, everything was perfect. And yet her 'performance' transcended mimicry; it was much more than the sum of its parts. There was a palpable sense of bear presence, a spirit in the room which was not the woman, but the woman-with-bear-spirit.

Equally remarkable work was done with a crow, a snake, and a squirrel. The participants found the work exciting, challenging, emotionally moving, and personally liberating, for work of this concentration drew on aspects of themselves they had not known existed. This sequence of workshops is the closest thing I have witnessed in a contemporary Western culture to a state of being in attunement with animal spirit. I found it exhilarating.

— Heeding the Crow Today —

A woman once approached me for advice on a disturbing experience she had had with a crow. One morning she had risen from bed, went to her living room window and opened the curtains. And there, lying on the balcony of her apartment, was a large, black crow, apparently dead. She was transfixed by the corpse of the large bird. Its very physical presence was upsetting, but it also seemed a harbinger of something, an omen, a terrible visitation from another realm. She dared not touch it, or even open the doors and go near it. She closed the curtains, willing it to go away, to be merely stunned or ill and undergoing recovery. But when she opened them again several hours later, it was still there, motionless.

She was not normally a superstitious person, she told me, and was rather shocked that she had been so gripped by the experience. She confessed her distress to her friends and colleagues, who had tried to comfort her by advising her to remove the corpse as soon as possible, and not to be haunted by the oracular reputation of the species. A friend disposed of the bird for her. But she still could not rest. She was agitated, nervous, and not at all her usual mature, professional self.

By the time she saw me, about a month had passed since the incident, and she urgently needed some help in exorcising the bird from her life. At first she thought that perhaps she might, with my encouragement, adopt some sort of ritual which would rid her of it. But the more I listened to her, the more I became convinced that the reason she was so locked on to the image of the dead bird and its possible oracular significance was because she was trying to reach, within herself, some knowledge that was hidden from her; crucial information about her life that she desperately wanted to obtain, but which was invisible. She wanted an oracle, an omen.

And when I encouraged her to see the bird as a gift, a messenger which had died bringing her important information, her attitude changed completely. The bird became an ally, not an enemy. But then, what if the information was bad: a portent of serious illness, or loss of a loved one? Doubt set in again. But we talked about the value of omens, whether they were seen, as with our ancestors, as information from another realm, or as we might see them today, as images or incidents which draw from within us knowledge which we already have, but which we cannot reach. She meditated on the bird's purpose, listened for a message, and heard clearly, she said, a portent of a threat to her health. It was quite straightforward. She went to her doctor for a check-up, was diagnosed as having breast cancer, underwent treatment, and was cleared of the illness.

When I heard the outcome, I asked her if she thought the bird had drawn bodily knowledge from her unconscious; that she already knew, deep down, that she might need treatment. She said, 'No.' She believes the crow came from another realm, and died bringing her information which saved her life.

CHAPTER FOUR

Mother Earth:
Freeing the Flow of Life Force

— Mother Earth —

For nearly two thousand years, a peat bog in western Denmark held the clue to one of the most remarkable rituals of ancient Europe.[1] Unearthed from the bog, where they had lain preserved for all that time, were two beautiful and intricately carved wooden two-seater carts. The carts had four slender wooden wheels, and a frame covered with symbolic carved details, expertly chipped and sliced from the solid wood. Also recovered from the warm, womb-like protection of the peat bog was a small alder-wood stool, which was the seat for the person riding in one of the wagons. Except that it was not a *person* riding in the wagon; rather, the wagons were occupied by the Earth Goddess. And buried with the sacred carts were a number of objects, such as clay vessels, and pieces from upright looms, which were characteristic of the tools used by women in their work . . . or even their rituals. This was not an isolated find, for similar carved and decorated wagons from ancient times have been discovered in locations all over Europe.

The procession in which Mother Earth rode in the wagons introduces our ancestors' concept of the feminine, and will lead us into an exploration of the nature of life force.

In the early years of the first millennium the city state of Rome, which was remarkably 'modern' in many of its perspectives, served as a kind of forerunner of the Western society we recognise today. They had an impressively advanced understanding of engineering and building, a rationally organised civil service system, and disciplined military. Their relationship to the inhabitants of the rest of western Europe was in some ways rather like a developed Western nation today in comparison with a Third World indigenous society, except that in those days we were the indigenous peoples, the 'savages' living on the untamed further reaches of the empire. Fortunately for us, attempting to weave together the wisdom of Wyrd from threads gathered at a distance of two thousand years, the Romans meticulously recorded in writing their observations and impressions of these wild people.

A Roman official named Tacitus was one of those charged with documenting the customs of the natives and, in his account called *Germania*, written in the year AD 98, he tells us that the Angli and other tribes living along the west coast of the Baltic, in what is today southern Denmark and northern Germany, participated in 'the common worship of Nerthus, that is Mother Earth'. *Germania* provides the fullest account of the early use of the symbolically carved wagons: 'On an island in the Ocean sea there is a sacred grove wherein waits a holy wagon covered by a drape,' writes Tacitus. 'One priest only is allowed to touch it. He can feel the presence of the goddess when she is there in her sanctuary.' This escort accompanies the wagon 'with great reverence' when at the appointed time of the year it is drawn from the island and pulled by oxen around the tribal lands.

Mother Earth, hidden in her wagon, was fêted wherever she went: 'It is a time of festive holiday-making in whatever place she deigns to honour with her advent and stay.' Clearly Mother Earth brought peace; wherever the wagon was pulled, 'No one goes to war, no one takes up arms, in fact every weapon is put away: only at that time are peace and quiet known and prized until the goddess, having had enough of people's company, is at last restored by the same priest to her temple.'

From Tacitus's commentary it sounds as if the goddess's stays in any one location were for a substantial period; certainly more than hours, more probably days, and perhaps even weeks, since 'no one goes to war' during her stay. The sight of these carved and draped wagons being wheeled about from village to village must have been common all over western Europe, presumably on days or seasons especially appointed for the ritual. We know that the Earth Goddess ceremony thrived in at least seven major tribal groups, reaching as far as south-eastern Europe where Cybele, the Syrian goddess of fruitfulness, was similarly borne round the countryside, and St Martin in the fourth century AD tells of Cybele's image, covered with white curtains, carried round the fields in ancient Gaul. So Nerthus and her corresponding deities transcended not only tribal groups, but also entire peoples.

The people believed that Mother Earth was in some way present, hidden in the wagon, and the role of the 'priest', more like a figure we would recognise today as a shaman, was to interpret her messages to the communities being visited.

Mother Earth embodies the power of the feminine. Or rather, she symbolises it, for she has no physical body. She is materially invisible. But she is imaged as a woman, and she is accompanied by a priest, not a priestess. It is the masculine, indeed the sacralised masculine of a priest, who ritually consults the goddess, and attends to her needs. She is kept in reserve in a secret place, an island, inured from the warring aggression of the masculine aspect of the cultural psyche. And when necessary, or more likely at periods in harmony with the moon calendar, she is literally wheeled out.

The Earth Mother is the ultimate power, and it is only when she is 'present' that the fighting stops. It is more than just a suspension of inter-tribal skirmishing, it is a change of mind, of heart, from the usual. Mother Earth seems to allow light into darkness; she is consulted by the masculine, and dominates it, reigns over it when she is present, so that the masculine vices are curbed, suspended.

Although Mother Earth is treated with 'reverence' by the escorting shaman and the advent of the 'peace' is greatly welcomed, it is not a po-faced and ultra-serious occasion; Tacitus says that it is a time of 'festive holiday-making' wherever Nerthus deigns to stay. Clearly the arrival of the forces of the feminine in such a powerful guise provokes celebration, almost as if the masculine-dominated world of war and battle craves it, and suffers from the curse of strife to be lifted only when the power of peace from the feminine is present. And at the end of the visitation, when by implication the forces of the masculine begin to dominate once again, one assumes that eventually the weapons reappear.

So what do we make of this image of the invisible goddess on a sacred 'round', accompanied by a priest serving her needs, and bringing peace wherever she stayed? First of all, she is clearly an extremely powerful force for peace, and she represents the feminine. There are two aspects to this. One is the archetypal, the mythological, in which certain tendencies and perspectives, energies and passions, are characterised as feminine or masculine, but which are present in all of us to varying degrees. The other is the identification of gender with the mythological principles. Certainly our ancestors did not shy away from the latter; they made clear distinctions between the genders in some elements of life. And the Earth Mother (rather than some concept of Earth Father) was the bringer of peace.

But we would be very much mistaken if we assumed that the nature of the Earth Mother in the psyches of our ancestors was that of a soft, quiet, yielding presence. Far from it. In granting peace, she also exacted her price. Tacitus tells us what happened at the conclusion of the festivals, when the wagon containing the Earth Mother was wheeled back to the island from which she originally travelled, her sacred grove. It was an incredible and awesome closing ritual: 'After which, the wagon and the drape, and if you like to believe me, the deity herself are bathed in a mysterious pool. The rite is performed by slaves who, as soon as it is done, are drowned in the lake. In this way mystery begets dread and a pious ignorance concerning what that sight may be which only those about to die are allowed to see.'

Clearly this is no ordinary cleansing, no mere washing of the dust and mud from the wagon and a freshening up of the cloth which drapes over the top of it. This is something much more important. Mother Earth and her wagon are bathed in a secret pool, a ritual cleansing, a cleansing spiritually of the contamination of the society she has visited, reanointed and sacralised. And there is a price to be paid for the peace-bringing visit of the feminine presence: the slaves who wash her clean are put to death by drowning in the pool itself, so that they cannot reveal her intimate secrets. It is as if the final act of the visit of Mother Earth is to put down the masculine literally; to kill it. The slaves are sacrificed in her honour.

We are used to the mass slaughter of today's wars being rationalised as 'in the name of God', from whichever religious source. But, perhaps because closer to hand and more intimate, the conscious sacrifice of people is more upsetting to us. The drowning of the slaves closes the ceremony with a disturbing and sobering act.

There was a recognition in the culture of Wyrd that the very same forces which brought peace could also bring violence; that those which brought life could also bring death. The ending of the Mother Earth ritual may be shocking to our minds, but is significant as an example of the balance of forces which hold all life together. Life force was something which was recycled. This does not mean of course that we would want to bring back such a ritual! But if we consider the procession of Mother Earth as an intra-psychic journey, a periodic visit of the forces of the feminine to counterbalance our masculine aggressions, what inner slaves do we have to sacrifice as homage to the insight, the recognition, the release brought about by the celebration of peace within ourselves? What do we have to give up in order to glimpse the essence of life, to experience the benefits and glories of her blessings?

Let us hold this question as we look at another aspect of the awesome responsibilities and significance of Mother Earth.

— Mother Earth as Lover —

We have talked about the presence of Mother Earth bringing peace, banishing war and replacing it with celebration. We have considered her presence as bringing blessings to the agricultural cycle: productivity and plenty. Today anthropologists sometimes regard the reverence, the rituals, the celebrations, the injunctions and taboos, the desiring to please and propitiate gods and goddesses in surviving indigenous societies as a 'superstition' fuelled by fear. Certainly for our ancestors the concept of Mother Earth was powerful and could induce fear, just as in the later Christian cosmology 'the fear of God' could strike people. But it was not a subservient, cringing fear which induced the indigenous peoples of early Europe to conduct their rituals which, after all, were sometimes referred to by the Roman writers and preaching clergy as 'celebrations' and 'festivities'. No,

Mother Earth: *Freeing the Flow of Life Force*   77

what our ancestors felt was the love of Mother Earth. Love was the currency with which Mother Earth dealt with all life.

Over the centuries the identity of Mother Earth changed from Nerthus and the other early tribal names. In north-west Europe she became a goddess named Frigg.[2] This name means 'love'. Frigg embodied Earth vitality; the nurturing, life-giving powers of Mother Earth. In fact, Frigg was so important a goddess, so all-embracing in her significance and influence over all aspects of life, that she had many other aspects, each representing her various responsibilities and qualities. She was like a multi-faceted crystal. Each facet had a different name and a different power: Saga, Eir, Gefjun, Fulla, Freya, Sjofn, Lofn, Var, Vor, Syn, Snotra, Hlin, Gna, Nanna, Sif and Idunn.

Scholars reckon that all of them represent aspects of Frigg or Mother Earth: seven of them are plainly so, while others are personifications of attributes of Frigg which derive from their names; for example Sjofn, from the Old Norse 'sjafni' meaning 'love-longing', and Snotra, from the Old Norse 'snotr' meaning 'wise, prudent'. It is possible that these goddesses so named represented Frigg at various stages of womanhood as the seasons of the year unfolded, appearing as virgin, bride, mother, matron, hag and so on.

Frigg means love, but the process was not Platonic. Frigg was also the goddess of sexual desire. The fecundity of nature was identified with sex, and 'frigging' is still, a thousand years on, a slang word in English for sexual intercourse. Carved and modelled images of Frigg were overtly and outrageously sexual and erotic. Clearly the quality of nature's productivity was seen through the pulsating perspective of sexuality. And lust played a practical role in people's celebration of Mother Earth, although it is very likely that expressions of that lust were sanctioned or encouraged under specific conditions; for example, on festival dates in celebration of communally approved goddesses and ceremonies. There is no suggestion in the literature or iconography that suggests lust should be indulged as an individual whim.

While the whole of life was seen as an aspect of sexuality, it was not at all like the twentieth-century modern Freudian concern with the psychological symbolism of everyday events. Rather, the Wyrd view seems closer to Tantra and other mystical and spiritual disciplines in which human sexual intercourse was experienced as symbolic of the greater forces of nature. In fact, love, lust and sex embodied the idea of freedom. To understand how this was so, we need to return briefly to the field ceremonies for crops.

The psychic world view underlying the ancient European shamanic celebrations is more understandable when we examine the significance of the crop, corn, which connotes an isomorphism between 'nature' and 'human'. This is one of the many connections, or even integrations, of the 'cosmic' with the 'personal'. It is a point at which the action of the sun, moon and the Earth to conjure life force, the 'spark' of life, was the same whether talking of crops and fields, or of people and human life.

The driving idea behind the symbolism of corn was that the 'seed' of new life was in the head, whether in the head of the crop, or the head of human beings. This is where the essence of life emanates from. This notion, now passed out of use, survived until very recently: a German idiom which has come down to us translates as 'he has groats [peeled grain] in his head,' meaning, 'he is intelligent.' So the grain is the seed, the essence of intelligent life.

It was a custom once widely spread in England and the continent to treat the last sheaf harvested as the 'corn spirit', representing the sacred essence of the crop, that which went beyond the merely pragmatic. The flower or fruit of a plant is called its head. The ritual was to cut it, 'beheading' or 'cutting the neck' of the corn spirit, and by this ritual claiming that part of the corn which sparked life, reaping and harvesting its power. Many ancient cultures practised rituals to go with the corn-planting and reaping which connect with this belief.

— The Binding of Life Force —

In the view of the tribespeople of Wyrd, just as life force coursed through fields, crops, wells and streams, all of nature, it also flowed within us, too. The life force was believed to be generated in the head, and flowed down channels in the spine and from there throughout the body and to the extremities and sexual organs.[3] Life force in a person was inextricably linked with self-expression, freedom and vitality.

Mother Earth: *Freeing the Flow of Life Force*

The free flowing of life force in a person was liberating, and the word 'liberate' stems from the root word 'libare', a 'pouring of a stream'. The word 'libido' used by Freud in this century to designate psychic energy is from the same source.

Slavery, which was sometimes a result of inter-tribal warfare, was a constriction, controlling, denial of life force. Slaves had their hair cut short as a visible sign that their life force was curtailed. Bands were placed around their necks to represent the controlling of the flow of the life force from head into the spine. The person responsible for placing the band was the one who controlled the energy so encircled. Emancipation from slavery was thus often called 'neck-loosing'.

It is interesting that in the contemporary Western world, and in the East, too, by imitation of the West, men in office jobs are often expected to wear a 'uniform' which includes the strange idea of a tie worn around the neck. It is such a widespread convention that we hardly notice it, and yet it is a very clear symbol of the constriction of the flow of life force. The company which employs the office worker 'owns' his freedom, as in a slave, and the open-necked, casually dressed employee may not be taking seriously enough the discipline of employment, the recognition that the company expects his energies to be devoted to their cause, and not something which might be more personal to him.

In the cultures of ancient Europe the very idea of freedom was related to the sexual act, to the liberty to participate in the fertility of life. Freedom was liberty to give expression to the sexual life force. 'Taking a liberty' with someone was, in Wyrd culture, meant literally. For example, the Anglo-Saxon word 'freo' not only means free in the social and political sense, but also means 'having desire, joy'. Freedom of spirit was celebrated by making love. And it was joyful. Life force flowed down from the head through the neck, and into the loins. The neck was the crucial channel for this flow of potent energy. From this understanding comes our contemporary term of 'necking' for kissing, for an Anglo-Saxon phrase to refer to one's lover was a 'neck bedfellow'! This places sexual energy and expression at the core of the idea of life force.

The concept of life force was spread all over Europe, finding expression in different but closely related ways in various tribal cultures. The Romans, for example, had a similar belief, a notion that the force of fertility and birth, the gift of life, health, vitality, was the same in nature as it was in people – and that this life force was separate from the human conscious self. And for the Romans, too, the head was the source of the seed of this life force in humans.

So Frigg, Mother Earth, in her sexual openness was providing life force, the life stuff of freedom.

— Lust and Fertility —

Later in the civilisation of early Europe, Frigg was joined by a masculine representative of love and sexuality. He was imaged in the pantheon as the 'brother' of Frigg's magical aspect, Freya, and was called Frey.[4] We do not know why this sex-change happened, late on in the first millennium, but since Tacitus tells us that just as no one fought when Nerthus was making her rounds on the circuit, so the introduction of Frey as a male counterpart in the warrior society was strongly counter to the fighting ethos of that subculture. The ban against weapons in Frey's temples, his anger when blood was shed on his sacred land, the taboo against outlaws in his holy place, all are in accordance with his character as a bringer of peace, just like Mother Earth, when weapons were put away and peace pertained in her presence.

The forces of fertility, of increase, of birth, peace and harmony rested with the female embodiment of Frigg. At some point in the second half of the first millennium, male culture tried to engage with this aspect of the cosmos. The first depictions of Frey may have been 'literary', that is, expressed through invention of the oral story-tellers and poets. But it obviously served a deep need since Frey was eventually established, at the end of this period in history, as the chief god of Sweden. But of course he was introduced partly at the expense of Frigg, so dividing the two aspects of the forces they represented.

It is just possible that what we are seeing here was an attempt to return to the values of peace and prosperity, harmony and love in a culture which by the Viking Age had become very embattled, with rival warrior leaders vying for power. A male version of Frigg represented a desire for peace, and a male peace and fertility god cut more ice within the closed world of elite warriors than that of a goddess. So Frey, or Frigg in male disguise, became the chief god of fertility in the late pagan period; he was the paramount god of the Swedes, and the divine ancestor of their kings. Snorri Sturluson describes Frey as 'beautiful and mighty. Frey is the noblest of the gods. He controls the rain and the sunshine and therefore the natural increase of the earth, and it is good to call upon him for fruitful seasons and for peace. He also controls the good fortunes of men.'

He is depicted in the sagas as journeying around the countryside to be present at feasts, as did Nerthus much earlier. And his overtly sexual nature mirrored the image of Frigg; Adam of Bremen reported in the eleventh century that Frey's wooden image at Uppsala, Sweden, was fronted by a gigantic penis, symbolising his powers of fertility and prosperous increase, and that the Swedes made sacrifices to him at weddings: 'He bestows peace and pleasure on mortals.'[5]

The consequences of shifts in the male/female embodiment of life forces in cosmological imagery is probably far greater than we realise. Although our individual gender does not necessarily conform to mythological notions of masculine and feminine, both aspects being present in everyone for potential expression, the imagery we employ for understanding life undoubtedly influences the ways in which we understand ourselves and each other. There are no detailed stories remaining of Frigg expressing her fertility functions in human terms, but there are some concerning Frey who, because he figured late in the development of the cosmology, had more of his stories recorded in forms which have survived until today.

Snorri Sturluson tells a story, which begins one day when Frey had dared to sit in Odin's High Seat, from where he could look out over all the worlds.[6] To the north, in Jotunheim, the land of the giants, he caught sight of a large hall, and while he watched, a beautiful young woman named Gerd walked up to it. When she raised her arms to open the door, they were so bright that they illumined the sky and sea, and the whole world grew bright from her.

Frey was thunderstruck. He crept away sick with longing for the woman. When he got home, he could not sleep, eat or drink. No one dared to address him, such was his mood. Eventually Frey's close friend and assistant, Skirnir, asked him why he was so downcast that he could not speak to anybody. Frey explained to him. He said that he had seen a beautiful woman and felt that he would soon die if he could not have her. 'Now you are to go,' he said to Skirnir, 'and woo her for me and bring her here whether her father wishes it or not. I will reward you well for it.'

Skirnir agreed to go, but asked Frey to lend him his sword to take with him, since the sword was such a good one that it fought by itself. Frey agreed to that and gave him the sword. Then Skirnir went and wooed the woman for him and obtained her promise that, nine nights later, she would come to a place called Barrey and there marry Frey. When, however, Skirnir told Frey the result of his mission, Frey complained:

> One night is long,
> long is a second,
> how shall I three endure?
> shorter to me
> has a month often seemed
> than this half bridal-eve.

This story has all the elements of a seasonal fertility myth. Gerd's name means 'field', suggesting that the fertility god has seen a field he lusts after. She is described as having arms so bright, and this suggests that she is a field covered with early spring frost.

Frey wishes to fertilise it, and he sends Skirnir to attract her (the field's) agreement. Skirnir means 'shining', and probably refers to the sun. He goes to woo her equipped with Frey's magic sword, and Gerd agrees to marry Frey at Barrey (meaning barley) in nine nights' time, a magic timespan which probably corresponds to a fertility ritual which lasts for nine nights. Icelandic writer Magnus Magnusson suggests that these rituals seem to have been 'played out in the Frey cult with scenes of sacred and ritualised intercourse',[7] though the participants would have had to wait, as frustrated as Frey was, until the ninth night.

Such acts of cosmic intercourse may be echoed later, and celebrated in the stone carved figures on medieval churches.[8] These figures vary from six inches to two feet in height. They take the form of a woman with a grotesquely enlarged vagina, usually held open with one or both hands. In one example (the eleventh-century church at Whittlesford, Cambridgeshire) the woman is flanked by a 'supporter' having an animal's head and a naked man's body, with stiff penis and testicles ready for action; he is not identified, but certainly depictions of Frey, or his equivalent in the local god and goddess names, may have been represented by a shaman in the dramatic, celebratory reconstructions of the event.

The vivid emphasis on sexuality and fertility of Mother Earth ran strongly counter to the official views of the Church, which through St Paul felt demeaned by 'earthly love', and had turned its version of the Earth Mother into the Blessed Virgin Mary.

— Sexual Metaphors —

Overtly sexual metaphors for the dynamics of the natural world seem alien to us today. We are now much more accustomed to scientific language in which the stories of nature are recounted in a more literal fashion. Science provides descriptions (which, if they are satisfying enough to us, we call 'explanations') of phenomena in language which meets fully the requirements of consensual validation, and seeks to minimise the subtleties and complications of poetic metaphor. But the scientific realm of discourse, while it has brought us knowledge of the functioning of the natural world and many practical benefits, proceeds from an 'objective' view. The environment being observed and accounted for is an object; the very process of scientifically encountering the world is to distance it from ourselves.

In mythological terms this is the masculine, analytic view. In restoring a consciousness in which we are once again connected to the Earth, I believe we can learn from our former ways of doing things by complementing our objective understanding of the natural world with poetic metaphor, artistic vision, dramatic involvement. We do this unconsciously, of course, in that much of our everyday 'art' has highly charged images of nature. But these images are confined to domains like advertising, in which emotive aspects of the natural world are used to connect with us in order to promote a product. We are dimly aware of the power of the images, but they are trivialised in serving solely commercial purposes.

And yet our responses and psychological connections to images of the environment are deeper and more powerful than we generally recognise. We do not normally probe the inner dynamics of our aesthetic appreciation of natural landscape. Joseph Sonnenfeld carried out a study with residents of Alaska, and showed the subjects slides which depicted landscapes varying on one or more of four basic dimensions: topography, water, vegetation, and temperature. The results revealed that males tended to prefer landscapes with rougher topography and with indications of water, while females preferred vegetated landscapes in warmer environments.[9]

We expect such preferences to be culturally influenced, of course, and it might easily be thought that the more rugged landscapes preferred by men are simply a predictable outcome of the male sex-role expectations and subculture in North America. But the results cannot be explained away as simply as that, for they also show that men, rather than women, show greater preference for water. As the American geographer Yi-Fu Tuan points out, in religious and psychoanalytic literature, water – especially still water – tends to be treated as a symbol for the feminine principle.[10]

It is possible that people are attracted to landscapes which express deep aspects of the opposite sex. But whatever it is, it is clear from these gender differences in landscape preference that there may well be deep and important psychological factors linking us with our perception of the Earth, even in our modern, insulated-from-nature world, which are akin to the poetically inspired and expressed images of the world of Wyrd. We need to balance the mythologically masculine principles of science with the mythologically feminine realms of the arts.

— Mother Earth Gives Birth —

Frigg was ruler over human productivity. Just as we have seen her role as Mother Earth in crop ceremonies, so also human reproduction was seen in the same light. People are 'nature' too, and they bore fruit. Birth in particular was the province of Frigg, and in the *Edda* poem *Oddrunargratr* Frigg is named, together with her magical aspect Freya, as a goddess to be invoked by women in labour. In Frigg and Freya's earlier Germanic form Frija they gave the name to Friday. It is intriguing to note that until recent times Friday was long considered in Germany to be a lucky day for marriages.[11]

So Mother Earth as Frigg represented love and, through its physical expression in people as sexual intercourse, then birth. It has always puzzled me that early anthropologists were so concerned with whether indigenous peoples recognised the connection between sexual intercourse and pregnancy/childbirth; whether they knew 'the facts of life'. For those indigenous peoples who bred and farmed animals could not fail to realise such a connection; even hunters who knew the life cycle of their prey animals would realise this aspect of the population of the species they were observing. But this mundane aspect of life and birth was subject to the sacred dimension. Sexual intercourse does not inevitably lead to pregnancy, and so, our ancestors assumed, there were other factors involved. Today we might regard these other factors as psychological (stress, desire) and biological (time of the monthly cycle of the female); for our ancestors these were more to do with aspects of the sacred (psychological state dependent on life harmony, and women's cycle connected to the moon). Certainly they may have been puzzled as to why we would consider this physical aspect of birth to be so important, when the spirit dimension was what really interested them.

Most so-called primitive societies have a much fuller awareness of women's cycles than we do today. The monthly bleeding of a woman was a significant event in early cultures, sometimes resulting in taboos which we would consider misguided today (for example, not eating with a woman who was menstruating).[12] But while we would not wish to duplicate some of the ways in which the awareness was expressed, it seems likely to me that most indigenous peoples understood the connection between intercourse and, nine months later or so, the birth of a baby. Certainly Frigg's role as Mother Earth presiding over love and childbirth suggests that our ancestors wished to make much more significance out of it than we do.

In recent years researchers have revealed a number of inscriptions which have survived from Roman times in Germany, Holland and Britain, and which are referred to as 'The Mothers'.[13] The ancient Roman culture had a parallel group to the Three Sisters called the Parcae, meaning 'to bring forth', and they were concerned with human birth and life. We know the importance of these women survived into this millennium: in the eleventh century Bishop Burchard of Worms rebuked women in general for their continued belief in three women known as the Parcae; he complained that it was a common custom (probably near the time of childbirth) to lay three places at table for them.[14]

But the potency of these rituals is not surprising; in those times, famine when crops failed or became diseased, or when human life was threatened and lost through plagues, were experiences close to home for many individuals. And a consequent deep sense of awe and gratitude at the coming of life must have counterbalanced the ease with which it could be snatched away.

Every tribal settlement then paid especial attention to fertility and motherhood, and underlined the importance of this aspect of womanhood.

— Dance of the Mothers —

Among our ancestors, motherhood, a state exclusive to women, was celebrated by women, and expressed, even flaunted, as a woman's way of knowing, a woman's mystery. Traces of their potent rituals survived until very recently in Europe. In the tribal groups of ancient Europe a birth triggered a communal response from the women of the settlement.[15] They ran wild. All the women, of all ages, danced and shouted their way to the house of the mother and, once assembled there, conducted some secret women's ceremonies. When these were complete, the women burst out of the house in a frantic race through the village; they all ran together, shouting and shrieking. In an account from the north of Schleswig, if they met any men they 'snatched off their hats and filled them with dung'. If they came across farm carts, implements of men's work, they broke them into pieces and set the horse at liberty. They went into houses and took all the food and drink they wanted, and if there were any men present, they compelled them to dance. This description is one of liberation, triumph, joy, freedom, and aggression.

We have no details from Schleswig of the secret ceremonies conducted by the women in the house of the mother who had just given birth, but an account from thirteenth-century Denmark provides a glimpse of what probably went on in similar forms all over Europe: 'the women gathered together in the house and sang and shouted while they made a manikin of straw which they called the Ox.' Two women danced with the Ox erotically, and sang secret songs. And then another woman began to sing in a deep, coarse voice, using 'terrible words' (the account is from the Christian reporter of the event, of course!).

These rituals surrounding childbirth (which, in those days, would have been medically supervised by a female midwife) are dramatic. Celebrations and secret, carousing rituals exclusive to women, followed by exuberant, exhibitionistic and even aggressive communal public behaviour which appear to claim a superior status to men who were abused, 'compelled to dance', and had their 'hats filled with dung'.

It is a radical contrast with the twentieth-century male-dominated world of obstetrics.[16] For the childbearing woman, as well as the village women, this experience must have been liberating and empowering. The men presumably went along with it, cooperated, respected the outpouring of feminine energy. They must also have felt threatened. The entire tone of the celebrations placed them firmly in deficit. These are connections with Mother Earth which men do not have.

Childbearing and menstruating are a kind of ongoing initiation, confirmation of belongingness to a world of mysterious knowledge for which men have no naturally occurring biological entry. The girl or the woman becomes conscious of a sanctity that emerges from the innermost depths of her being. For the woman the initiation is equivalent to a change of level, to the passing out of one mode of being into another. It is not the natural phenomenon of giving birth that constitutes the mystery; it is the revelation of the feminine sacredness; that is, of the mystic unity between life, woman, nature and the divinity.

Frigg, representing the Wyrd view of birth, clearly identified the union of sustenance (rebirthing) of the Tree of Life, the cosmological level of things, with the birthing and life-nurturing of individual human life. It represents, and reminds us, that motherhood is an expression, from within our own species, of a cosmological principle in which the birth of everything is a never-ending process. Medical advances in childbirth are a boon, but the formerly powerful role of Mother Earth, Frigg, reminds us to be aware of the cosmological, spiritual sense of awe and respect, excitement and gratitude at the miracle of birth.

Somehow the welcome advances of scientific medicine at one and the same time allow us to enhance the safety of mother and child at birth, but anaesthetise us to the miracle of the creation of life. In birthing all of creation, Mother Earth identifies childbirth with the deepest expression of all fertile creation, and recognises the spiritual significance of motherhood. Not merely the demanding, exhausting, important but nevertheless prosaic childcaring role, but a significance which can hardly be measured, such is its ubiquity. This is a powerful concept of motherhood. Mother Earth, motherhood, was sacralised in Wyrd culture as being both the basis and the pinnacle of life.

CHAPTER FIVE

Deep Waters:
Consulting the Wells of Wisdom

— The Sacred Power of Water —

Waterways were familiar territory for many people in ancient Europe, for whom boats and ships comprised one of the most effective forms of transport. Instead of travelling along highways, they went down rivers, across lakes, around the coastal waters for fishing and even across stretches of open ocean. They had plenty of experience of being out on the water, and this is reflected in their literature. One of the surviving fragments of text from our tribal heritage deals with the sea. It is in fact one of a collection of Anglo-Saxon riddles, in which the task was to guess what, or whom, is doing the talking in the riddle. The lines, written in their original form over a thousand years ago, translate as follows:

> Sometimes I plunge through the press of waves, surprising men, delving to the earth, the ocean bed. The waters ferment, sea-horses foaming . . . The whale-mere roars, fiercely rages, waves beat upon the shore; stones and sand, seaweed and saltspray, are flung against the dunes when, wrestling far beneath the waves, I disturb the earth, the vast depths of the sea . . . Sometimes I swoop to whip up waves, rouse the water, drive the flint-grey rollers to the shore. Spuming crests crash against the cliff, dark precipice looming over deep water; a second tide, a sombre flood, follows the first; together they fret against the sheer face, the rocky coast. Then the ship is filled with the yells of sailors . . . Tell me my name . . .[1]

The name is Aegir, god of the sea. These lines, oral poetry written down in England in the late 900s AD and rendered into modern English by Kevin Crossley-Holland, portray the sea storming, a personality with attributes, actions, powers, and leave it to us to name it.

This act of water is seen as a force with vitality, an active presence, and a sacred name, rather than an abstract meteorological process merely mapped and tracked objectively on satellites and computer screens. The storming water has a mana, a life force, a power of its own.

In fact, all tribal groups in ancient Europe seem to have recognised rivers and other water sources as powerful beings, sharing their life force as bestowers of life, health, and prosperity, and many of the main sources of rivers in western Europe were dedicated as sanctuaries, remembered in place names, borne out by the large number of consecrated offerings − figures, skulls, precious metals, weapons and domestic objects − that have been recovered from rivers and well sanctuaries.[2]

Many of the river names are feminine (although not all; the Mississippi is 'Ol' Man River', and the Thames is 'Old Father Thames'), and the names refer to the divinity or spirit presences who represent the mana of that river, as for example the Seine in France named from Sequana, goddess of its source. During 1964, excavations at this source revealed nearly two hundred pieces of wood carving, including many complete figure offerings, which showed that it was in use as a healing centre in the Roman period. The names of divinities of rivers and springs may be counted by the hundred all over Europe, and they seemed to embody specific images of their spirit: 'every spring, every woodland brook, every river in glen or valley, the roaring cataract, and the lake were haunted by divine beings, mainly thought of as beautiful females and associated with the Earth Mother.'[3]

Our ancestors saw reflected in their waterways not only mirrored images of their physical beings, but also metaphorical images of their psyches; essences of their souls, even, the very grounding of existence, the flowing of life in which they were a mere droplet in an ocean of meaning. Water washed, purified, and connected them with profound forces of life. Waters were sacred.

— Psychic Language of the Waters —

In contrast, today, most of us rarely think consciously about the significance of waterways. We know that it is necessary for life, of course, and that without drinking water we could not survive for longer than a few days, and that in some parts of the world, where drought occurs frequently, water is regarded as a precious commodity, obtained with great effort, and eked out sparingly. But in the technologically developed countries of the West we are used to water being piped into our houses, and use it with barely a second thought for drinking, cooking, washing, bathing, showering, flushing waste, cleaning cars, watering lawns, swimming, landscaping and so on. Water fountains spray attractively in our town squares, and fish swim hypnotically in the bubbling water of their tanks as palliatives in the dentist's waiting room. Our everyday encounters with water are intimate and frequent, but not mindful.

The people of ancient Europe, on the other hand, held it in a very different light. Not because water was in short supply, for the climate of ancient Europe included plentiful rainfall, and people lived near to rivers and streams, brooks and springs and naturally formed wells. They had other reasons for specially regarding water. For our ancestors, the people of the Wyrdtime, experienced the boundaries between self and the environment, between people and the rest of the world, as much more permeable than ours.[4] For us our skin is the dividing line between ourselves and everything else, defining the extent of our presence. Inside our skin resides the private self. Beyond our skin is the other, the not us. But in contrast, our ancestors regarded the external environment as essentially part of them, as a visible manifestation of the world of which they were an immutable participant. Even this is not going far enough. For in a sense the external world of nature was synonymous with their selves. Their skin was what joined them to everything else.

This connectedness was more than physical; it extended into the realm of the psychological, for the elements of the natural world were also the elements of their psyche. And, in remarkable contrast to our individualistic world view, their psyche was part and parcel of the natural world. A flooding river or a storm at sea was something which could devastate life in the material world; they had far fewer technological resources to cope with severe environmental conditions than we have (although conversely they lived simpler lives and so could return to normal more readily than we can). But apart from this, the very nature of waters, stormy or not, was a way of understanding ourselves. All features of nature were reflections of us, as we were reflections of them. Looking into the swirling waters of a raging river, feeling that immense pulsing of life, was the same thing as looking deep into oneself, into perhaps aspects of ourselves that are normally hidden from view, but lurk there ready to escape on rare occasions, with dramatic results.

Incredibly, even after centuries of science and a hundred years of industrialisation, with its consequent machine images of human functioning, some of these metaphors have remained with us, archaic ways of experiencing our selves as water, in language which has survived for at least a thousand years in our sayings, our folk talk. We say, for example, that we have a stream of consciousness, that we will brook no opposition, and we will pool our resources. Secrets leak out, and we plunge into things new. Or, at least, we dip our toe in the water. A wide-ranging alteration in a point of view is a sea-change. When we see an aesthetically pleasing aspect we drink it in, people are shallow or deep, and you cannot buck the tide. In fact, in dealing with life's issues, it never rains but it pours, and problems come in waves. We fish for a compliment, and throw the baby out with the bathwater. We overflow with emotion, and boil with rage. And, in going to a party, we hope to make a splash!

It did not take me long to construct this list of examples; you can probably think of others. But all these phrases express something of human behaviour and feeling, aspects of our lives, through the image of water. And in understanding those aspects of our lives through these images, we are seeing ourselves as at least metaphorically at one with water.

Why have these watery images survived in our folk-language? Why have they not been expunged in favour of images which derive totally from modern-day technology? I do not believe for a moment that these images live on in our langauge as a matter of mere accident, as force of habit; simply there because we have not yet got around to ridding ourselves of them. These are ancient images which flow deep in our unconscious, and which are there to tell us something, if only we could hear it. I believe they are there because they are natural to us; they are a way of reflecting our own natures in the qualities of our biological environment. After all, since our own bodies consist largely of water, it is hardly surprising that these images sometimes serve us better than more mechanistic language. As a scientist, I know that science is often not the right language; empirical concepts are invaluable but not for those aspects of our lives which require more subtlety of expression.

Water seems especially to be the metaphorical medium par excellence of the unconscious: deep images, flowing, receptive, swirling, still and calm, raging and torrential. Our conscious awareness of water is perhaps meant literally to be only 'the tip of the iceberg'; all that below the surface represents the depths of the unconscious.

However, the tide of opinion is changing; let us take a look at the science of water, with the Wyrd perspective in mind, and see what surprises have been landed.

— Healing Waters —

Water ran over the earth, bubbled up in springs, snaked across the countryside in streams and rivers, lay in pools, fell from the sky, formed in dewdrops; all this contained a nurturing energy which was transferrable to people and the land. Running water, especially, had healing power. An early Anglo-Saxon medical manual, in which the remedies and rituals of our ancestors are carefully scribed on to vellum leaves, tells us that to treat 'swellings', we should take a stick carved with healing runes, and throw it over the shoulder or between the thighs 'into running water'. The water carries the rune-stick, which has captured the sickness causing the swellings, back to the sacred source from which all things flow, including, of course, illnesses and swellings.[5]

Another remedy details a healing chant which, rather alarmingly to our anthropocentric ears, can be used with equally good effect for humans or horses! One line instructs us in a shamanic chant, and says, 'Sing this thrice nine times, evening and morning, above a man's head and in a horse's left ear, in running water, and turn his head against a stream.' The fact of its 'running' was a guarantee of purity. Stagnant pools caused disease; the water was still, it did not run back to the source. The flow of healing waters ranked so highly as a medical cure in ancient Ireland that it was required that any house in which sick people were being treated should have a stream of water running through it. This stream, poured from a bucket across the floor, hustled the evil, the sickness, out of the house and ensured a visible and recognised flow of life force near to the patient.[6]

When I first read these, and other, very ancient remedies, many years ago now, I was charmed by their colourful language. This was a particularly appropriate response, since I then discovered that these remedies were often called 'charms'. Their power lies in their ability to charm, to enchant, to coax from the patient a response to the treatment which transcends the mere physical, and attunes to the powers of healing beyond, in the psyche, and even in the spirit. Water was sacred, and to have it streaming through one's healing room guaranteed that whatever healing force resides in the placebo of psychological procedures would be there in buckets.

Of course, to refer to mind-body healing as placebo is simply to use an umbrella term of disguise; it covers up those many aspects of self-healing which we do not really understand from within the cause-and-effect models underpinning scientific medicine. Mind can influence body in remarkable ways. But I did assume that any healing benefit accruing from the water element of the procedures must be psychological, or even spiritual, rather than from the direct effect of the water itself.

But, remarkably, our assumption that science has somehow defined, labelled and contained the limits of the qualities of water is 'enchantingly' turned on its head by the biologist Lyall Watson,[7] who has pointed out that, in fact, water breaks all the rules of scientific principles. For example, it is more dense when it is in a liquid state than when it is chilled into a solid state of ice. Almost every other substance shrinks in volume and becomes more dense as it cools. Water follows this rule only until it has cooled down as far as 4° Centigrade. Then, Watson says, 'something weird happens.' As cooling continues, water begins to expand and to get lighter, until at 0° Centigrade, as ice, it has actually gained almost ten per cent in volume, and is less dense than when it was liquid.

Watson then considers the heating of water, and explains that it absorbs heat reluctantly. He gives the example of the all-too-common experience of burning oneself on a pot handle when the water inside that pot was still cool to the touch. Iron heats up, and cools again, nearly ten times as fast as water. But intriguingly, it seems that between the temperatures of 35° and 40° Centigrade, water is 'relaxed' and most easily warmed. And this narrow temperature range, in which water seems to want to respond to heat, to change and volatility, coincides exactly with the usual body temperatures of humans and most other active animals.

I find this fact to be one step beyond interspecies communication. Many of us have had, at some points in our lives, glimpses into the psyche of animals: a surge of empathy with the life space of our pet dog or cat; or, ranging further afield, a flash of insight into the experiential world of a wild animal. But when I read Lyall Watson's analysis of water states, I felt a flash of empathy with water; this ubiquitous liquid which has a natural 'body temperature' similar to our own, a shared level of optimal functioning, at least in terms of rate of heat transfer.

Lyall Watson concludes that far from being merely the pragmatically useful liquid with which we are familiar, the above-detailed characteristics of water, especially its sensitivity around normal body temperature, make it an ideal 'go-between'. He says that it renders water the supreme 'point of contact between ourselves and the cosmos. Something tantamount almost to a separate sense organ.' This summation by a contemporary scientist sounds very like the attitude to water of our ancestors, who were conscious of, attuned to and named its presence as a life force and medium of healing. I now turn to the source of water which carried particular significance for the people of ancient Europe: the well, for it went deep into the sacred Lowerworld.

— Honouring the Well —

In late May, the roadside banks and hedgerows in Cornwall are crammed with little flowers, glorious gentle colours coaxed from their hiding places by the warm sun in this most south-western tip of Britain. It was a warm day as Sue Bleakley, an artist who lives in Cornwall, drove me through this idyllic landscape heading for Sancreed Well, an ancient sacred site signposted off a narrow country lane near Penzance.

Walking down a well-trodden path, worn hard over the centuries by people who had come to this famous sacred site for personal meditation and spiritual blessing, the first thing we saw was not the well itself, but the thorn trees which stand next to it, their branches heavy with gorgeous blossom. And hanging from the branches were scores of coloured ribbons, rags, pieces of material, tied and knotted into place by streams of visitors over the previous months, or even years. The effect was stunning; quite eerie, in a way, for the rags were silent symbols, amulets, marks of significance for hundreds of strangers, people who had been at the site and had left this offering as an enduring connection with the spirit of the well. At least some of them had: undoubtedly a few of the emblems, in these secular times, were of the order of 'Kilroy was here'!

Old wells all over the country, all over the world, in fact, are sometimes accompanied by guardian trees fluttering with hundreds of rags floating from their branches.[8] In Britain the trees are often thorns, but also old 'blasted oaks', beech trees and others. The banners at Sancreed, drifting gently in the wind, were of all kinds and descriptions, small and large, some faded with exposure to the weather, a few very tattered and breaking up with age, many quite new, as people visit the well in the spring and summer in greater numbers than in the winter months.

The entrance to the well was a low stone archway cut into a large mound formed of earth covered with turf. The interior of the entrance glowed with soft, slanting sunlight and inside, stone steps descended steeply into relative darkness. Stepping carefully down the worn steps, I saw that the interior of the well was lined with stones, and formed an arched ceiling above. The walls glistening with beads of moisture, and at the bottom of the steps the water sat clear as crystal, as it had for centuries.

As I reached the bottom step, the outside world seemed to disappear, and I was cocooned in a timeless space. I crouched by the water, gazing into its depths, and slipped into reflection, literally and figuratively. It was so quiet in the well, so peaceful, so conducive to the floating of images in the mind, to plumbing the depths of one's thoughts, fears, and wishes. I felt protected in its cool, sparkling, softly lit embrace. I made my wish, and dipped my piece of cloth in the water, sending ripples shimmering across the surface. Afterwards, I knotted my cloth to a branch of the tree. I hope it is still there.

There are literally thousands of sacred wells still extant all over Europe; when Francis Jones studied those in Wales he identified twelve hundred in that small country alone.[9] Some of the wells show just how ancient are the rituals and ceremonies. At the thermal springs of Vicarello offerings have been found which date back to the Stone Age, continue through the Bronze Age, thrive in the days of Roman civilisation, and survive into modern times. One well of Celtic tribal origin was discovered in 1876 at the Roman fort of Brocolitia (Carrawburgh) on Hadrian's Wall, in the north of England. The well was dedicated to Coventia, almost certainly a local goddess adopted by the Romans. Over fourteen thousand coins, together with other offerings such as glass, pottery, and bronze figures, dating from pre-Roman times up to the fourth century AD, were found in the well, as were twenty-four altars, possibly hidden there when the shrine was attacked.[10]

These days, the sacred wells all over Europe are visited by many people each year. They come for a variety of reasons. Some visit just for the aesthetic pleasure, especially for city dwellers, of visiting natural landscapes; well sites are elements of the landscape which invite participation, literally an entrance into the landscape rather than merely observing, taking in the sights. There is also, for some, the sense of connecting with the old, with environment that has not been engineered anonymously to serve a pragmatic and temporary function, but instead a natural feature of the landscape which has been preserved, and into which thousands of people over many centuries have poured their hopes and dreams from the wells of their own imagination. And these days there are increasing numbers of visitors who come specifically for a sacred purpose, with meditative intent, to touch the deep underlying streams of life, waters that help us transcend the psychological and nourish us spiritually.

Celebration of the life force inherent in the waters of the well was recognised early by the Christian authorities, who were concerned to wrest spiritual control of such important sacred rituals from the indigenous shamans, and instead to invest the life force in the power of the Christian God and in their own intervention as His earthly representatives. They therefore caused laws to be enacted which made spiritual activity at wells unlawful, not allowing them to be used for the performance of cures until they had been blessed by the bishop and placed under the auspices of a saint: the twenty-sixth canon of Anselm, written in 1102, says: 'let no one attribute reverence or sanctity to a fountain, without the bishop's authority.'

So the power of the well was not denied, rather the connection with that power was appropriated, and the wells were changed in name to associate each of them with an Anglo-Saxon or Celtic saint. As in many other areas, the Church found that it had to accommodate indigenous spiritual practices and allow them to continue while claiming that they fell under the guise of Christianity. Many wells still bear the names of saints, and today, one and a half thousand years later, the belief in the health-giving life force of sacred wells persists, as for example at Lourdes in France, now under the jurisdiction of the Catholic Church.

At some well sites, more people walk past the adjacent church, along the little track which arcs into the field, towards the well than actually go into the church itself. In spiritual matters, these things come full circle.

— Keepers of the Well of Wyrd —

Wells, or natural springs, are formed by underground water trapped between two layers of impervious rock being forced up out of the ground by the build-up of pressure and released through a gap in the top layer of rock. Such a point of escape can occur naturally, or be engineered by digging or drilling a releasing shaft through the rock.

And yet these explainable water phenomena were accorded special status among the tribespeople of ancient Europe. Our denigration, or at least patronising, of indigenous people, only recently recognised and now undergoing rapid revision, has extended also to our own tribal ancestors, and in this vein it has been suggested that the ritual significance of wells was due to the ignorance of early Europeans about the laws of nature, and their simple wonder at the sight of water flowing 'miraculously' from the ground.

There is probably an element of truth in this; after all, we should not overcompensate for our cultural ignorance by romanticising our ancestors and according them engineering sophistication which they may not have possessed. Nevertheless, it seems to me to miss the main point completely. As we have seen, the tribespeople of ancient Europe regarded rivers, streams, and lakes with sanctity too. So it was not the wide-eyed marvelling at the appearance of a spring which directed such sacred thoughts, but rather the sense of connection with a realm more encompassing, transcending and imaginative than any that we may admit into our more secular lives today. Waters were, for the people of Wyrdtime, flowing from the very source of spiritual life.

In Wyrd creation mythology the original state of the cosmos was defined by two mighty regions of force, universes of energy, polarities opposing one another. One region was composed of fire, the other of ice. Between the two was a region of empty space, of nothingness. Then these two great polarities seeped into each other's territory, crackled together in the space, and exploded. The ice hissed, the fire spat, and between them they created a mist, a seething, swirling mist of potent liquid which filled three wells of wisdom, one of which was called the Well of Wyrd.[11]

The people of ancient Europe thought of the water in the Well of Wyrd as a spiritual force, a vital energy which permeated all aspects of the cosmos. Sturluson says that the water in the well 'is so holy that all things which dip into the well become white as the film which lies within the shell of an egg.'[12] The cosmology of Wyrd also featured, above the well, a central, unifying image: that of an enormous tree which was so high that it reached to the heavens, and with roots so deep that no one knew for sure where they ended. This World Tree formed an unimaginably vast organic map for the realms of the spirit, encompassing the upper worlds of the gods, middle worlds of people, and underworld of wisdom within the corresponding parts of the tree: upper branches, lower branches and roots.

And there, at the beginning, in the midst of this mythological narrative of creation, were the Wyrd Sisters, three all-powerful women symbolising the complexity and power of women's ways of wisdom. Stretching back at least six thousand years, all across ancient Europe, are references to these three Sisters of Wyrd, Daughters of the Night. In different tribal traditions they were variously called the Wyrd Sisters, the Nornir, the Parcae and the Moirai.[13]

The three sisters dwelled directly beneath one of the three massive roots of the World Tree in a cave by the side of the Well of Wyrd, a pool of great wisdom. And every night, under the glow of the moon, the sisters took water from the pool and, mixing it with clay from the banks, pasted the World Tree's root to keep it moist. Their splashing and sprinkling fell all the way to Middle Earth, and sparkled as dewdrops in the early morning mist. Snorri Sturluson describes it this way:

> there stands an Ash
> called Yggdrasil, I know,
> a soaring tree with
> white clay sprinkled;
> dews drip from it
> and fall into the dales:
> it stands ever green
> by the spring of Wyrd.[14]

Through this nightly task the three sisters are the nurturers of creation. The water in the Well of Wyrd comes from the beginning of time. The Wyrd Sisters nourished the World Tree with this water and thus sustained the sacred vision, the whole edifice of Yggdrasil. And it is this image, this vision of how the world was created in spiritual terms which leads to the special significance of deep, flowing waters. For emanations of water on the surface of Middle Earth were from the source, from the elements which nourish the sacred Tree of Life, the Well of the Wyrd Sisters. For this reason our ancestors regarded wells as sacred, because they represented in Middle Earth the great Well of Wyrd.

— The Voice of the Water —

Well waters flowed from the Well of Wyrd; they therefore were ideal sites for sanctuary, for meditations, celebrations, and blessings. Each well was considered unique, and had its own presence, its own way of linking the mundane world of psyche with the sacred world of spirit. Wells joined us to the Otherworld. And one aspect of this connection was that wells could help us to foresee events, to be 'far-seers', to gain a glimpse into the future.

The wells were oracles, answering whatever question the seeker held in mind, through a number of signs. The manner in which the water flowed from the well, or the height of the water level in the well, whether bubbles appeared on the surface of the water when an offering was dropped into the well, whether articles dropped in sank or floated: all these clues formed the nature of the well's response, and provided answers to the questions being posed.

In the earliest times the questions were posed and answers interpreted by the shamans and seers of the tribes. For example, in one of the ancient tribal stories, a man called Loddfafir declares: 'I've stood and stared into the Well of Wyrd, stared in silence, wondered and pondered. For a long while I listened at the door of the High One's hall. This is what I heard.' He then goes on to make prophecies for the people assembled through second sight, or shamanic seeing, and in his sacred reading of the well, Loddfafir has explained that the staring into the water, the wondering and pondering, enabled him to listen at the 'door of the High One's hall'; in other words, to eavesdrop on Odin, god of the shamans. So the crystal-clear waters of this well served rather like the crystal ball of later legend.[15]

We can understand today how meditation on a problem or question can be refocused by a psychological projection: the use of signals from the water, as from any such device like a pendulum or cards, to trigger a decision from deep inside oneself. But recently a German engineer called Theodor Schwenk has opened up a myriad of further possibilities by his studies of the communicative properties of water; possibilities that help us to understand more deeply our ancestors' regard for the waters.[16]

Schwenk suggests that water's sensitivity may be as great as that of the human ear. 'A gentle breeze blowing over the surface of water immediately creases it into the tiniest capillary waves . . . Water may be even more "impressed" by a stone thrown into it, and it passes this impression on rhythmically to its whole mass. The great rhythms of the tides are a response to forces which work in the interplay of Earth and cosmos . . . and from which, through its greater impressionability, the element of water is a receptive "sense organ".'

Schwenk goes on to describe water as 'the impressionable medium par excellence'. He sees its boundary surfaces as receptors, made especially sensitive by the presence there of complex wave patterns that turn them into structures with some of the properties of living membranes.

To document the extreme sensitivity of water to signals that we do not recognise through our human sense organs, Schwenk prepared a number of identical bottles of water and had them shaken mechanically every fifteen minutes in the time leading up to, during, and immediately after a total eclipse of the sun. When the eclipse was over, he introduced a fixed number of wheat grains into each bottle and allowed them to germinate without any further disturbance. The blades of wheat in water shaken at the time of the eclipse grew much more slowly than those in water agitated before or after the event. Somehow the water had been sensitive to this environmental factor, and had translated it into its ability to transmit 'growing force' to the wheat grains.

Biologist Lyall Watson points out that water commonly exists simultaneously in all three forms – ice, liquid, and mist – around a single winter lake or pool (or well), and that since water can transmute between the three states readily as a result of tiny variations in environmental conditions, such a system must, as a result, be tremendously sensitive, capable of responding to changes in the environment and perhaps even of recording such changes as patterns of information.

Similarly, Theodor Schwenk concluded that 'a stream, bubbling mainly over stones, forms countless inner surfaces and tiny vortices, which are all sense organs open to the cosmos', and that the 'impressions' so received it passes on to plants, animals and people.

So contemporary scientific research reminds us that there is a lot that we do not yet understand, and that we should keep an open mind about the sensitivity and communicative qualities of water. The seers and shamans of ancient Europe understood the language of deep waters without needing the confirmation of science.

— Women, Water, Wells —

The peoples of ancient Europe consulted wells for guidance on matters of personal importance. Particular wells were sometimes reserved for the exclusive use of women, or of men, because there were certain kinds of knowledge held within the depths of the waters which were for that gender only. One such example which survived until recently is on the Aran Island off the west coast of Ireland, where women prayed for children at St Eaney's Well, while men visited another well not far away.[17]

Wells which were for consulting by both men and women were often under the control of women. For example, in one account of a sick man attending a well for healing, he

> perambulated the well three times *deiseil* or sun-wise, taking care not to utter a word. Then he knelt at the well and prayed to the divinity for his healing . . . then he drank of the waters, bathed in them, or laved his limbs or sores, probably attended by the priestess of the well. Having paid her dues, he made an offering to the divinity of the well . . . and affixed the bandage or part of his clothing to the well or a tree near by, that through it he might be in continuous rapport with the healing influences.[18]

But more often the powers of the well were reserved for women, and the rituals served feminine knowledge rather than masculine. Women were more closely identified with wells than men even for pragmatic purposes. In many traditional societies, the physical retrieval of fresh water from the well – a daily routine – was usually done by women. The modern provision of water through underground pipes has taken away this daily reminder of the association of women with water; now that it is available with the turn of a tap, it is 'male engineering', technology born of the analytic, scientific culture which provides the water in the home.

Not that I am romanticising the carrying of well water; buckets of water are heavy and carrying them must often have been an act of hardship. Nevertheless, we no longer have a sense of the precious potency of water, pulled from deep within Mother Earth through the threshold of the well and into our life, but instead piped from reservoirs. Water has lost its importance as a metaphor for the energies of life, partly because its origins deep in the Earth are no longer reinforced by daily literal images.

For these were the sorts of images which enchanted the presence of water, so that the wells were not merely sources of liquid for mundane use, but also passageways into the depths of the Great Mystery. By divining at wells, women could tap into deep secrets, matters which concerned them as women, and which were not open to men to discover.

For example, at St Helen's Well, Rudgate, there is a legend that the original spirit of the well used to accept offerings from young girls in the form of pieces of their clothing hung on the nearby tree; obviously an early example of the ritual of cloth ripping and hanging on the Sancreed Well which I visited. In the legend the spirit of St Helen's Well, having received the offering, would then reveal to the girl, in a dream, the identity and image of her future husband. The Church rededicated the well to St Helen about eight hundred years ago, so this story refers to a period at least that old.

A similar legend attaches to Pin Well at Brayton, near Selby. A young girl going to the well for the same purpose would be turned into a fairy-sized being by the spirits of the place. In exchange for pins dropped into the well, to be used by the elves for 'elf-shot' which, as we shall see later, was a cause of particular kinds of illness preparatory to initiation into shamanhood, the spirits agreed to reveal a vision of the girl's 'true love'. The local clergy exorcised the well and rededicated it as the Well of Our Lady.

In addition to those wells which were foretellers of the future lovers of young women, some wells had the power of conferring fertility. Childbirth was an enormously important aspect of life in tribal culture, and women made pilgrimages to wells, drank or bathed in the waters, wore some clothing dipped in it, implored the spirit of the well, in order to have an easy delivery or abundance of milk for breast-feeding the child. The Bride's Well near Corgarff in Grampian was visited by the bride on the evening before her marriage. She would bathe her feet and upper body in well water to ensure that she would have children, and she placed a little bread and cheese in the well so that they would never go hungry.

The rituals carried out by the women in order to gain the favour of the well continued in some cases right up until recent times: in the late 1860s two men were by chance able secretly to watch a fertility ritual being practised at the sacred well of Melshach in the parish of Kennethmont in Grampian, and this account of the event is by J.M. McPherson:

> On the first Sunday of May, a keeper, accompanied by an expert from Aberdeen, set out for the moors to investigate grouse disease then prevalent. From a distance they spied a group of women round the well. With the aid of a field-glass, the men watched their movements. The women, with garments fastened right up under their arms and with hands joined, were dancing in a circle round the well. An aged crone sat in their midst, and dipping a small vessel into the water, kept sprinkling them. They were married women who had proved childless and had come to the well to experience its fertilizing virtues. No doubt words had been repeated, but the two observers were too far off to hear. . . . the remarkable thing is that the custom lingered so late.[19]

This was obviously a women's ritual, spied on by men, and I feel slightly intrusive even relating it here; to understand the practices of Wyrd we need to recover as much information as possible, but there are undoubtedly aspects which should be treated with particular respect, and in this case we are bordering on rituals which perhaps to men should remain a mystery.

All over the world, wells have long been associated with women. Mythologist Joseph Campbell suggests that this link of women's mysteries with water is essentially a connection between the waters of birth and that of the cosmos; the amniotic fluid is precisely comparable to the water that in many mythologies represents the elementary substance of all things. In early Europe, wells represented secret entrances to the body of the Earth Mother, the Underworld, all leading back to the Well of Wyrd. And because the life force of water came from the Wyrd Sisters it was particularly associated with the mysteries, the powers, the knowledge of women. This connection, this sacred bond between women and water is common to almost all traditional cultures.[20]

At the 'bottom' of the well are the Three Sisters. All wells had a tree next to them, as a natural world representation of the mysterious Well of Wyrd next to the World Tree. In the poem *Svipdaqsmal*, it says that the World Tree, nurtured by the sisters, has the power of women's healing. And that its fruits are to be burned in the fire and given to women in childbirth: 'that what is within may pass out'. This use of the World Tree imagery, the eating of 'burned' fruits to aid childbirth,[21] are women's ways of knowing.

Frau Holle, in the ancient Germanic tradition reported by the folklorist Grimm, is believed to keep the spirits of unborn children safe at the bottom of the well until needed. And at birth, babies were sprinkled with water from a sacred well in a naming ceremony which is the origin of the baptismal service[22] – water which was at source from the Well of Wyrd and therefore blessed by the Wyrd Sisters as they nourish the Tree of Life.

Chapter Six

Weavers of Destiny:
Changing Our Life Patterns

— Interlace —

In old-fashioned history textbooks, we were presented with an image of the peoples of ancient Europe as appearing rather drab, grubbing around with primitive agricultural tools in dreary peasant garb. We now know this to be an inaccurate stereotype, perhaps echoing the 'Dark Ages' label pinned to this period by historians. On the contrary, our ancestors were often dressed not only in beautifully coloured clothing, rendered into a wide variety of bright shades and deep, soft hues by vegetable dyes, but they also wore jewellery. Their hair, arms, fingers and clothes were decorated with necklaces, brooches, pins, arm and finger rings made with a variety of metals and stones. Circular clasps to fasten cloaks at the neck or on the shoulder were crafted from gold, silver and cheaper versions from bronze. Women wore ornate pins in their hair.[1]

The jewellers of those days used well-established methods. For example a Saxon craftsman, for his best work in gold and garnets, first made a base-plate of solid gold. He brazed or soldered gold wires to the base-plate to make a pattern of shallow holes. Into each hole he fitted a piece of gold foil, and then a tiny piece of garnet. The gold foil had a roughened surface which reflected light. This made each tiny stone sparkle brilliantly when light shone upon it. Some of the stone-cutting, and especially the shaping and craft-working of the objects, was magnificent. Everyday jewellery was made as many pieces to the same pattern. Jewellery for the king and other nobles was usually custom-made to unique designs; the finest weapons, shields, helmets and sword hilts of the warriors were often decorated too, and the tribal leaders, warrior classes and wealthy merchants wore intricate and sometimes stunningly crafted gold work.[2]

But the jewellery of the tribal peoples of ancient Europe is of more than aesthetic interest for us, because it is through the designs of these pieces that we can glimpse another important perspective on the world view of Wyrd. Any art reflects, of course, some aspect of the culture from which it arises, but in the European tribal cultures of a thousand years ago, and still today in some areas of the world, pieces of artwork are not merely for decoration. Rather, they represent ways of attuning to, honouring and celebrating the spiritual world.[3] They are aesthetically pleasing artefacts which are also sacred objects. And the twisting, enmeshed gold filigree of Wyrd artwork encapsulates in its design a central feature of the understanding of the nature of life, and death, of our ancestors.

This feature, common to Saxon, Celtic, and Viking artwork, consisted of ornate and detailed designs, often in gold strand, in which lines of decoration twist and enmesh within each other to form a seemingly unbroken connecting web of interlacing gold strings. It is an image of total interconnectedness. Everything involves and implies everything else as in an all-encompassing ecological system.

But there is a containment to the designs. They do not range randomly, but seem to have a purpose, a direction, a defined pattern. The ancient wood-carvings and metal work, whether representational or abstract, convey a similar impression of constant but controlled motion. The overriding impact is of tremendous vitality and energy contained within a finite universe.[4]

Images from the traditional stories about the creation and nature of life corroborate the impression given here, for everything in the mythological universe of our ancestors is in constant motion, rather like the action of atomic particles in contemporary physics.

The sun and moon are pictured in the stories as fleeing through the heavens, chased by howling wolves, jaws agape to swallow them. The World Tree, the central image around which all the cosmos is pictured, is being chronically undermined, with serpents and dragons gnawing at its roots and deer chewing and eating its branches. But the three Wyrd Sisters refresh and renew the roots of the tree each morning with potent liquid from a sacred well, for only by this incessant drenching can Yggdrasil maintain its life and strength. Meanwhile a squirrel scurries up and down the full length of the tree bearing insulting messages between an eagle, perched in the topmost branches, and the serpents, gnawing at the roots.

Mythologist Rosalie Wax says that the constant activity of this universe makes her feel as if she 'were watching an intricate ballet in which every entity follows its energetic but true path and fulfills its proper function. The heavenly bodies revolve, and, at the correct distance behind them, come the hungry wolves. The world tree is torn and gnawed, but its branches, nourished by regular applications of sacred liquid, always burgeon anew.'[5] So all the aspects, forces, beings and images in this universe move, not because they have been set in motion by some force external to them, as in our modern 'cause and effect' paradigm, but because movement or action is the very essence of their nature. It is a view much closer to the emerging chaos theories of today, in which underlying order is beyond our grasp if we consider individual elements, but may be visible to us if we attend to the overall pattern of activity.

In contrast to this, our traditional scientific and lay understanding of reality tends to be based on a universe of separate things, animate and inanimate, which act on each other as they 'move about' in empty space, and pass through a series of static states of change. Philip Rawson depicts the way we experience and measure time as dividing it up into countable moments, each of which is separate and, in an abstract way, identical to all others, however large or infinitely small we may choose to make them.[6] In our linear, uni-directional sense of time, these independent things 'cause' each other. This viewpoint has been invaluable in developing science and engineering; observable and repeatable sequences of events in the material world. But for anything more psychologically or spiritually sophisticated, this building-blocks image of the universe breaks down very early on.

But the viewpoint of Wyrd recognises that although concepts of things and states have an experiential reality (a door, for example, is experienced usefully as a thing through which we gain access to another space), the underlying world of Wyrd is also a seamless web of unbroken movement and change, interconnected at all levels (a door is a tree in transition, on its way to being firewood).

The twisting designs of the jewellery, with its seemingly never-ending intertwining of the gold strands, illustrates that the forces are in perpetual motion, and always in relation to one another. The balance between these forces is precariously maintained. Wax says:

> One slack moment on the part of any creature in the universe might lead to a pile up which would bring the whole of the system to ruin ... If the sun or moon paused in their flight they would be swallowed and light would disappear from the earth. If the wolves became fatigued and took time out, the natural progression of day and night would end. Similarly, if Thor relaxed in his battle against the giants or Odin in his quest for wisdom, Asgard, the citadel of the gods, would fall.[7]

The overall effect of this critical interrelationship of forces, balanced and intertwined, is dynamic, exciting, even exhilarating. It is in tune with the never-ending cycle of birth, death, and the essential vitality of life. Not life as a machine, but life in which each living, breathing, complex organism is inseparable from other organisms and the environment.

The mutual interdependence of each strand of jewellery, in which the knots of gold thread are impossible to unpick and a pull on any thread produces an inevitable and complementary pull on another, and similarly the demise of any aspect of the mythological web of forces entailing a loss of balance and the downfall of another, comprises a vision in which the forces of life are connected by a web of golden threads. These threads link absolutely everything: physical, social, psychological, and psychic events, objects, thoughts, feelings, the material and the ineffable, an interlace so sensitive that any movement, any thought, any happening, no matter how small, reverberates throughout the web.[8]

It seems that our ancestors had a sense of our being inextricably linked not only to the natural world, but to everything else as well, from the trivial and particular to the significant and universal. In this important respect we are still trying to rediscover what we once understood.

— Weavers of Destiny —

To explore further the significance of the intertwined threads of life I need to return to the Three Sisters, whom I introduced in the earlier chapter on sacred wells; they were all-powerful beings who had authority even over the lives of gods, and were unchallenged in their dominance as symbols of the cycles of life.

The Wyrd Sisters were common to all cultures in ancient western Europe: they were called the Three Norns in Scandinavian culture, the Parcae in Roman society and the Moirai in Greek mythology. It is a particularly strong, idiosyncratic image (there were no Wyrd Brothers) and had such far-reaching currency that it crossed over tribal language barriers which made the speech of one incomprehensible to another. So the Greeks, Romans and north-west Europeans had in common basic ideas concerning these three feminine powers, all-powerful figures of at least six thousand years ago.[9]

In an ancient Icelandic poem the Norns are described arriving at a place called Bralund, where they are attending a woman named Borghild who is giving birth to her child Helgi, a future king.

> Then was Helgi, the huge-hearted
> Born in Bralund to Borghild.
>
> Night had fallen when the Norns came,
> Those who appoint a prince's days:
> His fate, they foretold, was fame among men,
> to be thought the best of brave kings.
>
> There in Bralund's broad courts
> They spun the threads of his special destiny:
> They stretched out strings of gold,
> Fastened them under the hall of the moon.[10]

In this beautiful and comprehensive vision, the Wyrd Sisters arrive at night, by moonlight, and foretell the destiny of the child: that Helgi would achieve fame as 'the best of brave kings'. And then they spun the threads which would create his life's unfolding, bring to fruition their prognostication about his future. These threads, connecting and constraining energies, are imaged as spun and fastened strings of gold which, in their nature and the way they are fastened, create at birth a pattern of life for the newly born person. They are stretched out and fastened 'under the hall of the moon'.

Poetically golden, the image is arresting. Our destiny seen as a golden, glittering, lacy interweaving of fibres like a rudder fastened to the moon. Threads of gold stretching under the hall of the moon, perhaps even from the individual person to the moon, is a vision in which one's pattern of destiny can be seen in the night sky – like the slivers of light which obtain when one squints into the moon. Perhaps the pattern, the weave, was stretched by the gravitational pull of the moon; just as it moves the great oceans in tidal cycles, so it moves the liquid of our brains, our bodies.

But the image means something to do with the unfolding of each individual's life. The Anglo-Saxon word 'gewaef' means 'wove', and its cognate word 'gewif' means 'fortune'. Weaving and destiny, in the imagery of our ancestors, was one and the same thing. They imagined that we all have created for us in our inner nature at birth the frame of a woven pattern that sets our course, framed in golden strings by the Wyrd Sisters. The idea is based on the processes of spinning and weaving which were central to the life of tribespeople in ancient Europe.[11]

Certainly there is a similar conception to that of the traditional Kogi tribes of Colombia, whose inspirational cosmology has survived to the present and has been widely publicised in recent years. In Kogi belief, the Earth is a vast loom, on which the sun weaves two pieces of cloth a year. The top bar of the loom is taken to signify the apparent path of the sun through the sky at the time of the midsummer solstice, while the bottom bar represents its path at the midwinter solstice. The crossing at the centre is the point of intersection of the diagonals of the solsticial sunrises and sunsets.[12]

For our European ancestors, there seems to have existed a similar isomorphism between individual existence and the moving of the vast forces of the universe. The loom of life writ large was essentially the same as the loom of individual lives. The strings and strands of the sun and moon were intertwined inextricably with the strings and strands of our personal lives, forming our own unique patterns as our lives unfold. In the words of artist and writer Monica Sjöö, talking about indigenous world views in general, 'Cosmic mind and human mind are not essentially different, or separate, nor are cosmic body and human body. Everything is interconnected in a vast webwork . . . a universal weaving – in which each individual thing, or life-form, is a kind of energy knot, or interlock, in the overall vibrating pattern.'[13]

— Spinning and Weaving —

The making of jewellery was a craft, indeed an art, which was undertaken mainly by men, and we have seen how aspects of the designs open a window on the sacred world view of our ancestors. But another activity was equally central, equally significant in representing, through the materials of everyday life, deeper levels of understanding and attunement: spinning and weaving. And within this familiar process, the basis of cloth production for clothing, blankets, wall hangings and so on, lay a further stage to the idea of life being constructed like interpenetrating strands of fibres, as graphically illustrated in jewellery design. For the spinning and weaving processes, exclusive to women, implied the understanding that our individual lives are structured by the spinning of subtle strings of fibres at our birth, their turning and twisting threads holding us to a course, weaving for us a life pattern.

Of course, spinning and weaving are processes which have lost their impact for us as images for aspects of the deeper realms of life. The spinning and weaving of our textiles is done almost exclusively by industrial machine, thus removing it from direct observation and participation. It is helpful therefore, in considering the possible implications of spinning and weaving images for the ways in which we understand our own lives, to remind ourselves of the early techniques of spinning and weaving.[14]

The people of ancient Europe wore clothes made from flax or wool. Flax is a fibre made from the stem of the blue-flowered flax plant, which produces a light-coloured material still surviving in our contemporary language as in flaxen-coloured hair. But wool, mainly from sheep, was the more widely used material. Sheep-shearing was done mostly by the men. The women washed and combed the wool, then spun it into yarn and wove it into cloth. Spinning was performed by a woman turning the fleece into yarn by drawing it into a thread with her fingers. The yarn was then attached to a weighted stick called a spindle, which she spun so that it twisted the yarn, giving it extra strength.

The weaving looms were upright frames. The weighted threads of wool which hung down from the top are called the warp. Alternate threads of the warp were attached to a wooden bar called the heddle. The heddle had two positions. By moving it towards her the woman pulled forward the threads attached to it, so that they were in front of the others. She then passed the cross-thread from one side to the other between the two sets of warp threads. Next, she moved the heddle away from her. This allowed the threads attached to it to move to the rear of the others. Now she passed the cross-thread back in the space between them. She repeated these actions again and again, pushing the cross-threads upwards to add to the cloth she had already made.

Archaeological digs throughout Europe have unearthed many examples of the tools used by women in these tasks, including spindles, shears, embroidery workboxes and needles, and the loom-weights, rings of baked clay which were tied to the warp threads on the loom to keep them taut.

— Spinning into the Sacred —

But spinning and weaving meant more to these women, and the culture of Wyrd, than merely the making of garments and blankets, important though this was; their relation to the task was similar to that of many surviving indigenous cultures today. Among the Navajo peoples of North America, for example, the women weavers 'experience themselves as being directly inspired by the Great Spider Woman, the original weaver of the universe'. Their woven blankets are valued as organic expressions of the special powers of the makers. 'Each blanket with its inspired design has a spiritual significance, and is thought of as giving power and protection to the person who wears it.'[15]

In ancient textiles, a highly charged symbol language was used to communicate story and myth. Spinning and weaving were imbued with magic powers, and inscribed spindle-whorls are found in innumerable neolithic sacrificial pits sacred to the goddess. And in the cultures of early Europe the Three Sisters were the 'original weavers of the universe'. They were also known as the Daughters of the Night, and lived in sacred space in a cave by a pool whose white water gushed freely. The pool was at the base of the World Tree, where the Sisters spun at night by the light of the moon. The threads that they spun formed the destinies of individuals; they were the threads of life.

They had sway over the creation, measuring and ending of individual life. The Greek sisters were depicted as having separate functions: one who spun, another who measured the strings, and a third who cut them to lengths. It is likely that the Sisters of Wyrd were believed to operate in the same way: one creating the golden strings, another laying them out in ways which reflected and determined the life unfolding, and a third who cut them off to length and so determined the lifespan of each thread, and therefore each life.[16]

In the Icelandic myths, one of the three sisters had the name Urdr, which means 'Wyrd', life unfolding. Another was Verdandi, the present participle of the verb verda, which means 'be' or 'become'. Being, perhaps. 'To be' is half of the famous question posed by Hamlet: 'To be or not to be . . . that is the question.' This phrase, its fame and recognition far greater even than this celebrated play, seems to strike at the heart of an enduring human existential question; the very words, the posing of the polarities, has potency, even though supremely enigmatic. 'Being' in Wyrd is a state of life.

The third was named Skuld, which has the meaning of something owed, a debt to be settled, an obligation to be fulfilled. Sometimes these three great forces are represented in shorthand as Fate, Being and Necessity.

While the sisters are responsible for an individual's destiny at birth, so also they have dominion over the ending of life. Sometimes they are depicted ruling over the fate of men in battle. The obligation, the debt, of Skuld could represent death . . . the cashing in of one's life debts at the time appointed for death. In a story called *Njal's Saga* there is reference to death as 'a debt that all must pay'. Certainly an important aspect of the sisters appears to be the ending of life, and this strengthens the case for it. But a debt repaid to whom? The implication, and an intriguing one, is that life is a gift, or at least a loan, and it forms a debt to which we are subject, and which we eventually honour with our life or, rather, with our death. The givers of life are the Wyrd Sisters, and so it seems that the debt is repaid to them. And since the Wyrd Sisters represent forces of balance in the cosmos – the Earth and the sky – it is to this principle that we 'owe our life'. The life we lead has with it a responsibility, as in something owed. To the Earth?

So the interlocking threads which manifest the hidden forces of the universe are also woven into patterns of destiny for our individual lives. But this is a very different concept from the notion of free will which most of us unconsciously adopt in the Western world, leaving us uncomfortable with a notion which sounds rather like determinism. So what do we make of the life threads of our ancestors?

— Free Will and Destiny —

People naturally differ in the extent to which they ascribe influence over the events of their lives to the external world or to their own actions. But on the whole our everyday lives are conceived as the struggle of our free will to achieve goals which are within our compass. We fight the odds, struggle against social forces, seek to dominate inner doubts and fears. We feel that we have the free will to forge our own destiny, our fortune – and to accept the responsibility for our shortcomings, our failures, broken dreams.

This freedom can be cruel, punishing, life-denying. But we cling to it because the opposite we see as determinism, and that notion, that our lives are preordained and already set on a rigid path, is chilling; it leaves no room for our own action. Free will, for us, is the freedom to choose. And, interestingly, where we begin to feel that our lives are largely determined, that the forces ranged against us are overwhelming, that outcomes are inevitable and beyond our ability to influence, our psychological state is often labelled as depression.

Our notion that we have free will depends to some extent on the idea that we conduct our lives rationally, logically, making decisions by the effort of our conscious minds. Today, in the business world, the military, in education, we are increasingly drawn to trying to understand our lives by constructing models of this supposedly rational process by recourse to the language of the computer. We think of our cognitive functioning in terms of information processing, logical programmes, input and output, feedback loops, and so on. Computer imagery for understanding our own thinking reinforces our assumption that we are taking logical decisions based on practical information. And when we get things wrong, when our lives plunge off into directions other than those we have consciously chosen, we assume that it is because we had the wrong information, or not enough information, or failed to assess correctly the valence and degree of the little box marked 'emotions'.

But of course, another view is that our lives are anything but logical. We are ruled by deep passions, desires, fears and longings – powerful urges we barely acknowledge which sweep from the deep into our dreams and then back again. And while we might be aware of this, and take our decisions as best we can, we do not imagine that those cognitive functions of which we are aware are the sole or even primary processes which weave the pattern of our lives. But the division of life into free will or determinism is a black and white, yes-or-no artificially constrained mind-map of an immeasurably rich and complex landscape of interacting, flowing energies.

— Changing Our Life Pattern —

For the tribespeople of ancient Europe life was a complex negotiation between what is free and what is ordained. The unfolding of life patterns was subject to the intervention of shamans, and its imagery of spinning and weaving suggests that when we change aspects of our lives, ourselves, instead of changing our 'life-programme' (a terminology that is now current in, for example, management training and business psychology), we change our life-design: the shape, colour, texture, pattern, theme and so on. This imagery for the process of personal change recognises the integrity of a 'woven' design; the overall pattern of threads can be adapted, developed, rearranged – so long as it honours the basic theme with which it originated.

So using a weaving metaphor in which a life change is seen as effecting a change in an unfolding pattern implies that developing a new pattern for a life is to be accomplished in harmony with the original 'design', rather than in breaking a pattern abruptly and completely, as if inserting a new program into a computer. In the metaphor of weaving, this development of a pattern retains the integrity and strength of the pattern woven so far, but takes it in new directions, creates exciting changes in harmony with what has gone earlier; the pattern can alter and pick up on earlier themes and express them in very different ways. So the process of psychological change seen through the images of our ancestors has an organic and aesthetic feel, rather than that of our contemporary images which encourage everyday notions of psychological change more as a retooling or reprogramming of a machine.

The shamans of ancient Europe, in their healing work, created or attuned to a vision of the pattern of fibres entering individual persons to understand the complexity of forces and the nature of the pattern framing that individual's life.[17] Where appropriate I have worked with people using this idea of a life pattern framing an all-encompassing image of their life, sometimes with dramatic, releasing results. I shall describe here one example of using this framework, and you might feel encouraged to try something like it for understanding the pattern of your own life.

I was working therapeutically with a man who was at the time in his mid-thirties. He had many personal knots to deal with, many psychological doors closed. He had undertaken 'talking' psychotherapy, in which he had discussed with his therapist the nature of the issues in his life, and the possible predisposing experiences of his childhood. But in his case it had made little difference because he felt so utterly confused and paralysed by the multiplicity of his problems. So before dealing with the content and structure of any of the individual issues, we sought to obtain a clear vision of the pattern of his life, the strands that had been spun and the forms in which they had been woven together. We simply mapped them, and saw the design of his life, so that we could work in an artistically therapeutic way to redesign his life's unfolding pattern.

On a large notepad he listed events, people, issues, experiences, problems, strengths, weaknesses, friends, enemies, triumphs, failures. This work was done quickly; it is remarkable just how much information of this kind is retrievable, stored just below the level of awareness in memories. Each item he listed took only a key word or a few key words for him, for he was communicating the nature of the experience to himself and to me only; they did not need to be articulated at any length at this stage.

We then took a huge sheet of paper, pinned it to the wall, and he began mapping out the pattern of his life. He worked first with a pen, transcribing on to the new sheet significant people and events from his lists, and placing them where he thought appropriate on the new sheet. Some of his items did not seem to need any sense of chronological placing. Others were transcribed by him at a place on the paper roughly corresponding to taking the top of his sheet as the beginning of his life, as in weaving a fabric on a loom, and the bottom of the sheet as the exact moment in which he was working now. The large sheet represented the totality of his life as he had thus far lived it, and as he worked he began to represent it on the sheet.

Soon he was working with felt-tip pens, and then paints, using a different 'thread' colour for each category of items he was listing and marking on the paper. After a couple of hours, the sheet was a mass of colour, with dots, lines, blotches, streaks, curls and twirls, little faces and symbols and so on. And as we gazed at it, trying to take it in as a whole, he began to point to recurring designs, repeated motifs, connected structures and forms. When he found these, he worked on the paper with paint and pens to accentuate them, to make clear the patterns of his life. For him this was an aesthetically clear process; the patterns were strong and vibrant. Emotionally it was both exhilarating and draining. He required plenty of breaks from the work. But the entire process was completed in three long sessions spread over a week, apart from a few brief clarifications of the design which he made at our next session, two weeks later. In his case the finished work was aesthetically very pleasing, both to him and also to me, as an outside observer, but so long as patterns have been identified and made clear, the artistic merit of the pattern is not important for the process of therapy.

I was very struck by the potency both of the process and the finished pattern for this man's understanding of the sequencing, structures and connections of his life. He was so excited by it that he wanted to delay working on individual strands and motifs until he had had a chance to work more fully with the overall pattern; to appreciate and attune to it in as many ways as possible.

So we choreographed some movement work for him based on the flow of patterns he had created in his life and which were represented creatively on the paper. The first time he performed the entire dance sequence was tremendously cathartic for him, and each time afterwards was a centring, a state of presence within himself, a ritual act of faith in the integrity of his life pattern and, having articulated, painted and danced his way to understanding it, his ability to change it. People's life issues are complex, of course, and need to be addressed in detail in a variety of ways (including the 'talking therapy' with which he had begun), but this process of life-design analysis gave him such a vivid eagle's-eye view of his personal history and present situation, so that he could get his bearings, it gave him the impetus for the hard detailed work to unravel some of his twisted emotional strands. The transformation in his general wellbeing was remarkable.

CHAPTER SEVEN

Dwarfs: Transforming with the Web of Wyrd

— The Threads of Wyrd —

Changing the pattern of our lives necessitates an understanding of the nature of the golden strings, the threads that are 'fastened under the hall of the moon' by the Nornir. The threads are more than a poetic fantasy. They are a metaphor which carries and represents meaning. In the discourse of mythology, of shamanic states of consciousness, of dreamtime, the golden strings have been seen, experienced, touched and manipulated; so what is it that has been experienced in human lives that gives rise to such an image? And what may we learn from it today?

One answer to this question lies in a tale from the ancient tribal cultures of north-west Europe, recorded by the Icelandic historian Snorri Sturluson. My recounting of it below is based on Snorri's version.[1]

The story is about three gods and a wolf. The three gods were Odin, the magical, cunning, archetypal shaman figure and most dominant of the deities; Thor, the big, blustering god of the farmers who constantly went to battle with the giants; and Tyr, an ancient sky god, harking back to prehistoric times, and who was just coming to the end of his reign as a god and was to be soon replaced by other, newer deities.

The gods adopted the wolf as a pet. Called Fenrir, it was a beautiful and impressive pet, and the gods were proud of it. For a time, that is, while it was small. But as it got bigger and bigger, the gods began to become nervous of it. Soon only the ancient sky god Tyr had the courage to go up to it and give it food. The wolf gulped it down and grew even bigger.

Then one day the gods were alarmed to hear a prophecy that at some point in the future Fenrir was going to injure them. They said, 'We've got to do something about this wolf before he gets completely beyond our control, before we can no longer contain him.' So they formed a plan to make a really strong fetter, a chain which they could wrap around the wolf and fasten to the rocks so that he would not be able to chase them.

They commissioned a huge chain (which they named Loding) to be built, a very strong chain. When it was ready the problem was how to get the wolf to accept this chain without attacking them. They knew they would not be able to put it on by force. But Odin, who was vain himself, proposed they appeal to the wolf's vanity. Approaching the huge wolf nervously they said, from a little distance, 'We've got a new chain, Fenrir, and because you're such a strong wolf, we wondered if you'd like to test your strength against it?' Fenrir looked at the chain, which had taken months to construct, and laughed derisively. 'No problem. Wrap it around me.'

Eagerly they wrapped the chain around the wolf very tightly, banged it deeply into the rocks, and secured it very well. But as soon as Fenrir strained against the fetter, it snapped. He had escaped from Loding.

When the gods saw this they were very afraid. They knew they had to do something drastic. So immediately they commissioned a fetter twice as long, twice as thick, and twice as strong as the first one, the biggest that had ever been made, which they called Dromi. As soon as it was completed they dragged it back to Fenrir. The wolf was not too keen on this one. This looked like a serious challenge. The gods played on his vanity again: 'Fenrir, if you could break this really big chain, you would be ever so famous. Your name would go down in history.'

The wolf considered it. He reasoned to himself that although the fetter was very strong, he had grown in might since he had broken Loding. And, he thought, one has to take risks in order to achieve real fame. He allowed the gods to place the enormous fetter around him.

When the gods said they were ready, Fenrir snarled, shook himself, banged the chain against the ground and, struggling against it, dug his feet in so hard that the fetter burst into pieces that were flung by the

Dwarfs: *Transforming With the Web of Wyrd*

force far and wide into the sky where they formed the stars. They twinkled prettily but, unfortunately for the gods, Fenrir had now escaped also from Dromi. And his fame did, indeed, spread, as confirmed by the fact that I am telling you about him now.

The gods were terrified. It looked as if the dangerous and still-growing wolf would never be able to be bound. Reluctantly, Odin decided to send a messenger down to the Lowerworld to seek the help of the dwarfs. It was a humiliation for the mighty gods so to beg for dwarfish help, but there was no other course of action open to them. They were desperate.

Dwarfs were the blacksmiths of the Lowerworld; they forged magic jewellery and weapons. But they could also work with psychic and spirit forces on their anvils. And so the gods, rather embarrassed, explained to the dwarfs what had happened, and begged them to make a fetter strong enough to hold the giant wolf. The dwarfs drove a hard bargain, but when finally a deal was struck they agreed to make a fetter that would chain Fenrir and stop him from rampaging through the heavens.

But when the gods went back to collect their massive chain, the one that would really tie down the wolf once and for all, they were horrified and furious when they saw what the dwarfs had made. It looked like a thin piece of silk thread. 'We're not paying for this!' thundered the gods who, though they made a lot of noise, were not really in a very good position to say what would and what would not work.

'Just a minute,' cautioned the dwarfs. 'You don't yet know what this fetter is made of. It is a very special one. It is called Gleipnir.' Proudly they started to list the materials of their work: 'It's made up of six ingredients. One is the noise that a cat makes when it moves. The second is the beard of a woman. The third is the growing roots of a mountain. The fourth is the breath of a fish. And the fifth is the spittle of a bird . . .' The gods were beside themselves with anger; so far the fetter contained nothing of any substance at all. 'And the final thing is the sinews of a bear.' Which was actually the only material part of the whole chain.

'But what is the value of these ingredients?' bellowed the gods.

'Apart from the sinews of the bear, the ingredients are nothing at all!'

'Precisely!' retorted the dwarfs. 'And that is what gives it its power. Plus our magic of course.'

And then the truth dawned on the gods. The dwarfs had made a bond of spells. It was a magic fetter. 'Well,' said the gods reluctantly, 'we've paid for it, we'd better go back and try it on Fenrir.'

The gods took the fetter, which was as smooth and soft as a ribbon of silk, back to Fenrir. They felt pretty silly trying to explain to him that, although the fetter looked delicate, it was stronger than it appeared, and they passed it from one to another, each in turn attempting to break it to demonstrate to Fenrir just what a test of his famous strength would be this fetter. It was an unconvincing presentation. Fenrir was not impressed. 'I'm not being taken in by that thing. It's so slight a cord that I would gain no fame by breaking it.' The gods' hearts sank. 'And anyway,' concluded Fenrir, who was quite an intelligent wolf, 'if it has been made by magic, guile and cunning, it's getting nowhere near my legs.'

Poor gods. They banged their heads against the rocks in frustration and despair. They begged Fenrir to try to break the fetter, but he refused. Finally, they said, 'Look, Fenrir, if we put this on you and you cannot break out of it, we promise that we shall let you free immediately. Only a coward would refuse such a challenge.'

Fenrir's hackles rose, and his eyes glowered coldly. 'Rather than be accused of cowardice by you three,' he snapped, 'I'll do it. But only on one condition: that one of you place his hand in my mouth as a pledge that your promise is made in good faith.' This cunning device put the gods in a bit of a bother. They knew that, if the fetter did bind Fenrir, they had no intention of keeping their promise to free him, and so Odin and Thor did not want to risk placing their hands between Fenrir's huge jaws. But old Tyr thought that Fenrir's bargain sounded like quite a good idea. Tyr put out his right hand and laid it in the wolf's mouth.

Fenrir was surprised, but now had to go along with the bargain. Eyeing his teeth nervously, the gods settled the magic fetter tightly around the enormous wolf, and quickly scuttled back to a safe distance, the two who hadn't got their hands in his mouth, that is. When they said 'Ready!' Fenrir started pulling, tugging, digging his paws in, as he had done before with Loding and Dromi, trying to tear the cord free of the ground. It did not budge. He thrashed around, growling and howling, but the more fiercely he struggled, the more tightly tied he became. All the gods laughed in relief. All except Tyr, that is. He lost his hand.

— Chaos and Spontaneity —

There are a number of interesting possible meanings which lie behind this story. First of all, it is helpful to note the mythological 'identity' of Fenrir in the culture of our ancestors. In a way he is related to the god Odin, who was the dominant deity at the time of the story, and was taking over from Tyr as the inheritor of the powers of the sky god. Odin was a complex deity with many facets to his nature, each of which was manifested in the stories and cosmology by another named god who would accompany him on his adventures. But in understanding the meaning of the stories, one has to treat Odin as the chief protagonist, and the other gods as his aspects.[2]

One very important aspect of Odin was identified with a being who seemed to have god-like status, although was never listed as officially among the gods. He was called Loki. In the ancient stories of north-west Europe, Loki played the part of the trickster, who brought mischief and confusion into the world of the gods. His exploits challenged, and threatened to turn upside down, the natural order of things. There was nothing charming or amusing about Loki, as there sometimes is in trickster figures in other cultural traditions. Loki 're-ordered the cosmos' from time to time, and his actions often threatened to cause destruction to the harmony of the cosmos. He represented the forces of chaos, always shadowing the structured world of the gods like a hidden threat, and looking for any chance to strike.[3]

Loki had three children with a giantess called Angrboda. One child became the Middle Earth serpent, a binding and containing being who encircled the Earth; a second became the Queen of the Lowerworld, a spirit-woman who presided over the darkest recesses of the realm of the dead. And the third child was the wolf Fenrir. So as an offspring of Loki, the wolf Fenrir represented the always threatening forces of chaos, the potential destruction of harmony and order.

On the other hand, while Fenrir is a creature who is fettered, tied down, and restricted, his chaotic energy has within it elements of freedom, spontaneity, and vitality. He represents a part of ourselves. Fenrir reminds us that at every moment of our lives we are constrained and limited by the many subtle, unseen bonds we place on ourselves, which have settled into place during our lifetime. Our lives are necessarily involved with fetters, for every adjustment we make to life's demands, every psychological defence we erect, fear we avoid, temptation we succumb to, may constitute one of the dwarfs' fetters.

Of course, many of the fetters will always be there, and need to be in place. Some elements of the knot of fibres in which we each live provides a necessary framework to give pattern to our lives.

But fetters are all-encompassing. They restrict the ways in which we are able to deal with issues, and they are powerful, especially as they are so insidious as to be unseen. Identifying and removing, or shifting, or altering these fetters can be a liberating experience. Remarkably, to shift the pattern requires, sometimes, just a light and subtle alteration or refinement: the potent effectiveness of the most gossamer of spells, a revisioned perspective which can transform a life situation before our eyes.

In the mythology of ancient Scandinavia, the day came when Fenrir did escape from the dwarfs' fetters that bound him, and his escape to freedom marked the end of the world. Absolute chaos ensued, and the entire world fell to uproar and burned to the ground. And yet, out of this devastated landscape, in the myth, a new dawn arose. Life began anew.[4] So perhaps the Fenrir within each of us needs to escape once or twice in our lives. There are devastating results for a time, but then life is reborn.

— Using Dwarfish Magic —

But for life to be viable, for there to be a psychological and spiritual balance, we need to temper the spontaneity and joy of chaos, for it also carries with it the terror of destruction. In the story of Fenrir, the gods tried to do this, to contain the wolf they were afraid of by meeting force with force. But they were playing on the wolf's own home ground. He was too strong for their fetters. Of course, the gods are in this story enacting a scenario with which we are all familiar from time to time. When we face a problem, one which feels strong and potentially dangerous, threatening to bring chaos to our personal or professional arrangements, or relationships, or inner harmony, we often attempt to shackle it by fighting strength with strength, fire with fire. We attempt to deal with it, to take effective action, contain it, using the normal materials of everyday life. We wrestle with the problem, looking for a quick fix, trying to nail it down as the gods attempted with the wolf.

Sometimes this works; we are able to cope with the issue that has arisen. But sometimes the problem is more intractable than that. It does not go away. It resists, breaks through our attempts to contain it, and grows bigger. Panicked, we try again with more of the same. We give it extra attention, more of our time and worry; we try, try and try again. Extra struggle with the same materials. We wrap it in chains. But it rises up and breaks free with devastating effect. We are lost.

This is the masculine path to problem-solving.[5] To challenge, to confront, to defeat. It is redundant. A psychological tautology. Rather, to cope with an issue, to solve a problem, to alter the design of a life, requires us to find a way of revisioning the fibres, re-placing them around our problems, using subtlety and insight.

In the story, when this confrontational tactic did not work, the gods needed to turn to a different realm of action: that of the dwarfs. The dwarfs, as we shall see later, provided Freya, the shamaness goddess, with the bases of her wisdom. They represent the mythologically feminine path to magic, in which the intuitive and subtle is rendered as having great power. These are not necessarily gender-specific ways of approaching problems: both paths are open to each of us.

In the feminine path, rather than identifying the obvious obstacle, the ready-made remedy, one looks for underlying forces: the language of the threads. As with the powerful, magical fetter of the dwarfs, the ingredients of such an approach are subtle, even inconsequential in themselves, but are very potent in combination. By engendering an awareness of all the subtle forces impinging on an issue, a fetter can be constructed which is more powerful, and long-lasting, than a more dramatic and obvious 'fix'. Like drops of soft water falling on to hard rock, they wear away in time the most fixed of obstacles. To identify the threads in this way is to set aside the conscious mind, the controlling mind, and to use instead the resources of intuition and inner wisdom.

Note that the gods had difficulty in getting themselves to work intuitively. They felt humiliated in giving up their own sense of power, and even when they had resolved to seek the help of the intuitive mind, they had to have the insight and courage to realise the value of what had been revealed. Because the gossamer, magical fetter which finally chained Fenrir down looked insubstantial at first sight, the gods almost rejected it.

As a young adult I studied judo for some time. Along with certain other martial arts, this remarkable practice teaches that while pitting strength directly against a stronger opponent invariably leads to defeat, the use of the subtleties of speed, balance, insight, and a total concentration on the present, can lead to using the opponent's strength against him. The direction in which he is pulling becomes the direction in which he suddenly, inadvertently, will be propelled with a force which uses the momentum he was already generating for himself. Once this is mastered, larger and heavier opponents can be toppled and thrown with ease.

The story of the gods and Fenrir reminds us that psychological problems are often like this. In our lives, the technique of dwarfish magic is to look for the subtle problem which lies behind the obvious problem. The dwarfs realised that Fenrir could be fettered by wrapping him in something which used his strength against him, which tied him up as a result of, not in opposition to, his struggling. Most issues in our lives are not, as we know, unidimensional. There are underlying forces at work, hidden at first, not observable to the conscious, controlling mind, but identifiable through intuition, through recourse to the imagination, the subtle realms. And it is to these inner resources that we need to turn when we are faced with a challenge which is too strong, too complex, too deeply hidden within ourselves and others to face on its own terms rather than ours. Here we need the language of fibres and threads, dwarfish intelligence.

Spellcasting in Wyrd was often conceived of as placing or releasing bonds from a person. Odin was depicted as able to place binding spells on people, as the dwarfs did on Fenrir, and these were imaged sometimes as knots; also there are examples of memorial stones on which Odin is shown beside a kind of knot in the form of three triangles, linked together.[6] Odin had the power to lay bonds on the mind, so that men became helpless in battle. Symbols representing this knot of Odin are also found beside figures of the horse and the wolf on cremation urns from early cemeteries in East Anglia.

The power to bind was understood also by the early Christians in western Europe, as we see in the example of a Mercian king's warrior named Imma, who was taken prisoner by the Northumbrians after the battle on the Trent in 679. The chains by which he was bound continually burst open and so he was brought before his captors who asked him 'whether, through witchcraft or through runes, he brake his bonds?' Imma, who was a Christian, explained that this was not the reason, but that his brother, who was an abbot, believing him dead from his wounds sustained in the battle, was having masses said for his soul: 'the celebration whereof occasioned that none could bind him without his being immediately loosed again'.

Either Imma believed in the power of binding and the facility for spellcasting to break the bonds, as practised by the indigenous shamans, or he was a particularly quick-thinking man who told the pagans what he thought would scare them into granting him safety!

In workshops I have sometimes explored with the participants the many lessons to be learned from the story of Fenrir. Often we begin by enacting the story. It is exhilarating to dramatise, and the roles of the gods and the dwarfs are always highly coveted. Rehearsing and performing the story seems invariably to result in hilarity and helpless laughter at the conundrum facing the giants, their relations with the dwarfs, and the nature of the little people themselves. With larger groups of participants we can also create the chains Loding and Dromi, which explode with satisfying effect under the strain of

Fenrir's struggles. But the sheer exuberant energy of these dramatisations is grounded by an awareness that we are participating in one of those timeless tales that have deeper meaning, that can teach us something.

Afterwards we work in a variety of ways to establish connections between the dynamics of the story and the events of our own lives. Participants recall from their lives incidents, experiences, relationships, problems in which we committed the same mistakes as the gods with Fenrir: examples where we tried to fight issues of superior strength with our inferior strength. In individual work, or in groups where this sort of personal material can be shared, I ask the people with whom I am working to recount one or more of these examples in order to fix their awareness and deepen their perception of what sort of life situations are reminiscent of the gods struggling with large but breakable chains in attempts to contain a larger problem.

And then, in a more pleasant memory meditation, we recall examples from our own experience where we gained insight into the underlying energy of the problem, the deeper knots of threads which lead to a situation we wish to resolve, and the small shift in balance which allowed us to use the strength of the problem against itself, and to contain it with magical fetters. Reliving these latter examples is extremely valuable, for recognising them helps to resist the temptation to turn automatically to the controlling mind when facing a problem.

— Dwarfs of Transformation —

But the dwarfs can take us deeper than this. They were beings who ruled primarily over the transition from the mundane world of the psyche to the sacred world of spirit. Their domain extends beyond the psychological conundra of our everyday lives into the realm of the spiritual.

The dwarf is a transformational spirit being in many shamanic cultures; the idea of a dwarf who grants power or serves as guardian spirit is widespread in North America, for example, especially west of the Rocky Mountains in the tribes of the Plateau Groups (Thompson,

Shuswap) and in northern California (Shasta, Atsugewi, Northern Maidu, and Yuki).[7]

In European shamanic mythology the dwarfs lived in the Lowerworld as magical smiths. The Lowerworld was the realm of knowledge, and resting place of the dead. In a culture in which oral knowledge predominated, people took their wisdom with them when they died, which is why a shaman's journey to the land of the dead was highly prized, for it was there that answers to the most difficult questions could be obtained. Shamans engendered an altered state of consciousness conducive to the sort of journey or voyage which transported them to the spirit world, but the direction of the quest was not celestial, not towards the gods, but downwards, into the Lowerworld. The dwarf-smith's 'power over fire', and especially the magic of metals, have everywhere given smiths the reputation of sorcerers. Hence the ambivalent attitude towards them: they are at once despised and venerated. They used heat to transmute elements of the Earth into knives, swords, and beautiful jewellery. They created, and wove, fibres of beauty and strength in pattern-welded swords, and the fantastic and intricate swirling thread designs of Anglo-Saxon, Scandinavian and Celtic jewellery. Theirs was thread magic of a material kind.

But their greatest skill was in transmuting the souls and bodies of apprentices into shamans. The dwarfs were spirit creatures who were the catalysts for our own transformation.[8]

So how did the presence of dwarfs make itself felt in the shamanic world of our ancient European ancestors?

Myths all over the world feature apprentice shamans being carried into the Lowerworld by an animal spirit on his back, or holding him in its jaws, or 'swallowing' him to 'kill and resuscitate him'. The spirits come from every quarter . . . and speak through the shaman's voices. The dwarfs worked in this way, too. But they had many guises, secret identities.

Anglo-Saxon linguistic scholars have for example pointed out that the word 'dwarf' goes back to an Indo-Germanic form which is near the Greek 'serfos', a stinging or biting insect. And in Breton, Welsh and Cornish the word 'cor' also means both 'dwarf' and 'spider'.

Furthermore, the Swedish 'dverg' means not only 'dwarf' but also 'spider', and dwarfs in Scandinavian legend are specially associated with spinning. In other words the deep, original nature of the dwarf and the spider are identical. The spider was in fact a shapeshifter dwarf, who could spin the web of life anew.[9]

The Anglo-Saxon *Spellbook* contains an example in which the dwarf appears in the form of a spider creature and carries off an apprentice for initiation. The entry is listed as a 'Night Mare'.

— The World of Concealment —

Here a spider-creature came stalking in.
He had his bridle-web in his hand.
He said that you were his steed,
he laid his bonds on your neck.

Soon they began to set off from the land.
And as soon as they came off the land,
then their limbs began to cool.

Then the sister of the creature came stalking in
She made an end to it, and oaths she swore
that never this one the sick should harm
Nor him who could obtain this charm
Or understand how this charm to sing.

The spider goddess incantation, even when rendered into modern English as above, still retains some of the impressive imagery from its days in its native Anglo-Saxon, when it served as part of a tribal ritual for initiation into shamanism.[10] It is a spell which tells the story, in highly condensed and coded form, of the journey of an apprentice to the Otherworld, the world of knowledge, the initiatory testing grounds for a man about to become a shaman.

In all shamanic traditions, sickness was a gateway to wisdom. In the fevers of illness, the altered states of mind in which visions of another reality became possible, certain people were chosen by the spirits for transporting to worlds of knowledge. In recently surviving shamanic cultures, accounts of illness as a prelude to initiation reveal that the illness was sometimes sudden and severe, but it could also be a progressive change in demeanour and wellbeing, in which the future shaman becomes meditative, seeks solitude, sleeps a great deal, seems absent-minded, has prophetic dreams and even acute symptoms such as seizures. Dreams and visions experienced during the throes of sickness might determine a future shaman's career in a very short time, especially in the case of fevers in which the patient would see 'other worlds'.[11]

The spider-creature incantation probably occurred in a setting in which a 'patient', or sick apprentice shaman, is visited by a shaman who chants the lines we have in the document. These rituals were usually witnessed by an audience of at least family members and elders, and possibly by the whole settlement. As the apprentice is in a fevered state, and therefore open to journeys to the Otherworld, the shaman begins to offer visual imagery which helps to provide some structure for the visions. In the shamanic world of our ancestors, this soul journey was considered to have a validity at least the equal of the everyday state we call normal consciousness.

Some of the tribes of early Europe referred to this Otherworld, the realm visible and accessible only from altered states of consciousness, as 'halja', which means 'the place of concealment'. Halja was believed to have originated at the formation of the cosmos when ice and fire met to produce the highly charged mist of life. Some of the mist formed into ice-rain, and then into the shapes of giants, from whence came the Wyrd Sisters. But some of the mist remained – a very important feature of the mythological landscape, because it was here that glimpses of the true reality were possible; visions and shadows of original and eternal truth. Later, the Lowerworld of occult knowledge was called Niflheim – the first element of the word meaning 'mist' or 'fog'.[12]

Represented mythologically as a sacred space beneath the Earth, one way of understanding the Lowerworld today is to conceive of it as effectively a place in the mind. But this is not to say that it was merely in the mind, or only in the imagination; the Lowerworld was of sacred dimensions, and was equivalent in power to the concept of heaven which characterises Christianity and various other religions.

The Celtic peoples' image of this realm of concealment was very close to the everyday world. Enticing and yet threatening, it hung intangibly near, like a reflection in a deep, clear pool. Natural features of the landscape provided the dividing line between this world and that. They were also the points of juncture, the connections, the doorways into the Otherworld. Fords across the rivers, the ridges of mountains or high hills, the boundaries demarcating tribal lands – all these were charged with magical power and were points through which the mist of the Otherworld could seep into this world.[13]

Other liminal points at which the material world (Middle Earth) and the Otherworld (Lowerworld) came close included psychological shifts between states of consciousness, moments of light shift at dawn and dusk, turning points in the periodic waxing and waning of the moon, New Year's Day, the summer and winter festivals. All were occasions when the unseen powers from the Otherworld came very close, and were to be guarded against, unless one was preparing an intentional journey into those realms. At these times and in these places, powers from the Otherworld might disturb the expected unfolding of events.[14]

On Samhain (Hallowe'en) the interpenetration was mutual and open for all who sought successfully, for it was the night of celebration of the unity of the two worlds, which are really only separated by states of mind and appearance and actually coexist.

To reach this Otherworld in search of the wisdom which could be obtained there, one had to cross a normal wood, a hill, a river or a stretch of water. But entry to the Otherworld, the transition from normal to magical landscape, was dependent upon having been prepared for this sacred journey by passing some test to prove oneself worthy and, in so doing, ensuring that one was capable of entering and sustaining the states of mind and spirit that characterised the Otherworld.

Sometimes shamans would undertake prepared journeys to the Otherworld, shamanistic initiations, or quests for answers to questions of healing and divination. The mounds or megalithic monuments known as 'sidh' were opened and entered, or sat upon, by shamans, for they provided communication points between the two worlds.

The beings of the Otherworld could enter this world, and so could shamans.

The world of concealment, the halja, sometimes required powerful ritual experiences in order to enter it. For an initiate shaman, election by the 'spirits' for access to the secrets of the Otherworld was imperative, as was a journey to the Wyrd Sisters, who rewove his destiny as he changed from a normal person to a shaman.

After that, once someone has been allowed to see such things, as a shaman they are taught techniques for generating inner heat, and for entering the Otherworld at will. And it is in these states of consciousness that the invisible threads of Wyrd manifest. They are visible in the shaman's vision.

— The Spider Spell —

As with the rest of the Saxon *Spellbook*, this shamanic ritual was recorded by Christian monks or scribes, who were the only people in western Europe in those times, before the first millennium, to use secular rather than sacred writing.

The preface to the lines of initiatory detail is Christianised, as are elements of many of the spells, with the most blatant pre-Christian elements replaced with appropriate Christian terminology and ritual. Here the text describes a preliminary ritual, saying, 'You must take seven little wafers, such as are used in worship, and write these names on each wafer . . .' and there then follows a list of biblical names. This Christian introduction almost certainly replaces the carving of nine rune-sticks as an accompaniment, for the instruction then goes: 'and then let a virgin go to him and hang it on his neck. And do so for three days.' The number nine was the primary sacred number in rituals of the Germanic and some of the Celtic tribes of ancient Europe.

In the original version, then, the virgin brings to the person undergoing the ritual the rune-stave, cut with the appropriate runic message and then strung around the neck with a leather thong or piece of rope. The involvement of a virgin marks out that the power of this ritual is female magic. Indeed, it is likely that the woman who performed the presentation of the rune-sticks was originally a shamaness, with the requirement for a virgin being another Christian interpolation.

The instructions require the chant detailed at the beginning of this chapter to be sung over the initiate three times, in either ear and above his head. Three times three is nine, once again the sacred number.

— The Lines of the Spell —

The first lines of the chant are by the shaman to the patient, framing and setting up the apprentice's visions:

> Here a spider-creature came stalking in.
> He had his bridle-web in his hand.
> He said that you were his steed,
> he laid his bonds on your neck.

Harnessed by the bonds of the spider creature, the apprentice is about to be ridden. Now the shaman talks to the audience, describing the flight into the air of the apprentice spider:

> Soon they began to set off from the land.
> And as soon as they came off the land,
> then their limbs began to cool.

And then came the initiation by the Wyrd Sisters:

> Then the sister of the creature came stalking in
> She made an end to it, and oaths she swore
> that never this one the sick should harm
> Nor him who could obtain this charm
> Or understand how this charm to sing.[15]

Spirit helpers normally appear to the apprentice in response to the chant of the shaman . . . the words of power in this case conjuring a spider with a magic web. And once the apprentice had 'seen' this, and allowed it to be placed on him, he is bound to become a shaman. For the web is the very web of Wyrd, spun and woven by the Wyrd Sisters.

So the lines tell the narrative of the apprentice, hot from fever of illness, or from trance-inducing activity such as drumming, dancing, meditation, fasting, and perhaps drinking hallucinatory substances, being visited and 'captured' by one of the Three Sisters in spider form, wrapped in her fibres as a bridle, and ridden into the sky. As they rise into the sky 'his limbs begin to cool', and he is taken to a place where one of the other sisters comes in and proclaims that he is to be protected; he cannot be harmed.

The image of the spider, wrapping the initiate in a web and riding him into the sky is awesome. But what is intriguing is what happens to the apprentice after he is delivered, bound by the web, to the place where the sister 'made an end to it', protects him, and shows him the secrets of the charm? The sister is one of the Wyrd Sisters, and perhaps represents all three of them.

Mythologies from all around the world depict the ascent to the sky by the shaman-to-be, along with other images, in a spider's web. A parallel experience, in which the initiate can see the fibres and the other things that come with it, comes from the Australian shaman of the Yaralde tribe, who also have traditions closely paralleling Wyrd, which describes the initiatory terrors that accompany the vision of the spirits: 'When you lie down to see the prescribed visions, and you do see them, do not be frightened, because they will be horrible . . . If you get up you will not see these scenes, but when you lie down again, you will see them, unless you get too frightened. If you do, you will break the web threads on which these scenes are hung. If you see and hear these things without fear, you will never be frightened of anything . . .'[16] The web of Wyrd holds visions which are gateways to spiritual insights and transcendence.

Even more revealing, the spider spell has remarkable parallels with a recently surviving shamanic ritual from the Malekulan culture, a twentieth-century Stone-Age tribal society in the New Hebrides.[17] The parallel is separated by thousands of miles of land and a thousand years of history, but comparative research on shamanism has shown remarkable parallels the world over in initiatory techniques and narratives which seem to persist across time as well as distance.

Shamanic rituals tap an archetypal level of human functioning, basic ways of encountering the world psychologically and psychically, and so it should not be surprising that such parallels exist.

The narratives of the Malekulans can help us to see how the full story of the experience undergone by the Anglo-Saxon shaman may have developed beyond the few lines afforded by the ancient manuscript. The Malekulans have, at the centre of their shamanic initiation rituals, a labyrinth dance, in which the initiate must show that he is knowledgeable about the prescribed pattern of approach into a cave, wherein he is taught secrets. The dance is for men, and it is presided over by women, as goddesses of the labyrinth. The labyrinth is dedicated to the spider goddess Le-hev-hev, the spinner of fate who is also a 'Mother of Rebirth'.

For the Malekulans the newly 'dead' (apprentice shamans undergoing illness and ritual death), after being bodily abducted and taken into the sky by spider spirits, will arrive at a cave by the sea. There a labyrinth design is traced by Le-hev-hev on the sand at the entrance to the cave. On seeing the 'dead' person, the spider goddess obliterates half the design.

The apprentice has to show that he knows the pattern well, and dances the maze, completing the pattern in the sand. The guardian ghost of the cave, satisfied that the soul of the apprentice shaman knows its dance, releases the soul to join other ancestors in the depths of the cave, where it is taught great secrets known only to the dead. And then the soul is reborn, as the shaman, with knowledge, wisdom, magical powers and skills.

— The Goddess of Dwarfs —

Shapeshifting was quite usual for supernatural beings and, fortunately, the material in this spell is clear enough for us to be able to detect the various disguises. The spider creature was not exactly as it seemed. It had other guises, other identities. The Anglo-Saxon word in the spell translated as 'steed' is 'mearh', close to 'mere' meaning 'mare', or female horse. But the spells are of course handwritten, and it is possible that the word is really the Anglo-Saxon 'mare', which means 'a feminine goblin or succuba'. And this is confirmed by analysis of the spell by Anglo-Saxon linguistic scholars, which has focused on the word translated as 'spider creature', which is written as 'dwear'. This is closely related to the Anglo-Saxon word 'dweorg', meaning 'dwarf'. So if the spider creature also has the identity of a dwarf from the Lowerworld, it extends our understanding of the source of the initiation considerably.[18]

So the apprentice, in an altered state of consciousness, is taken to Le-Hev-Hev by a spider creature in order to be exposed to sacred teachings. But the web-spinning spider also represents the magic of a dwarf, who in turn is one of the Wyrd Sisters in transmuted form. Even more directly, the spider, as a shapeshifted dwarf, represents the powers of the shamanic goddess Freya, who was a later incarnation of the Wyrd Sisters.

In the mythology of ancient Europe, the dwarfs had a special connection to Freya. In fact, in some sense the dwarfs can be seen as doing the work of the sisters; they are an incarnation of the Wyrd Women. The dwarfs were, in the ancient stories, responsible for making magical objects for the gods and goddesses. The animal most sacred to Freya was the sow, and her nickname, Syr, means sow, and for her later male aspect Frey it was the boar, twin symbols which had originally been associated with the worship of the Great Goddess Mother Earth. The dwarfs made golden images of these animals on which the goddess and god rode. Freya's sow was called Hildisvin (Battle Pig) and Frey's boar was called Guillinbursti (Gold Bristled); they could outrun any horse.[19]

The goddess Freya is reckoned to have obtained a famous, or infamous, piece of sacred jewellery, the necklace of the Brisings. There is no doubting the fame and fortune of the necklace itself, a famous piece of jewellery in European mythology. One of the various references to it is in the Anglo-Saxon poem *Beowulf*: 'Never under heaven have I heard of a finer prize among heroes – since Hama carried off the Brising necklace to his bright city, that gold-cased jewel . . .'[20]

Scholars debate the identity of the Brisings, but many reckon them to be four dwarfs of the Lowerworld. And to obtain the necklace, Freya slept with all four dwarfs. It may have originally been that she had sexual relations with all four, simultaneously or over four nights. Indeed, Freya is represented in the later sagas as Thorgerda, and as consorting with trolls and evil creatures of all kinds. The Christian writers who document some of the stories about Freya are deeply disapproving of this aspect of her, and we get only fragments of her exploits as a result. Historians reckon that most of the myths, stories and ceremonies which concerned Freya were either not written down at all, or were written but later destroyed because of the often erotic nature of her mysteries; they were especially singled out for eradication by the monkish missionaries to the north. Even in normally tolerant Iceland, her poetry – the 'mansongr' (love song) – was prohibited.

But certainly Freya's sleeping with the dwarfs in return for the necklace seems to have been pivotal in her lascivious reputation. Brising is the name of some tribe or family; the word derives from the Old Norse 'brisingr', meaning 'fire'. So Brisings means 'fire-dwarfs'. Or the 'shining ones'. Either way it refers either to their gold-making or to the fire they use, or both. Although we are not sure of the identity of these four dwarfs, it has been suggested that they were Nordhri, Austri, Sudhri, and Vestri, identified elsewhere as being stationed at the four cardinal directions of the world, supporting the Upperworld. Recent Eskimo cultural traditions tell of four posts supporting the firmament, and when the posts go rotten they have to be renewed by the angekok or wizards.

In describing the cosmology, Snorri Sturluson also says: 'Four stags browse over the branches of the Ash and nibble at the bark. I'll tell you their names: Dainn, Dvalinn, Duneyrr and Duradrorr.' But Dvalinn is one of the dwarfs . . . so maybe these stags are the characters who taught Freya?

The necklace of the Brisings is much more than a pretty trinket. It is the all-encompassing fourfold cosmic ring, under the control of the great goddess Freya. It is the magical equivalent of the Midhgardh-Serpent that girdles the entire cosmos. The object is said to be worn either as a belt or as a necklace, depending on how the goddess wished to use its power. In any event, the result is the same: Freya gains control over the fourfold cycle of the cosmos and its generative and regenerative powers.

In the *Gods and Myths of Northern Europe*, Hilda Ellis Davidson writes: 'A necklace is something which is associated with the mother goddess from very early times. Figurines wearing necklaces found in the Mediterranean area date back to as far as 3000 BC, and small female figures wearing them have survived from the Bronze Age in Denmark and are thought to represent a fertility deity.'

From the above discussion, it seems likely that Freya's relationship with the dwarfs was an aspect of her initiation. She possibly had ritual sex with the four dwarfs as part of her quest for knowledge. In addition to their alchemical abilities as magical smiths, the dwarfs were depicted as having wisdom. For example, the myths tell about Alvis, a dwarf living in the World of Dark Elves. In a twelfth-century Eddaic poem he reveals some of his wisdom about the various realms of the universe. The name for night varies, he says, from one realm to another. The war gods, fertility gods and giants refer to it by its quality of a dark blanket (Darkness, Hood and Lightless respectively), and the elves call it Sleep's Soothing. The dwarfs, however, refer directly to the Magical Quality of Night, its use as a special, ritual time, its relation to their function as spinners of spells. They call it the Weaver of Dreams. And this is precisely what the dwarf/spider creature does in the initiation spell considered at the outset of this chapter. The content and nature of the dreams that are woven, wrapped in the threads of Wyrd, constitute the process by which the apprentice becomes a shaman.

— Altered States of Consciousness —

The vivid visions of the spider spell, in which the apprentice was gripped by a spider creature which rode him into the sky, cooling his heated body, landed him on an island, where he perhaps danced a pattern in the sand, thereby being admitted into the presence of the spider goddess, and then being given access to the secret knowledge of the dwarfs . . . this of course is the sort of experience which is concomitant with a radically altered state of consciousness; a mind-set very different from the reality-testing and conventionally focused cognition of everyday life. Indeed, if we had such visions as part of our daily life it would be impossible to function, and those people who undergo such powerful inner visions involuntarily usually suffer as a result and sometimes need treatment and support in a protected environment in order to be able to recover.

One name for the spider creature rendered into modern English is the Night Mare. Such images are not outside our own experience, therefore; almost everyone has at some point in their life experienced deep and disturbing dreams. So we all have the psychological capacity and the images to enter the world of the nightmare.

Today we generally regard such powerful experiences as being a by-product of brain 'over-activity' while we are trying to sleep; we have had a 'bad night'. In traditional societies, however, including that of our ancestors in ancient Europe, such dreamings were regarded as having special significance and value. They were an essential element of the range of human experience, and the images were seen as emanating from the deep, universal pool of the spirit world.[21]

Today the nearest concept to this that we have in the West is perhaps the collective unconscious, developed particularly by the Swiss psychiatrist C.G. Jung during the first half of this century. He characterised some of our deeper dream and art images as being shared among all humans, and expressing certain propensities to see the world in ways which were a consequence of our biological and neurological make-up. These deep dreamings were a dipping into a universal consciousness. Similarly, our ancestors thought that such images, such journeys as were undertaken by the apprentice with the spider creature, were as experientially valid as everyday material world activities. They were never regarded as 'just' dreaming. They were as important to the understanding of life and of ourselves as waking activity.

Interestingly, today we seem just as hungry for vivid imagery as ever, but for us it is provided in ready-packaged form for us to consume, rather than to produce. We spend significant chunks of our lives watching images on television, and in the cinema, at rock concerts and spectacles of all kinds. But these images, as well as being manufactured for us, are regarded as 'entertainment'. They are a break from the more serious business of the mundane imagery of everyday life. For our ancestors, the potential psychological power and insight obtainable from entering such imaginal worlds ourselves was developed to a sophisticated degree.

But dreaming is an involuntary entry into an image world akin to that of the spider creature, since most of us do not have direct control over the content and structure of our dreams. In cultures in which shamans functioned as 'dream doctors', which covers almost every traditional society there has ever been, their task was to set up for people, especially those who had been shown to be especially gifted in being able to enter the vivid world of the spirits, psychological journeys in which entry to and return from such worlds was created specifically and consciously.

In order to achieve this journeying ability, shamans themselves engineered their states of consciousness in a number of ways. Many of them undermined the supports which help us to maintain the everyday state of consensual reality. They would deprive themselves of sleep, staying up for marathon numbers of hours all through the nights and days, and most of us have experienced the disorienting effects of sleep deprivation from time to time. They fasted, thus setting aside the confirming, relaxing, comforting and conventionalising effect of eating food regularly, calming hunger pangs and maintaining a high blood sugar level. They went without drink, which soon releases the mind from the usual range of psychological states, and enables it to explore regions previously uncharted.

The shamans also performed marathon dances, so that the rhythmic bodily undulations and beatings of the feet on the floor attuned the mind-body to the rhythm of the spirits. They chanted and sang, shouted and called, intuiting the language of the spirits and using their voices to take them into other realms. Shamans also imbibed various concoctions prepared from selected plants to help to induce visions, glimpses of the Otherworld, sensations of flying, and a number of supporting experiences which empowered their travel out of this mundane world.

In many shamanic cultures, including those of ancient Europe, the shamans used drums to drive their journeying into the spirit world. The rhythmic percussion acts on the brainwaves to produce an effect that drives along the imagination, the flow of images, or perhaps opens up access to images coming from 'another realm'. It overrides the propensity of the mind to wander, to daydream, to lose concentration, to lack momentum in a vision journey; with the drums shamans can keep up a vivid spirit journey for hours at a time.

Of course, in traditional societies where shamans were present to supervise, advise, support and guide involuntary journeys which come from illness, or voluntary journeys which are created through ritual and technique, there is the opportunity for experiences ranging from mild to extreme, depending on whether one is simply a participant in a group tribal event, or whether one is training to be a shaman.

Such journeys in altered states of consciousness are best done under supervision, but there is another way to appreciate and use the idea of threads, the spider, the grip of life, a technique which is a gentle meditation from within the everyday state of consciousness: it can be done with ease and is a subtle but far-reaching way to alter one's idea of the forces and influences on one's life. I call it the Web of Wyrd.

— Mapping Your Web of Life —

I have described the way in which the tribespeople of ancient Europe held in their heads, hearts and artwork an image of a web of golden threads suspending, connecting, and integrating everything in life. The web was so sensitive that any movement, any thought, any happening, no matter how small, reverberates throughout the web, so that everything that happens involves everything else. The image can be a basis for revisioning the way in which we feel connected to other people, other influences and forces. I believe that the implications for our self-understanding are substantial, and it would take an entire book even to begin to explore comprehensively.

In order to find practical ways of working with this vision of our ancestors, I have explored a process of mapping personal webs of threads in which a series of tasks subtly shifts our usual awareness of others to a different dimension, a connected awareness which is akin in some ways to the Web of Wyrd. This process can entail many levels of elaboration and sophistication, and I have used it in working with individuals and in groups. But the basic idea is quite simple. It consists of creating an image of the ways in which our own personal world of relationships forms a web, threads of forces, of which we are a part. I shall describe the basic process here and you could adapt it for your personal use quite simply, as a sort of active meditation.

The first thing I ask people to do is to take a sheet of paper, and a pen, and to list the names of everyone they know. This sounds an impossible and paralysing task, for we all assume that we know thousands of people, far too many to list on paper from memory. And this is probably true, if we include absolutely everyone with whom we have ever come into contact. But the list of names should be those people in your lives now who have a positive emotional importance for you. Not people who have died (these are very important but are addressed in a separate meditation), or people you used to know, nor people you know but who are not significant emotionally, or those people whom you dislike or even hate. Only people who are positive and important to you now are included on this first list.

For most of us, listing people who mean more to us than mere acquaintances is not so difficult, the numbers not so great. In my experience, it takes people between half an hour and an hour to write down all the appropriate names, but this timeframe is meant purely for encouragement; you can take longer or shorter times than this. The important thing is to work at a speed which feels comfortable and enjoyable. And there are no right or wrong numbers of people: we differ enormously in the range of our personal contacts, and also in the cut-off level of intimacy we choose to determine whether a person is emotionally important to us. When working with individuals, I have found people keen to explore these aspects of the process in relation to their own lives.

The threads of our personal connections may be mapped in many ways, but the first web I ask people to construct is one based on 'material-world' geography. When you have completed the list of names, next take a large sheet of paper and draw a map. Usually for beginning work we copy a map of the world, or North America or Europe; a large-scale piece of the world which incorporates the country in which we live. For subsequent work more detailed maps may be appropriate. The map does not have to be exact, so long as it gives a reasonable sense of the geographical extent and location of those parts of the world you are going to incorporate in your meditation.

Mark on the map, with a dot, the place where you currently live, and which forms the geographical centrepoint of your activities. Then, taking your time and working carefully and accurately, and using a different-coloured pen to before, mark on the map the homes of each of the people named on your list. For most of us, this process results in some names being dotted far and wide around the world, and a far greater number being marked nearer to our own home location. But everyone's map is different, there are no 'right' or 'wrong' maps.

The final stage of this task is very carefully and accurately to draw straight lines from the dot representing our own location to each and every other dot on the world map. This can be done in one colour, or using different-coloured pens or pencils for the lines, depending on the nature of your relationship with the person.

You now have a geographical representation of your 'significant other' network, depicting the lines of positive energy that come your way from people who mean a lot to you. It is a map constructed in physical, geographical space, of where we are in our personal universe; the map looks like a huge spider's web, and we can see our position in it; it is a map of supporting threads, keeping us safe.

Apart from those closest to us, with whom we live or share our lives directly, most of us think of the special people in our lives only occasionally, usually one at a time; rarely do we encounter a representation of their sum total. The people with whom I have worked on such webs are often surprised by the cumulative effect of seeing all those threads coming to them from around the country, or around the world. It is a map of encouragement and support, of strength sustained by others, an extended view of one's own emotional territory. A number of the people who constructed these webs have made them into wall-charts; much more directly affecting than ordinary maps of the world!

There are various elaborations you can make even to such a simple web as this: for example, you might find it interesting to join to one another the dots of people in your web who are close to each other emotionally, forming cross-threads in the web. Again there is no right answer; some people have a very integrated web in which many dots are connected to each other, whereas others have a more separated web, in which the lines of personal influence come directly to the mapmaker's location, but do not join up between themselves very much.

As an image of love connections, this basic web is a nice start. But then the real work begins. For it is in using the web of fibres as a meditation which yields the deeper elements of this whole exercise, and begins to edge a little closer to the tremendous range and meaning of the original vision of our ancestors. For with the web ranged in front of you, you can take your time to rest your eye on each dot (most people who have practised this meditation quickly achieve recognition of the identity of each dot without needing to consult the list of names), and allow an image of that person to fill your mind's eye. It is not only a visual image, of course; these are people who are special to you, and so it is also a heart image.

Meditating on these maps is an exhilarating, warming, comforting, and moving experience. It can last anywhere from five minutes (which can be long enough if you are concentrating on one person only at each meditation) to perhaps half an hour or more. But no matter how few or how many people are visualised at each meditation, the session should finish with a contemplation of the whole; the complexity and unity of the entire web is what you should take away with you at the conclusion of each of these times.

From here there are many possibilities. We can abandon physical space maps, and instead construct maps, sometimes three-dimensional, in which we paint images of the threads penetrating our own lives, starting with those influences of which we are consciously aware – people, events, hopes and fears – and then moving on to fibres which can be apprehended only through meditation and inner visioning. These psychic maps are tremendously clarifying, both in their construction and in meditations on them, for they provide a vivid alternative to the jumble of thoughts with which we often attempt to conceptualise the myriad influences operating upon us at any one time.

If you are feeling low, discouraged, or lonely, this simple meditation can be very supportive; you can construct, for example, a web of allies, a web of guardians, a web of companions, or even a web of love.

Chapter Eight

Seeress:
Divining Through Deep Intuition

— Thorbiorg's Seance —

We have considered some of the beliefs and practices of our ancestors which address the capacity for intuitive living. This valuing of the ability to open our ways of feeling and thinking to a broader and deeper reservoir of experience than can be carried in our conscious processing went further even than everyday levels of ability, for the tribespeople of early Europe had individuals who had been selected, divined, chosen by the spirits, trained, initiated, for the express purpose of being able to enter deeply into the intuitive mode. They were men and women. But those who specialised in using, directly, deep intuition in order to be able to see into the future, were almost always women (men more often used spellcasting for this purpose). Seership of this kind was considered, in ancient Europe, to be a feminine power, used on occasion by men, but essentially practised by women.

A thousand years ago, in Iceland, an account was written of the work of one of these women; it is one of the most vivid descriptions of early European shamanic ceremonies and affords some detail in envisioning her divinatory rituals, and in gaining a closer understanding of the gift of deep intuition.

The saga *Erik the Red*, written in the late thirteenth or early fourteenth century in Iceland, depicts the lives of people during the so-called 'saga age' of 930–1030.[1] It includes an account of a seeress named Thorbiorg. The saga is set in Greenland, but historians think it likely that the shamanic tradition documented in the tale thrived in Norway in the tenth century and before. It is possible that Thorbiorg was a historical person. In the account it is clear that she was widely renowned; she was nicknamed Little Sibyl, and was known as the last of a group of nine 'sisters' who were all seeresses, and who journeyed around the country offering advice from the spirit world.

In the saga Thorbiorg is performing divination seances during a great famine. The year preceding her visit had been one of critical food shortages; men who had gone out sealing and fishing had come back with very little and, because of bad weather, some had not returned at all. Late that winter the leading farmer of the area, Thorkel, was given the responsibility of inviting Thorbiorg to prophesy when the terrible famine would end. Many of the local community gathered in his farmhouse, and 'A good reception was prepared for her, as was the custom when a woman of this kind should be received.'

Thorbiorg's appearance was dramatic: she wore a black lambskin hood, unusually lined with white catskin, a long cloak, and catskin gloves which were furry and white on the inside. Shaggy calfskin shoes were laced with long leather straps ending in big brass balls. She carried a tall staff adorned along its full length with brass, and topped with a brass knob surrounded by 'magical' stones.

She removed her cloak to reveal a blue tunic, fastened at the front by leather straps, and sparkling with precious stones all the way down to the hem. Around her neck glowed a necklace of glass pearls, and around her waist a tinderbelt from which was suspended a large animal-skin pouch in which 'she kept the magical stones, feathers, implements and objects of her craft'.

Thorbiorg was greeted with great ceremony. She was served a specially prepared ritual meal created from 'the hearts of all living creatures obtainable', along with a porridge of goat's milk. She ate with her own implements: a brass spoon and copper knife with a hilt of walrus teeth, clamped together by two rings around the handle. Afterwards, she explained that she needed to sleep in the house overnight before embarking on the seance.

Preparations for the spirit seance were completed the following day, and by evening everything was ready, including a ritual 'high seat' topped by a cushion which had to be stuffed with hen feathers. At the appointed time, 'Master Thorkel took her by the hand and led her to her special seat.'

She asked if there was anyone in the hall who could sing the necessary charm to bring the spirits, and at first it appeared as if no one knew the necessary spells. But a young woman called Gudrid knew. 'I am unversed in magic, nor am I a prophetess,' said Gudrid, 'but Halldis my foster-mother taught me in Iceland the chant which she called Varthlokur.'

'Then you are wise in good time,' said Thorbiorg.

'But this is a kind of proceeding I feel I can play no part in,' protested Gudrid, 'for I am a Christian woman.'

'Yet it might happen,' said Thorbiorg, 'that you could prove helpful to folk in this affair, and still be no worse a woman than before. But it is Thorkel I must look to, to procure me the things I need.'

Thorkel, the host of the seance, persuaded Gudrid to help Thorbiorg. The women formed a circle around the platform on which Thorbiorg was seated, the men around the edge of the room. Gudrid recited the chant so beautifully and well that 'no one who was present could say he had heard a chant recited by a lovelier voice.' The seeress thanked Gudrid for the song, said that it was sung well, and that 'those which before would have turned away from us and given us no hearing; but now there are many matters open to my sight which before were hidden both from me and from others'.

When she was ready, Thorbiorg said that she was prepared to answer questions, for the answers had been given to her by the spirits. According to the saga, the farmer asked her about the outcome of the famine and accompanying plague.

'I can easily see many things that were previously hidden both from me and others. I may say that this year of dearth will not last longer than this winter; in the spring everything will be better. The plague, which has been raging for a long time, will cease sooner than you think.'

Then others asked about personal fortunes and misfortunes, possibilities, troubles, anything they wanted, and Thorbiorg answered all the questions. For example, in reply to one young woman who had enquired about her fate, Thorbiorg replied, 'I now see thy fate clearly. Here in Greenland thou shalt get that marriage which is the most honourable, although it will not be lengthy, for thy ways go to

Iceland. And from thee will come a kindred which will be both great and good, and over thy descendants there will shine a bright light. But now, farewell, and good luck, my daughter.'

The saga manuscript says that she was most willing to impart information, and concludes with: 'and it was only a little that did not happen of what she said.'

— The Women Diviners —

This wonderfully detailed account of an ancient ritual shows Thorbiorg undertakes the divination on behalf of the community, as well as individuals. She contacts the spirits in order to gain knowledge concerning the destiny of the people gathered in the farmhouse.

Certainly, all through the heritage of ancient Europe, such women who possessed the powers of deep intuition, of reading the future, were honoured and revered. The tradition was a long one, and we have written records of it stretching back in time at least a thousand years before Thorbiorg.

The Roman historian Tacitus, writing in the first century AD, recorded many valuable observations about the lives of the indigenous peoples living at the frontiers of the Roman Empire.[2] He sums up the attitude of some of the tribes succinctly, writing: 'They believe that there resides in women an element of holiness and a gift of prophecy.' Divination of this kind was originally, in the culture of Wyrd, a mystery known especially to women. Certain women had the capacity, the gift, of being able to receive inspiration from the powers beyond the earthly realm, and they were very greatly honoured for this talent. Tacitus writes: 'In the reign of the Emperor Vespasian we saw Veleda long honoured by many Germans as a divinity; and even earlier they showed a similar reverence for Aurinaia and a number of others.' This esteem obviously went beyond mere fame or social and political status; these seeresses were regarded as sacred.

Veleda was a famed seeress of the tribe of the Bructeri in the Rhineland, where she practised her divinatory arts nearly two thousand years ago. She 'enjoyed extensive authority', Tacitus writes, 'according to the ancient German custom which regards many women as endowed with prophetic powers, and as the superstition grows, attributes divinity to them.' The name Veleda is from 'veles', 'seer', a word related to the Irish 'file', 'poet', and it is likely that these were sacred, shamanic names pertaining to their spiritual attainment, as the Celtic Merlin was the name awarded to the most highly acclaimed wizard-shaman in the romantic literature that has followed from the early traditions of that tribal culture.[3]

The Roman writers explain that Veleda's enormous popularity among the Germanic tribes was largely due to her divinatory visions which predicted the outcome of battles, and especially her foretelling of the unexpected German destruction of the Roman legions in the German revolt of AD 69. Incredibly, when the Romans wanted to agree peace terms with the Bructeri, it had to be done through Veleda. The representatives sent by the Romans were not allowed direct access to the seeress, who remained isolated, sitting in a high tower constructed for the purpose of her divination: 'One of her relatives chosen for the purpose carried to her the questions and brought back the answers, as if he were the messenger of a god.'

We have this invaluable information about Veleda, but she was by no means unique; in early Europe, many tribes venerated such female seeresses, and Roman chroniclers made references to others including Ganna, a priestess of the Semnones, and another 'wise woman' of the Chatti tribe.

The term used for such women in ancient northern Europe was 'spakona', meaning 'a woman with prophetic gifts'. A more precise term for a woman practising divination was 'volva' usually translated 'seeress', and for this there is no masculine form. The divination rite in which the volva took part was known as 'seidr'. The etymology of the word seidr connects it with the large group of terms based on the Indo-European root 'sed': a seidr, then, was literally a seance; a 'sitting' to commune with the spirits.[4]

In the sage of *Erik the Red,* Thorbiorg was said to be the last survivor of a company of nine women, and the sagas elsewhere present the seeresses going about in groups. Possibly at an earlier time than that represented in the sagas isolated seeresses were less common.

The rites they carried out were bound up with the fertility of the land and also with the rearing of a family and the giving of young girls in marriage. It is a tradition in which women were able to participate fully, both as celebrants and as audience. But it went much further than that, for the practice of seidr magic was reserved for women only, and presided over by the goddesses Frigg and, especially, Freya. Both appear at times as the beneficent goddess helping women and girls at the times of marriage and childbirth, as well as shaping the destiny of children. Freya's name is specifically linked by Snorri Sturluson to a special kind of witchcraft known as 'seithr', for he states that she was a priestess of the Vanir who first taught this knowledge to Odin – an event we shall consider later. The volva were really spirit mediums on missions from the goddess Freya, the earthly representations of her great power.

We are told of one volva in the story *Landnamabok* who is said to have worked sorcery so that a sound should fill with fish, which means that she took an active part in the bringing of plenty to the land. The seeresses thus sometimes went beyond divination, and mediated the power that created new life and brought increase into the fields, among the animals, and in the home. They brought also the power to link people with the unseen world. Besides divining concerning the fruits of the earth and the baby in the cradle, they also offered wise counsel granted through divination concerning worldly events. And they offered also the collective experience of sacred ceremonies where the spirits revealed mysteries, and the power of Freya was incarnated for all the participants to witness.

— The Seeress's Art —

The account of Thorbiorg's seance contains a number of interesting objects and processes, a kind of structure through which work could be undertaken in the divinatory arts. They represent a template upon which we may see the way we are living our life in regard to the divinatory impulses within us.

THE POUCH

The saga reports Thorbiorg as having a tinderbelt from which was suspended a large animal-skin pouch in which 'she kept the magical stones, feathers, implements and objects of her craft'. In *The Mound People* archaeologist P. V. Glob describes a prehistoric Scandinavian medicine pouch (a millennium older than that of Thorbiorg but perhaps relating to the practices of Veleda and other early seeresses), noting that thirty of these bags have been found in Bronze Age Danish graves. They must have been similar to the pouch strapped to Thorbiorg's belt. Glob lists the contents of one bag, which gives us an impression of the sorts of items Thorbiorg might have been carrying:

> Inside the bag were the most extraordinary objects: a piece of amber bead, a small conch shell . . . a small cube of wood, a flint flake, a number of different dried roots, a piece of bark, the tail of a grass-snake, a falcon's claw, a small, slender pair of tweezers, bronze knife in a leather case, a razor with a horse's head handle . . . a small flint knife stitched into an intestine or bladder, a small, inch-and-a-half-long leather case in which there was the lower jaw of a young squirrel and a small bladder or intestine containing several small articles . . . the contents of the bag had been used for 'sorcery or witchcraft' and had in fact belonged to a medicine man.[5]

This fascinating collection of objects is in essence the tools of the trade; combined with the knowledge, intelligence, skills of the practitioner, they add up to a way of working with deep intuition. Some of the tools are probably of immediate practical benefit: the 'slender pair of tweezers', for example, could be for making things, or for extracting injurious materials from the skin of a patient. The 'small flint knife' stitched, presumably for safety, into a bladder bag, might also have been of direct practical importance.

But the others are resonant with symbolic meaning, with magical action, and with connection to the spirit world which is the medicine man's Otherworld: the piece of amber bead, for example, does not have an obvious practical use, but may have been part of the paraphernalia of a spell, and amber could have had properties important to the healer. Since it had been constructed into a bead, with a hole drilled through it, the piece of stone had already been intervened with for some purpose or other; alternatively it may have been from the personal decoration of someone important, significant in the healer's life.

The small conch shell may have been for listening to, for hearing voices and advice from the spirits; the small cube of wood may have been from a tree of particular significance, a tree struck by lightning, a tree with which the healer feels an affinity and gains power from, a tree which represents the World Tree, the structural image which joins together the spiritual worlds of the Upperworld and the Lowerworld with the world of everyday reality, Middle Earth. The piece of bark may have had a similar connection, and could indeed have been from the same tree as the cube of wood.

The different dried roots were presumably either for the power of their connection with the plants from which they were extracted, or may have had a direct benefit in being used to make drinks or potions, perhaps from scrapings of the root mixed with water or other substances.

The tail of the grass-snake, the falcon's claw, the horse's head handle on the razor, the lower jaw of the young squirrel: all these could have symbolic referents. The World Tree, for example, has in its classic image a squirrel scurrying up and down its length, crossing between the world of Lowerworld, Middle Earth and Upperworld, exchanging insults between the bird of prey (falcon) which stands on its highest branches, and the serpent (snake) which devours its root. These three objects could have been talismans of the World Tree, along with the piece of wood and bark, all adding up to the calling card of a Wyrd shaman.

This is all speculation, of course, and does not directly relate to the objects in Thorbiorg's bag. But there are plenty of parallels when we remember that her bag is reported to have magical stones (the amber bead), feathers (relating to the falcon's claw), implements (like the tweezers, flint flake and small flint knife) and objects of her craft (objects of her status, her role as a diviner, and perhaps corresponding with the World Tree objects I have just outlined).

The bronze knife in a leather case could have had simple practical usage, although it is intriguing to remember that Thorbiorg had a special copper knife with a hilt of walrus teeth, clamped together by two rings around the handle. The saga account says that the point of the blade has been broken off, possibly in a different sort of ritual. In the Anglo-Saxon *Spellbook*, a short charm to protect against being 'shot' by invisible arrows from elves also requires the use of a knife with a yellow horn handle, and mounted with three brass nails. This implement, too, might be similar to the special knife with which Thorbiorg eats her ceremonial meal, with the walrus teeth representing the same defensive, weaponry function as the brass nails.

All this paraphernalia, easily carried in a leather pouch attached to a belt, sums up the calling card, the essential implements, the weapons and sacred objects of the seeress's, or shaman's, mission. Working practically with deep intuition, making the realm of the inner imagination manifest for the purposes of healing or otherwise, required these special objects.

The Ritual Meal

When she arrives, Thorbiorg is served a ritualistic meal, devised to intensify animal-spirit power. Stephen Glosecki's translation of the narrative indicates that the meal included not goat's milk, but rather colostrum, a sustenance more concentrated than ordinary milk, full of antibodies as well as nutrients, secreted for a few days after birthing to fortify newborn mammals in the weakest phase of their lives.[6] He says that the colostrum of goats is yellow-orange, thick, and very strong-flavoured: 'nowadays, at least, people tend to recoil from it.' Along with this drink, Thorbiorg takes as her meat the hearts of all animals in the vicinity. Her eating of the hearts of a variety of wild animals, using her own special implements, suggests that she needed to integrate their essence into herself in order to gain their strength and help in contacting the spirits. Tribal people often consider the heart a source of spirit strength. By imparting animal power, the meal strengthens her for her ecstatic journey.

The Brass-Knobbed Pole

The ceremonial pole carried by Thorbiorg is common in cultures in which the shaman carries a staff which is placed on the ground foot down, knob up, and represents the World Tree.

Carrying a ceremonial pole was symbolic of these journeys. The fact that Thorbiorg's staff was decorated with brass all down the side, ending with a brass knob adorned all round with magical stones, suggests that the brass decoration may depict the journey she makes to the spirit world. The 'magical stones' which decorate the top of the staff perhaps represent the worlds of knowledge of the Wyrd cosmology.[7]

As the symbol of journeying, or 'flying' to the spirit world, the staff also represents a means of flight, a symbol of spiritual transportation. Centuries later in the European female shamanic traditions, when the surviving practices were labelled as 'witchcraft', the witches were depicted as flying on staffs in the form of broomsticks, which for them represented spirit travel.

THE HIGH SEAT

For her divinatory ceremony Thorbiorg was placed on a high seat or stool, and in an account of another ritual it was recorded that one of the volvas was seated when making prophecies, and was very angry when people crowding around her inadvertently pushed her off her seat. Seidr divination rituals invariably employed a high seat for the seeress, probably representing the shamanic flight to the spirit world which she was about to undertake, and placing her in an elevated position from which she could receive visions of worlds beyond.

The volva's journey to the spirit world was often depicted as being like flying as a bird. Thorbiorg's high stool was required to be topped by a hen feather-filled pillow. And Freya, the archetypal shamaness represented by Thorbiorg, was reported in the stories as being able to adopt a 'feather' or 'falcon' shape, and when she flew she shapeshifted into a bird and travelled vast distances. Also, the myths suggest that she had a kind of flying bird shamanic costume which she lent to the male gods so that they could fly.

Sometimes, as the volvas 'flew' to the spirit world by sending their souls out of their bodies, people would claim to have 'seen' them, usually in the form of women with hair streaming out behind them as they flew. But it was a dangerous journey, because if the soul was wounded or killed on its travels in the spirit world, the body of the seeress showed corresponding wounds or even died.[8]

— Singing the Spirit Trance —

In other, more fragmentary accounts of seidr rituals it is implied that the seeress obtained her knowledge while in a state of trance; she was said to gape, to fall down as though dead, to be roused with difficulty, to be utterly exhausted when the ceremony was over, and so on.[9] In some accounts of similar divinatory rituals, seeresses travelled with a number of singers trained in the incantations necessary for the spirit work. But at the time this saga was set, Christianity was the official religion, and Thorbiorg had no singers with her.

In the early north-west European female tradition, seeresses such as Thorbiorg seem to rely on voice chanting, or song. Another account of seidr describes a lone seeress called Heidr, who travelled to divinatory ceremonies with thirty trained singers, half men and half women, taking this trance-inducing and spirit-catching function to a sophisticated level. The effect of having so many chanters performing in a farmhouse, singers able to exploit the potential of human voice, in range and volume, would be overwhelming. And the soundscape is created live, for the very first and last time in its precise formation; a unique performance which has the immediacy of performance art, rather than the safe, contained effects of a sound trapped in a recording on tape or disc. The singers accompanying shamanesses were chanters.[10] They sang songs in a magical way. The skill of drawing in the spirits depended upon pitching and rhythmically pulsating the air in a manner which enabled the trance-entering of the seeress, and opened the doors of heaven for the entry of other forces.

While the shaman journeyed to the spirit world, and the songs catalysed this transformation, he also needed song to induce a receptive and appropriately creative state of consciousness in the audience, who after all were participants rather than mere observers. It is important that they were 'taken out of themselves' so that the audience became as one, was literally and metaphorically 'in the spirit' of the occasion, in the beginnings of sacred intoxication, and therefore ready to receive the messages to be transmitted by the shaman from the world of spirit.

While the rhythm of drumming or chanting may induce altered

states of consciousness relevant to the rituals being carried out, the words of chants can also carry significance. Hilda Ellis Davidson explains that the title of the spell-song required by Thorbiorg for her ceremony is related to the Scots dialect word 'warlock', or wizard, and the meaning is thought to relate to the power to shut in or enclose.[11] She suggests that this might be interpreted in two ways: first, the song could attract and hold the helping spirits who enabled the volva to obtain the knowledge; alternatively it could mean that the song had the power to arouse the volva from her state of trance and summon back her wandering soul from the spirit world to return to the enclosure of her body.

In Thorbiorg's ceremony, the song used was obviously one generally known to elicit the spirits. But in all shamanic traditions, reference is made to songs which are unique to shamans, and which sometimes play a part in their initiation. Certainly they have a quality different from melodic entertainment. German ethnopsychologist Holger Kalweit reports a shaman from a more recent tribal culture describing the way songs take him over, how the words are induced by other forces:

> Songs are thoughts, sung out with the breath when people are moved by great forces and ordinary speech no longer suffices. Man is moved just like an ice floe sailing here and there out in the current. His thoughts are driven by a flowing force when he feels joys, when he feels fear, when he feels sorrow. Thought can wash over him like a flood, making his breath come in gasps and his heart throb. Something like an abatement in the weather, will keep him thawed up and then it will happen that we, who always think that we are small, will feel still smaller. And we will fear to use words. But it will happen that the words we need will come of themselves. When the words we want to use shoot up of themselves – we get a new song.[12]

This gives us a glimpse of the experience for Thorbiorg and other volvas of the power of their songs.

In many cases, the spirit songs are connected with the initial experience of spirits which occurs before initiation begins, and it is likely that Thorbiorg must have had at one time such a primary encounter. And there is invariably a time also when the shaman is able to summon the presence of spirits by a song, even though there may well have been 'involuntary' encounters with the spirits earlier in life. The shaman's role is to mediate between people and the spirit world, and therefore had to include the conscious raising of spirit energies.

To see and hear in a totally different way is what happened in the case of a shamaness from the north early this century, a woman who may well have had a similar shamanic path to Thorbiorg's of a thousand years earlier. She was called Uvavnuk.[13] Knud Rasmusson, an explorer, heard the story of Uvavnuk's initiation. He reports that one evening she had gone out to pass water. It was a dark winter's evening, and suddenly a shining ball of fire showed in the sky. It came down to Earth, directly towards the place where Uvavnuk sat. She wanted to run away, but before she could do so she was struck by the ball of fire. 'She became aware all at once that everything in her began to glow. She lost consciousness and from that moment on was a great summoner of the spirits. The spirit of the fire ball had taken up residence within her . . .'

Apparently, Uvavnuk went running into the house, half unconscious, and sang a song which since that time became her magic formula whenever she was to help others. As soon as she began to sing, she became delirious with joy, because the people she was seeking to help became cleansed of all that burdened them. 'They lifted up their arms and cast away everything connected with suspicion and malice. All these things one could blow away like a speck of dust from the palm of the hand with this song.'

Rasmusson gives the words of Uvavnuk's song:

> The great sea has set me in motion,
> Set me adrift,
> Moving me as the weed moves in a river
>
> The arch of sky and mightiness of storms
> have moved the spirit within me,
> till I am carried away
> Trembling with joy.

It is clear that this song is a transcending, exhilarating, cleansing, relieving, tension-banishing song full of love and joy. Perhaps the songs sung by Thorbiorg and her trained singers were similar, songs that transcended the entrapment of everyday 'suspicion and malice', and instead induced a sense of love 'delirious with joy'. This is indeed a healing state, as we know from the evidence of complementary medicine in training people to meditate and envision the body healing itself from illnesses.

— Divination Today —

The gift of divination brought by the volva was a mysterious and magical one, essential for an understanding of the forces at work in the world. In subsistence economies, as that of the indigenous Europeans, attunement to the most subtle nuance of weather, crop production, childbirth, health and warfare determined whether or not survival was possible. They were issues of life and death with which we no longer grapple so directly, on a daily basis, in the contemporary Western world. The volvas represented Frigg and Freya, goddess descendants of the Wyrd Sisters, and people paid service and homage to their powers of fertility.

But what of its relevance to us today, a thousand years and more later? Colourful though it seems as a tradition, we no longer place such high value on deep intuition, on 'reading' the future, or so it seems. Should we think differently on this matter? Could we recall the spakonas to our society? Should we?

To my mind, it is less a question of reinventing something that supposedly no longer exists, but rather recognising something that takes place all the time, but gets ignored because it is not the rational, logical thinking that we are used to. We are making predictions, prophecies all the time about what is going to happen in the future. The enormous gambling industry across the Western world depends on such judgements, of course, where people are placing bets on their predictions of which random numbers will appear in a lottery, which horse will win a race, which dice will land wherever on a roulette table. All are staking small or large pieces of personal disposable income on judgements of the future; 'seership'.

Equally, in business, many executives use 'seership', deep intuition, even divination, in their thinking; in projecting sales, in working on commodities markets and in currency dealing, in investment of all kinds. These are realms in which judgements about what will happen are beyond the simple formulae allowed by the processing of information which can be logged. There are too many uncertainties, too many permutations of events, for us to process the likely outcomes, even on computers. We need to make a judgement. Successful business people are usually the ones who manage to do this, although for the most part they will put it down to 'experience', rather embarrassed to lay claim to being good at something as unlogical, unrational, unmasculine as 'intuition'.

But it is in the less acquisitive regions of our personal lives that we constantly practise our seership, our attempts to weigh the outcomes of situations, conversations, happenings and events, courses of action. Our lives are dominated by such continuous activity, and our daily reverie consists largely of rehearsing possible future scenarios, from the simple to the complex. In this context, rational thinking plays but a small part, even though we may convince ourselves, individually and collectively, that we are logically working through the possibilities. In fact, judgements are much more dependent not on tapping the information we have passing through our conscious minds – where we all have a strictly limited ability to process information – but on 'listening' to the processing, below awareness, of information that we have taken in and 'digested'.

Occasionally we all use our deep intuition, our reservoir of inner knowledge which is not directly accessible to the conscious mind, but which is 'in there'. We know things 'in our bones', we can 'feel it in our waters', we 'play hunches' and 'follow our nose', thereby acknowledging the possibility of living more in touch with this deep intuitive power.

If we are inspired at all by Thorbiorg's story, by a culture in which people trusted intuition, then we should consider what the lessons of the story are. How can we learn from her in dealing with the realm of deep intuition?

I think we can understand more fully how Thorbiorg and her fellow seeresses could envisage the intuitive mode, and were able to take in information from the 'outside' in the way that they thought about the connections between themselves and the rest of the world. They allowed 'outside' information, forces, influences, to come 'inside' them, rather like a medium.

But when the seeresses talk about journeying to the spirit world to gain information, they sound as if they are somehow about to go outside their skin and travel in thin air. This was the depiction of such women several hundred years later than Thorbiorg, of course, when in a Christian Church-dominated Europe they were talked of as 'riding through the sky on broomsticks' while their physical bodies lay in their houses in a sleep so deep that they seemed to be in a trance, or a coma.

The essence of the way in which we encounter this idea is the relation we have with the boundary of our selves and the world around us. In the Web of Wyrd exercise we were depicted as having an extended psychological self. And if you think about it for a moment, it is quite possible there is at this very instant someone, somewhere in the world, thinking about you; so you are not only in the physical location where you are reading this book, but also somewhere else, at least as a psychological presence.

This sense of being an extended presence can go further than the merely cognitive. The descriptions of shamanic journeying in tribal societies are physical ones, a sense that the body is really being left behind, bringing another dimension to the extended sense of self. The sensation of filling more space than just our physical body, of experiencing something more akin to the space we fill psychologically, was surely only a part of what Thorbiorg did, but it is an entry to her world, a small step outside the limiting visions of our own.

For most of us the sensation of operating from a centre within the physical body is paramount. We think of ourselves as an individual entity quite separate from everything and everybody around us. We live according to the assumption that our identity is coterminous with our body, and that 'I' am 'in here' while everyone else is 'out there'. This viewpoint is so deeply ingrained in the way we are brought up that it conditions every other perspective we develop in life. It comes as a shock when we hear of people who believe it could be otherwise, that the self can exist outside the body, as we did in ancient Europe.

Our sense of a 'self' located in the head is for most of us the control box from which we live, from where we make decisions about our behaviour. This sense of self dominates – it is thought of as in a proprietal capacity relative to the rest of the body. We speak, for example, of 'my arms' or 'my legs' as if they were somehow separate from, but owned by, the self. Yet the self cannot escape the body. We are limited by physical boundaries. And because this body-bounded view of our selves is so fundamental, it underlies all other aspects of how we live.

At the Royal Academy of Dramatic Art in London I explored the process of extending the sense of the body boundaries in a meditation with an actor called Kirsten Hughes. She lay on her back in the middle of a very large rehearsal room, her eyes closed. I talked her through a relaxation procedure which slowed her breathing, relaxed her body and cleared her mind. Each succeeding breath becomes slower and deeper than the one before.

I asked her to imagine that with each succeeding breath she was taking in a colour, any colour she chose. With each intake of breath a ball of the coloured light formed in her body; a bright, vivid ball of light at her centre, the core of her energy, her body, her mind. This psychological process, in which a colour visualisation concentrates the mind, is a very effective meditation.

I then asked Kirsten to imagine a pebble being dropped into her ball of colour, as if into a pool of water. Ripples spread out and around, and the colour passed through her skin and gradually spread around the room. She continued to breathe deeply and strongly. The colour ebbed and flowed until it filled a huge space outside her body. She continued to work, to breathe, until the colour filled the complete interior space of the theatre. The colour, I suggested, was her extended self. The room was filled with her energy. Her body and my body were inside her extended self. We were both inside *her*.

At this stage I asked Kirsten to stand up, but keeping her eyes firmly closed. Taking her by the arm, I led her around a tour inside her newly extended self. She discovered the environment, the space, inside an extended self. It is huge. We walked faster. Her eyes were tightly shut, and I was leading her at a good walking pace, and I asked her to begin reporting to me her sensations — where it felt warm, where cold. And to tell me when she felt she was passing through the centre of the space, from where her energy had arisen.

Kirsten began to feel at home inside herself. She was striding around confidently in the space. I let her arms go and she walked with no guidance, safe because she was not walking in alien territory. Everywhere she went was space that was hers. Her self. No longer confined by her body. Extended. Expanded. Exhilarated. The boundaries were stretched. Until she walked near a wall and I shouted 'Stop!' for her boundaries of self were now coterminus with the huge room rather than with her body. Then she set off in a different direction, continuing the voyage inside Kirsten.

Eventually, she began trotting across the space, her eyes still closed. I guarded the edges and shouted when she was in danger. She was running inside herself. She ran again, and again, faster. Soon she was running at high speed across the room, with me to meet her near the boundaries. It was terrifying and thrilling to watch. And the sense of exhilaration and liberation that came from her running uninhibited, blindfold, in extended inner space, was incredible. She was ecstatic. Her feeling of freedom, of influence, of taking in so much more, of being able to see further, even with her eyes closed, was vivid.

Eventually, I guided Kirsten back to the centre of the room. She lay down again, and I directed her breathing back to normal. Shortly afterwards she had to leave to go straight on to a rehearsal for the production she was in. Her fellow actors, who knew nothing of her experience of an extended self, told her they were stunned by her work at rehearsal. They had never seen her performing with so much confidence, spontaneity, intuition, vision.

Extending the sense of self is not the same thing as seership, of course, but I believe that it is part of that process, a small glimpse into the inner world of Thorbiorg. A small step backwards in time, towards the experiential world of our indigenous ancestors.

Chapter Nine

Heart of the Wolf:
Transcending Warriorhood

— Odin —

The divinatory seance of Thorbiorg provides a close encounter with the work of a mystic from the world of our ancestors. And the clues in the magical medical documents, stories, sacred poetry and archaeological research which I have described in earlier chapters make it possible to begin to pull together the threads of wisdom of Wyrd, even on occasion weaving them into some sort of pattern which might begin to resemble the original, a thousand years ago and more.

But there is one particular body of material that I have not yet described in any detail. This is the sacred poetry collected together by Snorri Sturluson referring to the initiatory experiences of the god Odin. These accounts, written in the thirteenth century but from material of centuries earlier, afford a glimpse of the first-hand experiences of a mystic of Wyrd as he enters the 'sacred realms'.

When Wotan sings across the opera stages of the world, at the centre of the *Ring* cycle of Wagner, his stories are dramatised in the manner befitting grand opera. But the stories are more than the dramatic creations of Wagner. They go back a thousand years. They represent some of the key themes of ancient shamanic Europe. The stories, like so much else of the traditions of the forest peoples, lie just beneath the surface of modern-day culture, so that we are still breathing our ancestral knowledge, stirring archetypal patterns, when we think we are merely enjoying an evening's entertainment! Not only opera; I believe that many of our artistic and cultural activities, be they theatre, dance, film, fine art and so on, provide overlays upon overlays, mirrors, masks and disguises which enable us to stay in touch with ancient themes of our sacred past amid the secular settings of modern-day society.[1]

Wotan, as he was known in ancient Germanic cultures, was called Woden in Britain, and Odin in Scandinavia. Most of our knowledge about his original nature stems from this latter tradition, for these far reaches of north-west Europe were Christianised later than the mainland and Britain, in some cases not until the beginning of the second millennium; Iceland became officially Christian in the rather neat historical niche of 1000 AD. And so in Scandinavia the sacred stories of deities and spirits survived longer, and were admitted into post-Christian life more fully than before by missionaries keen to engage the last outposts of 'lost souls' into the messianic mélange of the organised Church.[2]

The thirteenth-century Icelandic historian Snorri Sturluson, writing from oral tradition and written sources now lost to us, describes the Norse god Odin's appearance: he has only one eye, the other being sacrificed during his quest for visionary initiation. He travelled among people, and in human size and form, wearing a wide-brimmed hat to avoid recognition. He has a blue cloak, and carries a magic spear called Gungnir. A traveller carrying a spear would not have been unusual, though on Odin's shoulders ride two ravens, called Huginn and Muninn, which must have been rather more of a giveaway. The names mean, roughly, 'thought' and 'memory', and each day the sacred birds cover the world for him as visionary seers.[3]

Snorri Sturluson explains that Odin was originally a mortal being of great wisdom and knowledge.[4] His exploits became legend, then myth, and finally he was recognised in the form of a god. As a deity he was acknowledged and celebrated widely across tribal Europe, from the northernmost reaches of Scandinavia to the eastern steppes of Germany, south into the Celtic lands of Breton and west to Ireland, where his identity was represented by the Celtic god Lugh.[5]

The god's very name ties him to the beginnings of the shamanic traditions of Europe. The etymology of the Germanic name Woden relates it to 'wut', meaning 'high excitement, fury, intoxication or possession', and the Old Norse adjective 'odr', from which Odinn, the late form of his name in Scandinavia, is derived, bears a similar meaning of 'raging, furious, intoxicated'. These words, conjuring an image of extreme emotional arousal, mental and physical inspiration, a crucible for great 'possessing' forces, describe the state of mind, body and spirit of the shamanic trance.[6] They are virtually identical to the etymological meaning of the term shaman, which derives from the word 'saman' of the Tungus people of Siberia, meaning 'one who is excited, moved, raised'. So in the ancient languages of north-west Europe, it seems likely to me that Odin/Wotan/Woden is a title meaning 'shaman', a professional designation, a name to be awarded and assumed upon completion of the initiatory process of inner discovery. Indeed those stories about Odin which have survived depict him as possessing a wide range of shamanic abilities, including healing, spellcasting, shapeshifting, and the knowledge of sacred signs and symbols. In addition, Snorri Sturluson says that: 'Odin . . . had the gift of prophecy, and by means of this magic art he discovered that his name would be famous in the northern part of the world, and honoured above that of all kings.'[7] As we have seen, divination was regarded as the province of female magic. Odin's knowledge of divination was a gift from Freya, the goddess of seeresses, and he transcended the gender division of initiation to become the most gifted shaman of all. His acquisition of women's knowledge was highly controversial as I shall soon explain.

Although Odin/Woden/Wotan was conceived of as the 'original' shaman, this is highly unlikely in the linear dimension of historical time. Such archaeological clues as we have in, for example, the cave paintings of Lascaux, suggest that the practice and artistic depiction of shamanic activity would have long predated the person of Odin as he was imaged in the so-called Dark Ages.[8] But the traditional cultures of Europe saw time not as a historical sweep of linearly ordered events connected inexorably by chains of influence, but rather in cycles and rhythms. And this concept of time lent itself to ritual in which the participants were able to 'stop' time and to create, by means of activities rich in symbolic significance, a timeless state in which the original event could be relived.[9]

These rituals celebrated Odin's identity as being the original shaman. When he took the shaman name of Odin, he would have inherited all

Heart of the Wolf: *Transcending Warriorhood*

previous wisdom as if it were his own. The people of Wyrd were probably aware of ancient shamanic practice from stone monuments which had survived all over Europe from aeons ago, and they would have incorporated this awareness into their own sacred life.

In this sense Odin/Wotan/Woden is truly the 'First Shaman'. As Wotan sings Wagner's music on the opera stages of today, he is giving us only a glimpse of what he knows.

— The Lesson of Death and Rebirth —

> I mind the folk war – the first in the world –
> when they pierced Gullveig with their pointed spears,
> and her they burnt in the High One's hall;
> she was three times burnt and three times born,
> over and over yet ever she lives.
>
> Heidr men call me when their halls I visit,
> a far-seeing witch, wise in talismans, caster of spells,
> cunning in magic, to wicked women welcome always.[10]

It nearly did not happen. Any of it. For Odin had to learn a crucial, life-changing lesson from Freya, the goddess of magic, before he could take the first step of his initiation. The lesson was about death, rebirth, and the power of the feminine.

It is a remarkable story. The poetic lines above are from the *Elder Edda*. The narrative reveals how Odin was led into shamanic realms, indeed on his wisdom quest, by a woman, a seeress already versed in the powers of the spirit world. The incident which impels this to happen is embedded in poetic lines which contain the visions of a seeress presumably very like Thorbiorg. I have taken these visions to be those of a single seeress, and put them together in the account below, moving back and forth within this vivid material. In particular, I have included a section of the poem dealing with a seeress's vision of a war which ends the world within the seance conducted by Heidr and Gullveig, in the lines above. (Gullveig and Heidr, names which mean respectively 'Shining One' and 'Gold', are identical names for one and the same person.)

So the story opens when Odin, as a powerful warrior and chieftain, is leading a tribal community across western Europe and into Scandinavia, and 'taking possession of much of the land', in Snorri's account. They arrived in what is now Sweden, and their travels were 'attended by such prosperity that, wherever they stayed in a country, that region enjoyed good harvests and peace, and everyone believed that they caused this, since the native inhabitants had never seen any other people like them for good looks and intelligence'. Since Odin struck such a fine figure, I suspect that this is well before he lost an eye, bought the large-brimmed floppy hat for disguise in the 'lands of men', and had two ravens riding on his shoulders and leaving droppings on his cloak.

According to *Visions of the Seeress*, a woman called Heidr came to Odin's great hall, a woman who could see into the future, cast spells, manipulate magical objects and charms; an impressive volva rather like Thorbiorg. 'Outside I sat by myself . . .' she said,[11] 'by myself, when you came, terror of the gods, and gazed in my eyes. What do you ask of me? Why tempt me?'

'Terror of the gods' refers to Odin's power in the realm of the warrior gods: 'and gazed in my eyes' is interesting: perhaps he took a long, close look into Heidr's eyes to see if she really was a seeress.

She does not come readily: 'What do you ask of me? Why tempt me?' It seems that she wants Odin to say it, to ask for her wisdom, to name a price. He does so: 'Arm-rings and necklaces, Odin, you gave me to learn my lore, to learn my magic.'

Heidr, a far-seer, conjures a vision into the future, and offers Odin a prophecy, a glimpse of her occult knowledge: 'Odin, I know where your eye is concealed, hidden away in the well of Mimir: Mimir each morning his mead drinks from Allfather's pledge.' Allfather is one of the names applied to Odin, and she seems to be prophesying the initiatory encounter he will have with the wisdom giant Mimir, when he will be granted knowledge of spells of power in exchange for his sacrificing of an eye and embarking on a terrible beheading game.

'Well, would you know more?' Heidr is obviously telling Odin the sort of thing he wants to hear, and at this point Odin may have given her more gold in exchange for another vision. She goes on: 'Of Heimdahl, too, and his horn I know, hidden under the holy tree? Down on it pours a precious stream from Allfather's Pledge.' Heimdahl was a god who accompanied Odin in his consultations with Mimir – he is even perhaps an aspect of Odin – and so she is relating further detail about Odin's initiatory encounters with Mimir. 'Well, would you know more?'

But then, abruptly, her narrative changes, and she seems to address the beings and spirits that are clamouring in her entranced mind:

> Silence I ask of the sacred folk,
> Silence of the kith and kin of Heimdahl.

With this exclamation she has banished from her mind the visions of Odin's initiatory future and starts to tell of something else.

At Odin's request she recounts ancient knowledge: 'At your will Allfather, I shall well relate the old songs of men I remember best.' Heidr tells, at length, of the beginning of time, how Earth and sky were created out of chaos, and how the first man and woman were created out of driftwood on the shore. She recounts how the gods established themselves in Asgard, and lived in contentment around the World Tree, naming created things, making tools and fine treasures, building halls, and sitting in counsel to establish the laws which governed the worlds.

This is not prophecy, because it is something which presumably has happened already (although with cyclical time one can never be sure), but it is occult knowledge, secret information about the beginnings of time. Either Odin already knows it and she is establishing her credentials by proving that she knows it too, or it is new information, and he is learning from her. I suspect that it is the latter, because it seems unlikely that Odin would be bribing her with arm rings to tell him things he already knows.

She then tells Odin what was his role at the beginning of time when he came to the Earth and found ash and elm trees which were feeble, faint and with no destiny, no breath, no blood or senses, no language or life colour. And it was he who was able to give them these things.

She then returns to prophetic visions: 'I know an ash-tree, named

Yggdrasil . . .' and begins to describe the sacred tree on which Odin will undergo his initiatory tests, where it stands in the mythological universe, and then tells of the three Norns, the Wyrd Sisters, who determine the lives of men and fix for ever their fate.

This is where things take a dramatic turn for the worse. Presumably up to now it has all been acceptable to Odin. He keeps wanting to hear more. But suddenly, Heidr switches the attention to herself, and delivers shocking lines, predicting a war which will result from the attempts of Odin and his warriors, right there in the great hall, to pierce her with spears and attempt to burn her to death in the fire-pit. But that she will be reborn. We can imagine the stunned reaction.

The seeress plunges into visions which prophesy tragedy, bad fortune, and catastrophe. She tells about war breaking out between the different races of the gods: the Vanir, fertility gods (of which she is a representative) and the Aesir, warrior gods (Odin's tribe). She also predicts greed, oath-breaking and treachery: 'Oaths broken, binding vows, solemn agreements sworn . . .' and delivers a crushing image of a war to end the world. Since this comes much later in the poem, it may be more a forewarning of the worst that could happen if the imminent war between the races of gods was not contained. It must have made for pretty apocalyptic reading: omens and portents preceded the end, Odin's son Balder will be slain, and the monsters which the gods had held secure (remember Fenrir the wolf?) will break loose to join the frost giants in an attack on Asgard. In the final battle both gods and monsters will perish, and raging fire and overwhelming seas engulf the Earth. She recounts her vision of the future: 'Earth sinks in the sea, the sun turns black, cast down from heaven are the hot stars, fumes reek, into flames burst, the sky itself is scorched with fire.' It is a deeply disturbing vision, even now. Far too like a nuclear holocaust for comfort.

Her prediction about the war between the races of gods was borne out. Other sources in the ancient sacred literature show that the mythological war did happen, despite initial attempts to negotiate a settlement. This means that Odin and his warriors did try to burn Heidr/Gullveig. The gods had lived in peace until Gullveig's visit to the stronghold of the Aesir. The myth explains that after the

Aesir tried to kill Gullveig, the Vanir met to decide whether they should demand a wergild, a fine in punishment for their hostile actions. But their deliberations were cut short when Odin hurled his spear into the kingdom of the Vanir in the well-known signal that war was to begin. In the myth it was described as the first war ever.

Christian writers blame this on Gullveig, and a later version of the story, written after the north had been firmly Christianised, reflects the Christian aversion to feminine magic. The 'heroic lay' of the verse Edda called *Volsungakvitha* dates from after the year AD 1000; that is, after the introduction of Christianity to Iceland:

> Thou wast a Valkyrie thou loathsome witch
> evil and base in Allfather's hall;
> the Champions all were forced to fight
> for thy sake thou subtle woman.[12]

But, eventually, in the myth the fertility and warrior gods called a truce. And at this cessation of battle, the gods held a peace conference and arranged an armistice this way: they each went up to a pot and spat their spittle into it. When they parted, the gods took that peace token and rather than let it perish they made of it a man. This man is called Kvasir, so wise that 'nobody would question him about anything at all without his knowing the answer'. So the outcome of the war between the masculine and the feminine principles was wisdom.

What does this incident mean? What can we make of it today? There is so much here it is difficult to know where to start. It has to be, I think, with the identity of the seeress.

— The Presence of Freya —

To begin to unlock some of the significance of this tale, we must stay with the myth a little longer, and begin by examining again the identity of the seeress.

Gullveig and Heidr, the two names of the seeress, both mean, essentially, 'gold' or 'bright as gold'. But in the myths generally it was Freya, the archetypal shamaness, revered as a deity, who was the primary image of a 'golden goddess'. She wept golden tears, gleamed with golden decoration including the famous necklace of knowledge called Brinsangamen, and embodied gold as a symbol of wisdom. Not only that: Freya was also deemed to be in charge of the powers of divination, magic and witchcraft. She owned a falcon skin which enabled her spirit to take the form of a bird, travel to the Lowerworld, and come back with prophecies and knowledge of destinies. And so Gullveig and Heidr are identified by some scholars as being Freya in disguise.[13]

Why would Freya be in Odin's hall? Snorri Sturluson has the answer, for he tells us that it is Freya who teaches Odin the secrets of divination, the special kind of sorcery that was a woman's mystery.[14] Her appearance at his hall as a diviner drew him into her power. I believe that, as Snorri says, for Freya to initiate Odin into the mysteries of the seeress's art (the most powerful magic there is, according to Snorri), she needed to get him to make a commitment to embarking on such a transition. He said that he wanted to learn some of her lore and some of her magic, and he paid Freya in gold arm rings for her divinatory seance. But there is, of course, much more to it than that.

At the outset of the encounter Odin acted as though he could 'buy' the seeress's knowledge with gifts of gold: 'Arm-rings and necklaces, Odin, you gave me to learn my lore, to learn my magic,' she says. In fact, Freya does not give much indication that she is keen to 'sell' her knowledge to Odin. At first, she wants to know why he is trying to tempt her with gifts, as if she doubts his motives. And she continually tests him during the seance by asking him to confirm whether he wants to 'know more', as if she is not sure that he is yet ready to hear more. But then, in the divinatory seance when she finally tells him what he does not want to hear, Freya knows that when Odin hears about the dark, shadow sides of his future life he will be so enraged by the bad news that he will try to rid himself of his doom-laden future by killing the messenger.

We also know from a couple of mythological sources that Odin did indeed start the war that the seeress predicted: in the *Vision of the Seeress*, right after the Gullveig story, come the lines:

> Odin hurled his spear into the army of enemies:
> so came for the first time war into the world,
> the walls crumbled of castle Asgard;
> the raging Vanir trampled the earth.[15]

The same incident is related in the *Ynglinga Saga*: 'Odin moved with his band of warriors against the Vanir (the race of fertility gods of which Freya was a member), but they knew the attack was coming and defended themselves, so that neither were able to overcome the others. Each devastated the lands of the others and caused much damage. When they had had enough of this warfare, they agreed on a peace treaty and exchanged hostages.'

So Odin initiated the attack, but his battle strategy failed. In the peace treaty in which they exchanged hostages, the fertility gods sent Njord (Freya's father) and his son Frey (probably originally Freya herself, before the cultural changes in gender of the gods, which I discussed earlier in the book). In exchange for Frey (Freya) and her father, the warrior gods sent Hoenir (often the trusted companion of Odin on his travels) and the wise giant Mimir (who was to be Odin's mentor in his shamanic initiation). This deal produced a fragile peace; broken once, almost right away, but then restored.

— Freya Comes Back to Life —

So why did Freya, in the guise of Heidr/Gullveig, visit the hall of Odin and prophesy his attempt to kill her and the subsequent war? Some writers on mythology have concentrated on the notion that she 'caused' the first war, and that that is the significant dimension of the story. But for me the overriding image which comes from the incident is not the predicted war, but Freya's coming back to life three times from death. This process of death and rebirth lies at the heart of shamanism and the sources of many of the great religions. I think that Freya wanted to demonstrate to Odin her shamanic powers of death and rebirth to draw him into his own process of development, of transcendence of his status as a warrior and on to a new identity as a shaman.[16] In fact, in mythology, Odin eventually becomes the archetypal shaman on whom mortal shamans based their sacred visions and rituals. The dramatic encounter in his hall marks, I believe, the beginning of Odin's journey into deep inner knowledge.

Of course Freya, as Heidr/Gullveig, was conscious that she already possessed shamanic knowledge and abilities. The central lines of the whole poem depict her nature: 'A far-seeing witch, cunning in sorcery'. We have to recognise that these words from a pre-Christian era have acquired, over the centuries, a negative connotation. For many people 'witch', at least until the recent renaissance of women's spirituality, reeked of rituals evil and forbidden. Now it is more widely recognised as a term designating a practitioner of 'wicca', an aspect of the spirituality of ancient Europe.[17]

Similarly, 'cunning' is a quality which is nowadays regarded with suspicion. It is synonymous with 'sneaky, scheming', and certainly 'not to be trusted'. And the word 'sorcery' implies action of a malevolent quality and dark forces. But in the context of the ancient European shamanic tradition the words are actually descriptive rather than disapproving. Gullveig was a witch; that is, a practitioner of pre-Christian spiritual rituals. And 'cunning in sorcery' in the original meaning of the words means 'clever in divination',[18] or in the manifesting in the material world events conjured from the spirit world. 'Far-seeing' simply indicates that she was a diviner, a person who could 'see' far into the future.

There is no question that Freya had shamanic powers if she survived being burned 'to death' three times, and as Eliade points out, all over the world shamans of more recently surviving tribal cultures are considered to be 'masters of fire'. During the festivities at the 'ordination' of an Araucanian shaman the masters and the initiates walk barefoot over fire, without burning themselves or setting fire to their clothes. Throughout northern Asia and North America the shamans are able to swallow burning coals or to touch red-or white-hot iron.[19]

'Spirits' are distinguished from mortal humans by their incombustibility, their capacity to endure the heat of live coals, so shamans who have mastered fire are believed to have passed beyond the bonds of normal human condition and to be able to enter the spirit world. The mastery of fire expresses in sensory terms *a transcendence of the human condition*, and the ability to become a spirit. The apparent ability to survive the physical effect of flames is tantamount to transcending the sensorial realms altogether; it 'anticipates the experience of death ... (the shaman) can exist, in his capacity as a "soul", without its separation from the body being fatal to him'.[20]

Holger Kalweit points to the substantive significance of the belief that shamans transcend the limitations of the physical body: 'The belief, the knowledge, and even the experience that our physical world of the senses is a mere illusion, a world of shadows, and that the three-dimensional tool we call our body serves only as a container or dwelling place for something infinitely greater and more comprehensive than that body.' This is a central concept which characterises recently surviving indigenous cultures, as well as that of ancient Europe.

More generally, Freya's death and rebirth echo a process at the heart of all shamanic cultures. The shaman was believed to be able to journey to the land of the dead and back again. These journeys were perilous, but the shaman garnered information and knowledge from the Lowerworld, and was able to pass it on in rituals of healing, initiation or spiritual celebration. The initiation of a shaman invariably involves an intentional journey to the limits of physical endurance, a ritual in which the body, mind and soul of the apprentice are sacrificed to make way for a totally new identity, that of the shaman. The extreme physical challenges enable the apprentice to enter visionary mental and emotional states, and to make possible journeys into the spirit world.

In more recent times initiatory shamans are often depicted as having survived physically dangerous and life-threatening conditions. Some of the feats are humanly impossible, but are actually mimicked in ritual circumstances which may be arduous, but fall short of fatality. For example, an account of an initiation ritual from early in this century tells of the Caribou Eskimo shaman Igjugarjuk, who was initiating a pupil called Aggiartiq. In this case the form of dying was by drowning. 'Aggiartiq was tied fast to a long tent pole and carried down to a big lake. A hole was hewn through the ice and Aggiartiq was lowered, fully dressed, to the bottom of the lake and left there for five whole days. When they pulled him up he was as dry as if he had never been touched by the water. After this, he obtained guardians, and became a shaman.' This process of death and rebirth by which traditional shamanism has marked the transition from mortal human to sacred shaman certainly underlines Freya's status as a shaman.[21]

So the story of Odin and Gullveig confirms that Freya, a goddess representing the powers of the feminine, knew the secrets of divination before Odin did. And she taught them to him. She also had magical abilities to withstand fire, and other hardships (including spears being thrust through her), and to die and be reborn. These capacities, characteristic of the shamans and mystics of many recently surviving indigenous peoples, demonstrate vividly that for our ancestors, the tribespeople of ancient Europe, the deep secrets of Wyrd magic were held in the depths of the feminine. Although feminine forces are part and parcel of both women and men's psyches, I think that it also probably means that the people of Wyrd believed that women were practitioners of central aspects of shamanism before men.

All this was something that Freya knew Odin needed to see. Freya was capable of divination, which Odin wished to know, and would pay arm rings in order to hear. But she was also capable of resisting attempts to kill her by spear and fire; she knew that this would terrify Odin, but intrigue him utterly once he had recovered from the shock. His initial reaction would cause ructions, but by the time he was involved in an 'exchange of hostages', Freya knew that Odin would be well on the way to exploring deeper layers of magic. He had had to acknowledge the special power of her sorcery, secrets that he would certainly want to 'know' for himself.

— Feminine and Masculine Polarities —

But, impressed though he must have been by Freya's show of magical prowess, Odin did not immediately find a way to integrate with it, to approach it, to be open to learning it. He struck out against it. Why was this?

One way for us to understand better the significance of this war is to consider more closely the nature of the two 'races' of gods, the Vanir and the Aesir. The Vanir (of whom Freya is a leading goddess) are depicted by Snorri as being fertility deities. They are the older gods of earth and vegetation. They are peace-loving and have a great sense of art and beauty. Theirs is a world in which women play a prominent role. And they possess the most powerful magical techniques of all: the powers of divination. The Vanir represent the forces of the feminine principle.

The Aesir, on the other hand (of whom Odin is a leading god), are warriors. They are the younger, less mature gods of war. They are patriarchal gods of conquest. They command a different magic: that of words and spellcasting. They all categorically reject the magical knowledge of the Vanir as being 'shameful for men' – that is, with the exception of Odin who, as we see, learns this magical art from Freya.[22]

Further, the myths and cosmology represent Frey and Odin as having a close relationship, even though they are from different races of deity. And yet we have just seen a story in which Odin tries to burn Freya to death.

I believe that the dispute between Odin and Freya is that between 'masculine' and 'feminine' principles. This of course is not a gender distinction, but a delineation of 'forces', 'energies', 'tendencies' within each of us. The cosmology of the ancient Europeans emphasised polarities of forces, as in the creation of the world through opposites akin to fire and ice. Earlier, when we considered the attempts of the gods and the dwarfs to tie down Fenrir the wolf, I discussed the intuitive capacities of our feminine principle as one way of approaching the world, and the masculine propensity for analytical processes as another way.

But this time it is emotional, deeper streams than the problem-solving of the Fenrir story. And it is a battle within the psyche of Odin. The warrior god, representing the masculine principle, wants more intimate knowledge of feminine magic, represented by Freya the fertility god, embodying the feminine principle. He offers to pay for it in gold. She shows him something of what she knows, but then 'reads' in her vision disastrous aspects of the dark side of Odin's future life. She knows that he will not, at his level of personal development as the masculine principle, be able to deal with such a threat as her powers. She also knows what he will be driven to do about it: he is going to try to 'kill' his feminine aspects. These are the very aspects of his psyche which he needs to know if he is to become a shaman, like Freya. Part of him knows that, which is why he is seeking feminine divination in the first place. But he is not mature enough to follow it through, and 'war breaks out'.

In one sense, this war is a mythological one between tribes of deities. In another sense, it is warfare within the psyche of Odin, a battle between the warrior state of his masculine forces, and the hidden, repressed but beckoning potential of his feminine aspects.

The masculine and feminine polarities in nature, in people, and as expressed in the cosmology of our ancestors are not necessarily gender-based. As men and women we may all find ourselves going through a psychological and spiritual process of coping with, negotiating, attempting to mature through the constraints and dynamics of these forces. But Odin was trying to take a big step from warriorhood to mystic, and his struggle is probably a process which characterises some of the issues faced by men, both in his time and in ours.

— Warriorhood —

Odin's reaction to the prophesying of Gullveig was brutal. Not the sort of reaction one would like to see in an idealised 'apprentice mystic'. But the story is there. We need to try to make sense of it, and see what we can learn from it.

It could be said that he was acting as a warrior in the Viking tradition, and was therefore a 'product of his time'. Perhaps, in other words, his brutal clinging to his warriorhood was something which happened then, but not now. But it has been suggested recently by psychologists that the role of warrior functions as an archetype which is expressed mainly in men, although can of course also feature in women's psychology. If it is indeed an archetype, a deep-seated and ever-present way of dealing with the world, it is not restricted to any historically specific culture: it roams the psyche just as readily today as a thousand years ago.[23]

Heart of the Wolf: *Transcending Warriorhood*

There is not much doubt that at the time of Freya's visit to his hall (in the guise of Heidr/Gullveig) Odin was embodying the warrior archetype in its pure form. This is his role, of course, as a mythological figure; if humans find themselves embodying any of these great polarities in anything approaching pure form then we are in deep trouble psychologically, for they are meant to be balanced, flexible, interpenetrating, organically evolving, moving forward, returning. But Odin as a god embodied extreme states of the great polarities.

Today we are concerned about the apparent expression of pure warrior in the world, in wars and in macho self-presentation; aggressive energy in all its forms is regarded with suspicion and apprehension. Women in particular are disturbed by it, and this is hardly surprising since they are often the victim of it, either psychologically or physically.

Jungian writers Robert Moore and Douglas Gillette take the view that 'We can't just take a vote and vote the Warrior out. Like all archetypes, it lives on in spite of our conscious attitudes towards it. And like all *repressed* archetypes, it goes underground, eventually to resurface in the form of emotional and physical violence.'[24] But they go on to say that a mature, balanced person does not live the fully formed, extreme polarity of warrior to the exclusion of other major archetypes without suffering badly psychologically.

And there are advantages to a mature warrior archetype, when not lived exclusively and therefore fanatically: 'The Warrior should not be identified with human rage in any simple way . . . Aggressiveness is a stance towards life that rouses, energises, and motivates. It pushes us to take the offensive and to move out of a defensive or "holding" position about life's tasks and problems.'[25]

Odin is at a stage where he has achieved fame and fortune as a warrior. He needs to move on to another stage in his evolution. But such a step, a step into inner knowledge, magical awareness, shamanic wisdom, is threatening, because he has to reach new parts of his inner self. This threatening situation, exacerbated by Freya's devastating show of magical power, tends to bring to the fore the unhealthy aspects of his warrior archetype, the 'shadow' side.

There is a deep-seated apprehension in the male warrior archetype in its pure form, if unleavened by expressions of other crucial archetypal forces, a clinging to control with a desperation born of fear. It is sometimes manifested as an obsessive compulsion to attempt to suppress anything that is not within the warrior's realm of understanding, and thus offers a threat: 'The Shadow Warrior carries into adulthood the adolescent insecurity, violent emotionalism, and the desperation of the Hero as he seeks to make a stand against the overwhelming power of the feminine.'[26]

Moore and Gillette propose that the man unable to live the warrior archetype in a balanced way finds himself still battling against what he experiences as the inordinately powerful feminine and against everything supposedly 'soft' and relational. Even in adulthood, he still feels terrified that he will be swallowed up by it. His desperate fear of this leads him to wanton brutality. This sounds very like Odin.

One aspect of such men's fear of the feminine is, as Archetypal psychologist Alan Bleakley points out, a sense of inferiority, of lack, in comparison with what is perceived as the woman's 'greater binding to Earth, and under-earth'. It is partly the Middle-World rational ego, which fears the irrational, dark Underworld, and therefore fears that without exerting control there might be a dreaded 'reversal to dark, chaotic, uncontained nature, to a permanent dream-time'.[27]

But this clinging to the securities of the extreme warrior archetype plays against Odin being able to open himself up to the sacred power of Freya's knowledge; instead he is terrified by it and reacts violently. It is clear that Freya understands all this. She knows the warrior archetype, and predicts how Odin will react to her, and the outcome.

— Transcending the Feminine and Masculine —

But she also knows that Odin is ready to take this step into the feminine aspect of himself. How does one know when it is time? Alan Bleakley says that in understanding the integration of the feminine with the masculine we must beware of thinking that what we want is for 'men to be like women. The fatal mistake of the androgynists is their rejection of what is positive in the archetype of gender.'[28] A too-early integration of the feminine is dangerous.

As Archetypal psychologist James Hillman suggests (dipping into Greek mythology to illustrate his point): 'In serving the feminine, in letting the feminine rule, there is one essential caution. Hercules serves Omphale only after the twelve labours are done, and Ulysses abides with Circe only after the ten years in battle are passed. A certain masculine position must evidently have already been won.' He proposes that this might mean that first there must be an ego that has accomplished something. And if so, it implies that one is best to be past mid-life, otherwise one has too little awareness, too little strength, and the ego abandons its position too easily: 'Then it is no sacrifice, no real reorientation. Then it is merely a regressive serving of the Mother, separation from whom was the aim of all the labours and the battles.'[29]

We know that Odin was a successful warrior first . . . and Freya's judgement was that he would integrate with the feminine only after lashing out, defending his position, protesting, resisting. She knew she had the power to withstand his mistakes.

She describes war. But she also describes the hostage-sharing between masculine and feminine forces (not strictly gender, as we see, since men and women are exchanged across the boundaries of the archetypes). I find it fascinating that in the hostage exchange, Odin allows Freya, and her father, into his territory, his main area of the psyche, as symbols of the feminine he is integrating with, and he yields up to the feminine (the Vanir) principle the being who is to be his mentor in shamanic initiation, the giant Mimir, and his companion in travel, Hoenir.

This is like an interchange of energies within the person: a sacrificing of the protective, exclusive boundaries of the warrior element of the masculine polarity in order that an integration might take place, a rebalancing, an opening to new potentials. Perhaps the story of Odin and Heidr/Gullveig/Freya is one which speaks to all of us.

— The Heart of the Wolf —

I want to bring us back briefly to the encounter between Odin and Freya (Gullveig) because, intriguingly, the sacred texts provide an alternative ending to the incident. It closes the action at the point of the seeress being burned by Odin and the warriors for the third time. In a tiny piece of poetry from the *Short Voluspa* is the following:

> Loki got the wolf with Angrbotha . . .
>
> Loki ate the heart which lay in the coals, half-
> burnt he found the heart of the woman;
> Loptr was fertilised by the evil woman:
> thence in the world came all the wolves.[30]

It is likely that these lines refer to the episode between Odin and Gullveig, either literally, or so closely in mythological terms that they may be taken as the same story. It appears that the 'evil woman' (another charming epithet for a witch), now called Angrbotha, had been burned by persons unnamed, but her heart remained undestroyed. Loki represents the trickster aspect of the gods and sometimes accompanies Odin in his wisdom stories; if we regard Loki as representing here the trickster aspect of Odin, the part of him that 'turns upside down his normal world', we see that Odin's trickster self ate the burned heart of the woman from the embers.

Immediately the seeress with was him. He knew, without her having to tell him, that he had made his commitment. He was to leave the hall of the warriors, and go with her into a new realm, to learn the mysteries of divination and the wisdom of the Wyrd.

Alan Bleakley reminds us that when C.G. Jung, the psychiatrist and mythologist, visited the Pueblo Indians, he wrote of 'discovering new approaches to age-old knowledge that has been almost forgotten'. In his conversations with Ochwiay Biano (Mountain Lake), he encountered the 'Red Man' who spoke from the heart, who spoke with what Amerindians call 'Perfect Speaking'.

'See how cruel the whites look,' said Ochwiay Biano. 'They are always seeking something . . . We think that they are mad.'

Jung asked him why he thought the whites were all mad.

'They think with their heads,' he replied.

'Why, of course. What do you think with?' Jung asked him in surprise.

'We think here,' he said, indicating his heart.[31]

Such 'thinking' is alien to a culture that represses the heart. Like our culture today, in which the discipline of our minds has created the scientific and technical capacity to feed the world. And yet we do not do it. If we could also think with our hearts, perhaps we would do it.

In eating the half-burned heart of the seeress, Odin/Loki is learning to think with his heart. And in eating the heart he became 'fertile', or productive, and from that came 'all the wolves'. It is interesting that in the ancient mythology Odin is depicted as having for constant companions two wolves. They were important beings, guardian spirit animals called Geri and Freki. Odin was believed to give them all his food, needing only wine for himself. He sometimes adopted wolf form and wolf characteristics. So the reference to 'all the wolves' might refer to Odin's guardian spirits; in other words, not only the physical animals, but also the spirit animals of shamans.

— The Nature of Wolves —

It is appropriate that Freya 'gave with her heart' the spirit of wolves to Odin, two wolves as guardians, for she was to teach him divination, or 'far-seeing'. Today we tend to think of wolves as fearsome animals, rather like large guard dogs. But wild wolves are very different. They are beautiful, sensitive, perfectly of this world but also otherworldly.[32]

I remember vividly the first time I encountered timber wolves. There were two of them, owned by the animal behaviourist John Fentress, and they lived in a wood, a large fenced compound, in Oregon. One day I went with him to visit them. As we walked along the narrow track into the wood, we rounded a bend and there, standing stock still under the trees and watching us closely, ears erect, were the wolves. They started moving about as we got nearer, and their wonderful camouflage coats made them appear like skittish ghosts, spirit visitors from another realm.

And then I heard a sound I shall never forget. Not a howl, nor a growl. Rather, a soft whistling; the repeated 'wshee, whee, wshee . . .' that people use when they are whistling their dogs to come to them. I glanced at John, but he was watching the wolves intently as we approached, and his mouth was closed.

'What was that whistling?' I asked.

'The wolves!' he replied with a grin. 'Remarkable, isn't it?'

And then I heard it again. It was a greeting cry from the wolves, one that must have been picked up by humans hundreds, or more likely thousands, of years ago. We learned their language, or a tiny snippet of it, in times long past.

We can gain a glimpse of how wolves might have been regarded by our ancestors from the views of more recently surviving tribal peoples. In North America, the Pawnee saw the wolf 'as an animal who moved like liquid across the plains; silent, without effort, but with purpose . . . he could see "two looks away" . . . he could even hear the clouds pass overhead.'[33]

Perhaps this is how Odin travelled to distant places in spirit, to 'see far'. In fact, the wolf often appears in the legends of the Native American as the great long-distance traveller, a messenger or guide to the spirit world. Blind Bull, a famous Cheyenne shaman, was reputed to send and receive messages to various places in the real and spirit world via wolves. And a Cherokee embarking on a long winter's journey would first, as psychological and spiritual preparation, call on the help of the wolf spirit by rubbing his feet with ashes to grey them, singing a wolf song, and moving a few steps in imitation of the wolf.

There is another quality to the wolf which became appropriate for Odin: the wolf is often considered to be an 'outsider'. As in Hermann Hesse's famous novel *Steppenwolf*, about a man who lives on the fringe of society but reaches great insight into it, so the stepping from the world of the warrior into the realms of the shaman meant for Odin leaving behind some of the security of being 'one of the men'.[34] To obtain his knowledge from Freya he took an extra step, he ate her heart, he fought an internal war and negotiated a peace with a hostages exchange between his masculine and feminine polarities.

Sometimes to go deeper, to know more, to grow, one has to leave behind the security of the familiar. And it can happen that one is berated for it by others who cling to that security, who will not or cannot take the steps to learn from their other aspects. It happened to Odin when he learned from Freya the arts of divination and magic.

— Odin Becomes an Outsider —

Odin's reward for integrating his feminine is to learn the hidden secrets of Freya's 'feminine magic', the system of divination as practised by Thorbiorg, Heidr, Gullveig and Freya herself. He has to buck the expectations of masculine culture in order to do this. It was a step too far for most men; they could not manage it.

Snorri Sturluson says: 'Odin knew and used that craft, from which the greatest magical power followed, and which was called seidr. By this he could know men's fate and things to be.' He also says that seidr (the oracular ceremonies of Thorbiorg and Freya) gave the power over other people 'to bring about their death, misfortune or disease, deprive them of sense or strength and give it to others'.[35] This sort of power, if Freya/Gullveig held it and the warriors did not, would be great cause for fear, and would explain why they tried to kill her.

But the fear ran deeper than that, for Snorri Sturluson makes it clear that the knowledge was really the province of women, and was not considered suitable for men. Odin had therefore taken a grave risk. Snorri Sturluson again: 'But when this sorcery is exercised there follows from it such turpitude that men seemed not to be able to use it without shame.' As a result, says Snorri, Freya taught seidr to women priestesses only.

The seeresses who practised seidr were treated with great respect, but men who tried to learn or practise it were castigated. There are stories of men who dabbled in the divinatory magic of seidr, but they seem to have been looked down upon, disapproved of, and sometimes became outcasts. North-west European kings sometimes had them put to death, or banished from the country.

One of the early chieftains, Harald Fairhair, had a son called Ragnvald, who was said to have worked seidr with a company of eighty followers; some of them perhaps chanters. His descendant Eyvind also practised seidr, but there was great hostility against these two men, and both were killed in the end by members of their own family, and are condemned in Snorri Sturluson's *Heimskringla* for their wickedness.[36]

Seidr was the province of the goddess Freya. As the centuries unfolded and the Viking culture became more militarised and male-dominated, the god Freyr was introduced to represent a masculine aspect of Freya. But this caused confusion in the practice of seidr. Saxo Grammaticus, who wrote a history of Denmark in the late twelfth century,[37] refers to the worship of Freyr accompanied by 'effeminate gestures' and 'clapping of mimes upon the stage', together with the 'unmanly clatter of bells'. This implies some kind of performance which was part of the seidr rituals of Freya, but when they were incorporated into the new cult of Freyr, to Saxo and the Danish heroes whom he describes appeared unmanly and debased. In order to celebrate the powers of Freyr/Freya, men had to behave effeminately. Or, perhaps, acknowledge and express their own feminine aspects?

In the *Elder Edda* even Odin is reviled in the following words:

> But they said that thou madest *seidr*
> on Samsey island
> and drummedst on the cove (or drum) as sorceresses;
> like a sorcerer
> didst thou run over the world
> and I thought that unmanly.[38]

The indigenous peoples of ancient Europe believed that there are secret wisdoms that only men can know. And secrets and wisdoms that reveal themselves only to women. But also, on the path to initiation, there are paths which transcend this divide, where men are led by women and women by men. Odin transcended the divide, and was initiated into some of the secrets of the opposite gender.

Freya was considered in the cosmology of ancient Europe to have a special relationship with the god Odin. For one thing, the ancient texts tell us that she was married to a god called Odhr. A number of scholars propose that Odhr is Odhinn (Odin). The name Odhr indicates the force of ecstasy, of the magically inspired mind, and writer on Norse mythology Edred Thorssen suggests that it is to this ecstatically seeking, spiritually inspired aspect of Odhinn to which Freya is married.[39] This shamanic inspiration is, as with Odhinn, the main object of her own strivings.

In the myths, Odhr is said to take many journeys, and Freya weeps golden tears for him, and even wanders in search of him. But given that Odin is seeking powers which Freya already has, it suggests that she is weeping for him because he cannot find his initiatory path. And she is weeping gold. Not merely material gold, either, for she is the goddess of feminine shamanism. She weeps tears of golden alchemical inspiration. Odin is the one who is lost. And when Freya teaches him seidr, Odin finds himself through his feminine aspect. So Freya and Odin may have been lovers, or even married, but their love was probably sacred, tantric, and their marriage alchemical, magical. But one thing is clear: she was a mentor for some of his journeys into the wisdom of Wyrd.

A price Odin paid for his transcendent insight was rejection by those men who could not take the step with him into deeper knowledge. But his reward was elevation as the greatest god. Perhaps somewhere between those two extremes lies the destiny of all of us who attempt to gain a foothold on a deeper knowledge, including the wisdom of Wyrd.

Chapter Ten

Vision Journey:
Riding the Tree of Knowledge

— The Sacred Poetry —

Learning from Freya the secrets of divination was just one of the experiences Odin underwent in his quest for knowledge of Wyrd. In the lines of an ancient poem called *Havamal*, included in the compilation known as the *Elder Edda*, and written in a form so condensed it is practically a hidden code, are clues to his other ventures into mystical consciousness.

The *Havamal* narrates Odin's own description of his initiation, his exploration of his inner worlds, and the map of the cosmos he revealed during his spirit journeys. The concentrated core of Odin's vision quest for shamanic knowledge is distilled in the following lines:

> I know that I hung on the windswept tree
> for nine full nights,
> wounded with a spear and pledged to Odin,
> offered, myself to myself;
>
> The wisest know not from whence spring
> the roots of that ancient tree.
> They did not comfort me with bread,
> and not with the drinking horn;
>
> I peered downward,
> I grasped the 'runes',
> screeching I grasped them;
> I fell back from there.
>
> Nine lays of power I learned
> from the famous son of Bolthor,
> father of Bestla,
> and I got a draught of the precious mead,

Vision Journey: *Riding the Tree of Knowledge*

> mixed with magic Odrerir.
>
> Learned I grew then, lore-wise,
> waxed and throve well:
> Word from word gave words to me.
> Deed from deed gave deeds to me.[1]

Each of these lines refers to a whole world of symbol and significance, and they need to be opened up, expanded, and explained in order for us to understand the world he is depicting. But the bare outlines are clear, and generally agreed by scholars: in the myth Odin climbed into a sacred tree, and stayed in the tree for nine days and nights with no food and water. Under these conditions of privation and intense focus, he entered states of consciousness in which the tree changed into an enormous white, eight-legged horse, on which Odin rode through the sky and down to the Lowerworld to the nine Otherworlds of Knowledge.

During this journey he met, at a magical spring bubbling up by the root of the World Tree, a wisdom giant called Mimir. Odin's remarkable encounters with Mimir yielded incantations and powers to help him in his quest. He then journeyed to far-off realms where he had to fight, use his wits, trickery, shapeshifting and other powers acquired from Mimir to obtain the source of sacred inspiration which was stored in three vast cauldrons of mead, and hidden in a cave in the centre of a mountain. It was guarded by fearsome giants, and Odin nearly died in the mountain. But triumphantly he fulfilled his quest, and brought back to his fellow gods, and the human inhabitants of Middle Earth, the secrets of life contained in the mead of wisdom. His quest for visions of wisdom formed an archetypal template for mortal shamans to follow in the Wyrd traditions of ancient Europe.

Let us explore the inner meaning of Odin's visions by reference to the lines in *Havamal*, beginning with the tree.

— Yggdrasil —

> I know that I hung on the windswept tree . . .
> The wisest know not from whence spring
> the roots of that ancient tree.

These lines conjure an evocative image of a mysterious tree. Such images lie at the heart of all shamanic visionary activity, and Odin's journey on the World Tree echoes an apparently universal experience of shamans in all cultures, and all times. In recently surviving tribal cultures, apprentice shamans acquire their helping spirits, those 'beings' which advise, give healing powers and assist in journeys to worlds of knowledge, in highly ritualised and sacralised retreats into remote areas of the wilderness.[2]

In all traditional cultures, there were particular places which were favourable for such first encounters with the spirits, places which existed in the material world but which had extraordinary significance as entry points to another world: literally and metaphorically doorways into the spirit realm.[3]

The physical nature of that special place depended on the terrain in which the tribal culture lived. It could variously be in the vast lake area of Siberia, the mountains of the East, the desert plains of the western United States, the snow plains of the Sami or the rainforests of South America. For the apprentice shamans of early north-western Europe, it was usually on a hilltop, perhaps on an ancient burial mound left by previous civilisations, and preferably high in a tree selected for the ritual.

In all these locations, the initiate shaman entered an altered state of consciousness and plunged into the imaginal depths of the collective unconscious. This state of mind was far from the mundane, everyday state, more a 'dreaming with open eyes'. Nevertheless, the sacred process was framed within the material world, the physical, for shamanic inspiration is largely the sacralisation of the familiar, not merely escape into some other reality. Seeing the familiar with new eyes is the gift of the shamanic journey. So the shaman climbed a real tree in order to undergo a journey of the imagination as colourful and intense as can be imagined, one which engendered the arrival of spirit forces which would come upon the shaman in the guise of visions, sounds and the material form of animals.[4]

In an example from a recent tribal culture, a Siberian shaman thought of the World Tree as represented by a birch. He explains that in preparation for the initiation ritual, or 'on the way to the ancestral

Vision Journey: *Riding the Tree of Knowledge*

shaman', the master shamans arrived with him at a tree believed to be possessed of powerful life force. The initiate shaman rested at the foot of the special tree and examined the individual markings placed by various shamans over the years. By carving his name into the tree and vividly calling to mind the names of his shamanic ancestors, the newly initiated shaman shared the sacredness of the tree and acquired additional knowledge.[5]

Odin says that he hung on a 'windswept' tree, which suggests an exposed position on high ground; almost certainly a sacred tree on a sacred mound, either growing naturally, or cut down and re-erected on the mound. At dawn or sunset, on the horizon, trees on high ground look as if the top branches are reaching high into the heavens. The tree represented a ladder to other worlds, other realms, other states, and climbing it physically was a metaphor for his journey from one realm into another.

Many psychological and spiritual traditions have used the tree as a central symbol, and the Swiss psychiatrist C.G. Jung, after studying the tree's symbolism and comparing it to the spontaneous pictures of his patients, proposed that the tree formed an image of psychological individuation, in which the roots represented unconscious material, the trunk conscious realisation, and the crown of the tree the goals of life and personal integration.[6]

Of course, all archetypes, the World Tree included, yield images of a deeper level of reality. They do not 'stand for something', like a logo of a company. Their meaning is within the image itself, encompassing myriad nuances and subtleties that can be apprehended by our imagination but beyond the capacity of the conscious mind to process cognitively.

For the tribal peoples of ancient Europe, all creation arises within and from the image of the World Tree. This belief gives rise to a cosmos with a sacred dimension from every aspect, like light shining through a complex crystal, in which each detail also represents and incorporates the whole so that everything is an image of everything else.[7]

The World Tree in which Odin undertook his vision quest was named in the ancient manuscripts as Yggdrasil. This name is a compound of two words: the stem of 'yggr' is 'ygg-', the 'frightening' or 'awe-inspiring one', a nickname for Odin; 'drasill' is a literary word meaning 'horse'. So the name identifies the tree as the means of Odin's 'ride' to the spirit world, his transportation for the quest.[8] I surmise that the name Ygg is Odin's identity *before* he undertook his initiation in the World Tree. The name Odin, as I explained earlier, is so close to the root meaning of the word 'shaman' that I suspect that Odin is a title acknowledging his new status. And when he first went to Freya, disguised as Heidr/Gullveig, as she waited outside his hall, she referred to him by the same 'pre-name' of 'terror of the gods': that is, Ygg.

— Sleipnir —

During the course of his nine-day fast on the tree, Odin's image of the tree transformed into that of a horse. In fact, the conception of a tree as a horse for journeys into the spirit world reached into all areas of life. When criminals were hanged, the gallows were also known poetically as a 'horse', upon which its victims 'rode' to their deaths to the Lowerworld where reside the souls of the dead.

The World Tree transformed into a magnificent white, eight-legged flying horse called Sleipnir. This visionary animal carried Odin on a journey around the sacred cosmos to the nine worlds of knowledge. And Sleipnir, being eight-legged, had a leg for each of the worlds, with Odin the rider forming the centre point . . . the ninth world. For nine days and nine nights Odin rode Sleipnir to the Otherworlds.[9]

But although we talk of Odin climbing into the World Tree, the tree transforming into a horse and carrying Odin to the worlds of knowledge, it is also important to reverse this process of imagery. It is just as true to say that the process of Odin and his horse journeying to the spirit worlds created the World Tree. In other words, the World Tree is a construction of the mind and soul, the very threads of Wyrd woven through the imagination.

The eight-footed horse is the principal shamanic beast in many cultures in northern Europe, including the Siberian. Historian of

Religion Mircea Eliade, in his detailed study of shamanism throughout the world, relates the story of a Buryat shamanka from central Asia. She was married to a human husband, but she had for her 'second husband' the ancestral spirit of a shaman. One of her husband's mares gave birth to a foal with eight legs, and he cut off four of them. 'Alas,' cried his wife, 'that was my little horse on which I ride as a shamanka,' and after that she left him and disappeared from among men, becoming the protective spirit of her tribe.[11]

In ceremony, shamans sometimes would incorporate an effigy of a horse. Buryat shamans, for example, use a horse-headed stick in their ecstatic dances, and in later ritual the eight legs of Sleipnir are mimicked by hobby-horses and steeds with more than four feet which appear in carnivals and processions. Hilda Ellis Davidson also points out that a dead man is carried on a bier in the funeral procession by four bearers; borne along thus, he may be described as riding to the Otherworld, the world of spirits of the dead, on a steed with eight legs. Confirmation of this is found in a funeral dirge recorded among the Gonds in India. It contains reference to Bagri Mare, the horse with eight legs, and it is clear from the song that this means the dead man's bier. One verse of the song runs:

> What horse is this?
> It is the horse Bagri Mare.
> What should we say of its legs?
> The horse has eight legs.
> What should we say of its heads?
> This horse has four heads . . .
> Catch the bridle and mount the horse.[11]

Odin's hanging on the tree of Yggdrasil was metaphorically the first ritual of its kind, but apprentice shamans have been performing this process ever since, all over north-west and western Europe, and far east until it turns into the Asian steppes of Siberia.

The external, material world structure which supports the shamanic visions, such as a remote sacred site or tree, serves as a framework enabling the imagination to be liberated from the mundane, the Middle World, and to roam in the realm of the spirit. The structure of the shaman's imagery follows the structure of the tree, with its roots and branches in different realms, and then in Odin's case transforms into a horse, an eight-legged beast which can fly through the sky to all the worlds of knowledge.

In our contemporary discourse we would conceive of these worlds as being located in our psyche, perhaps deep in the unconscious. The imaginal structure of the World Tree, and the process of journeying on the tree as it transforms into a magical horse, would be tools and techniques for accessing areas of the unconscious which might otherwise be closed to us except in the most deeply symbolic dreams.

But for the peoples of ancient Europe, the imaginal was a realm not physically bounded by the body, and not conceived of as 'only' an internal event. For them, the significance of the imaginal was that it allowed humans to encompass elements beyond the material world. For our ancestors the everyday, logical, analytical, material world was a tiny microcosm of the magnificent, boundless imaginal world.[12] Shamans were expected to be able to journey, and act, in the latter on behalf of the community.

Today our human-centred, separatist view has brought us great benefits through science and engineering, but it has brought also great disadvantages, not least in our poorly developed sense of self-understanding.

To attempt to pursue the quest for self-understanding from the perspective of 'objective science' will simply compound the problem. We need to understand ourselves once more in relation not only to the organic environment from which we have separated ourselves, but also from the sacred dimension accessed through our imagination. We all need to ride Sleipnir to the Otherworlds of Knowledge.

In some ways, we still can.

— Journeys on the Tree of Life —

The sun dipped behind the mountain peak, and splinters of light shimmered across the grassy plateau on the Rigi Mountain in the Swiss Alps. The small plateau was dominated by a magnificent, heavy-branched beech tree which seemed to force its way into existence from an upraised outcrop of rock in a stupendous show of life force.

Vision Journey: *Riding the Tree of Knowledge*

Curling around the thick trunk of the beech like a coiled snake was the twisting trunk of a small conifer, and at the base of the trees their exposed roots crawled intertwined across the rock like dragons' claws. It was the ideal site for attuning to the spirit of the World Tree.

The root system of the two trees projected ten feet above the plateau before the entwined trunks began to rise above the rocks. Many marvellous holes, openings, crevices and cracks disappeared into shadowy tunnels beneath the trees. We crawled around and over the roots, each person charged with the task of finding a tunnel which drew them, appealed to them, excited them.

When everyone had found their entry into the World Tree, we spread out over the plateau and there the participants in the Wyrd workshop, practitioners of medicine, psychotherapy, business and government, stretched out on their backs and prepared for a journey. For modern seekers of this Wyrd awareness, there needs first to be an acclimatisation, a stretching of the imaginal muscles to encompass the ambience of the spirit world.

When they had relaxed, attended to their breathing, centred, they turned their concentration to the sounds going on around them. The mountain air crackled and hummed, and as they listened I asked them to form a vivid image in their mind of the entrance to the World Tree they had chosen among the rambling roots of the beech and the conifer.

I began to beat a large drum in a regular and slow rhythm. The drum beat holds vivid images in the mind, moves them in action scenarios, and enhances their intensity. The moment I struck the drum hard three times in quick succession, the vision seekers were each to imagine that they were travelling down the hole, burrowing under and into the tree, and along a tunnel inside the mighty plant heading underground, into the Lowerworld. There they would see and hear spirits.

I hit the drum three times, paused, and then resumed rhythmic drumming at a faster rate. In shamanic cultures around the world, entrances to the Lowerworld commonly lead from the World Tree into a tunnel which eventually opens out upon bright and marvellous Otherworld landscapes. From there the shaman travels wherever he desires for minutes or hours, finally returning back up the tunnel to emerge at the point where he entered.

Such a journey is described by Rasmussen for the Iglulik Eskimo of Hudson Bay:

> For the very greatest (shamans), a way opens right from the house whence they invoke their helping spirits; a road down through the earth, if they are in a tent on shore, or down through the sea, if it is in a snow hut on the sea ice, and by this route the shaman is led down without encountering any obstacle. He almost glides as if falling through a tube so fitted to his body that he can check his progress by pressing against the sides, and need not actually fall down with a rush. This tube is kept open for him by all the souls of his namesakes, until he returns on his way back to earth.[13]

And on *his* journey, Odin's horse Sleipnir 'rode nine days and nine nights down ravines ever darker and deeper, meeting no one, until he came to the banks of the river Gjoll which he followed as far as the Gjoll Bridge; this bridge is roofed with burning gold.' The bridge was the fantastic bridge of fire known as the Rainbow Bridge; it was the transformational gateway to Otherworlds of Knowledge.[14]

This group had done journeying work with me before. This time we were creating a more shared framework for the imagery. The drum began to beat a little faster, and as we had prearranged, they walked down a pathway in their individual landscape towards a hut or small house. Carefully they approached the building, reaching for the handle, and swung open the door. Inside the building it was dark. They entered the room and closed the door behind them. And after a while their eyes adjusted to the dark. And there they could see, in the room, their guardian spirit.

They waited long enough to see whether the guardian had anything it wanted to tell them. A message. A hint. A word from the unconscious. Or from the expanded universe of the dream world? Eventually the drum shifted pattern, and speeded up. They were on their way back, through the tunnel, out of the World Tree and back into their bodies.

We sat on the plateau and talked of what they had seen.

Some of the participants had seen animal-like creatures. Some had encountered human forms. Still others had heard sounds or voices communicating with them, but not seen a manifestation. 'I felt myself to be underwater. As soon as we came out of the tunnel, I was floating, but underwater. My eyes were open. I could see around quite easily. It was very beautiful. Everything was green and glowing.' The person, a German medical practitioner, explained that she had never dived underwater in the sea or a lake, only in a swimming pool. But the vision she saw was like something she had never before experienced.

> I floated forwards without effort, past brightly and indescribably beautiful fish and other creatures. I could hear the drum beating, and I knew that soon I should see the cave or dwelling where my guardian spirit should be. But I just kept floating. Finally I decided to just stop there, underwater, and wait to see what happened. I could see colourful plants around me, and so thought I must be near the bottom of whatever water I was in, but I could not see the bottom. I was able to keep quite still, suspended upright in the water. Then a large fish cruised by, silent, with a round, blue eye watching me carefully. It was a wonderful creature. It had a black stripe down its side, and silvery scales which seemed to move and glitter in the half light. It glided past, watching me with its deep, deep eye. And then it told me something, but without speaking. Its thought came into my head as a thought. It was like seeing inside my own life with a bright torch.
>
> Then I heard the drum beating for us to return. The big fish was disappearing, and so I moved back through the water, faster and faster, and was swept back up the tunnel to here.

The woman was obviously very moved by the experience. I asked her how she felt about the large fish. 'I love it,' she said immediately. 'I feel very close to it, and I love it. It was beautiful, and it came so close and looked at me so carefully.'

Others talked of their experiences, though I asked them to be discriminating about what they revealed of messages, lessons, personal insights. Even with such relatively simple preparation, such imaginal journeys can be surprisingly affecting and important. Under such evocative conditions it is common for people to be surprised with what comes up. The nature of the images they see can be thrilling, revealing, shocking, transcendent.

Journeys can be open-ended into Otherworlds, or to specific worlds, selected according to the issues in the individual's life, the psychic and sacred spaces they wish to explore. Ambitious initiatory journeys can be accomplished with the help of fasting, and we talked about Odin's remarkable journey on Sleipnir to the nine worlds of knowledge; the 'original vision quest'. We talked also about how he had prepared for that experience, and meditated on his sacrifice of nine days and nine nights without food or drink. And then to recover from this meditation we went and had a very good and very large meal!

—The Sacred Nine—

> For nine full nights . . .
> nine lays of power I learned.

A person undergoing a shamanic initiation enters a time out of time, a sacred time set aside for the purpose of attuning to the trajectory between this world and the spirit realm. This altered experience of time transcends the everyday linear progression of minutes, hours, and days. Of course, the two time dimensions exist side by side; while Odin was journeying in sacred time, he was still existing in mundane time. But the experiential realities of the two dimensions, just as in our dreaming and waking states, are very different.

In the Celtic myths a very short time in the Otherworld may correspond with a very long time in this world. Alwyn Rees and Brinley Rees, scholars of Celtic literature, recount from medieval texts journeys into the spirit world in which a man returns after a seemingly brief sojourn and finds that his contemporaries are dead and that his own name is but a memory. And then when he touches the ground or embraces a now ancient grandson or nephew or tastes the food of mortals, he 'moulders into a little heap of dust as though he had been dead for ages'.[15] On the other hand, a long time in the Otherworld sometimes transpires to have been but an instant in this world. For example one character, Nerta, after three days in the Otherworld, returns to find his companions at the same meal as they were preparing when he left them. So Otherworld time can be both longer and shorter than the time of our world.

In the lines of the *Havamal*, Odin tells us that in the course of his initiatory ordeal he hung in the World Tree for nine nights. Given that the experience of the initiatory world of 'altered states' can be very different from the linear time we are used to associating with 'nine nights', it is possible that the literal duration of his journey was nine hours, or even (although unlikely!) nine minutes. When I first read of Odin's long ordeal I doubted whether it could literally be true. It seemed that such a long ordeal would end in death, for nine nights without liquid refreshment is in medical opinion very difficult to survive physiologically.

However, I then found out about the remarkable marathon monks of Tibet. These are Buddhist mystics, people who live in the mountains and who are embarked upon a training of many years leading to enlightenment, and recognised status as an initiated monk. Part of their training involves the nightly performance of a marathon: a journey of about thirty miles on foot, usually accompanied at a fast walking pace, wearing sandals and carrying a staff. At various points on the journey the monks stop to perform a simple ritual of meditation, and then they continue their long trek. This nightly marathon walking goes on for several years, during which time the monks suffer physical stress to the ankles and joints of the legs, but of course otherwise build up a phenomenal level of fitness and stamina.

At the end of a prescribed period of marathon walking, usually five years, the mystic is entitled to undergo the ordeal which sanctifies them as monks. It is an ordeal which in some ways parallels that of Odin and the traditions of our ancestors in ancient Europe, for it involves nine nights of privation. The would-be master is given a last meal, and then taken to a hut set aside for the purpose of the ritual. There he sits and meditates during the day. At evening, he is escorted from the hut by other monks, observers, and people from the community, along a path to a stream, where he fills two pails of water, sets them on either end of a pole, and carries them with the pole across his shoulders back to his meditation hut. He is then enjoined by the ritual to drink none of this water. Instead, as he prays, and meditates, he gradually pours away the liquid as a sacrificial offering; an offering which becomes more and more of a sacrifice as the nights progress and the monk becomes ever more thirsty.

Each evening, he is escorted again to the stream to fill the pails of water, and back to the hut. On the first night of the ordeal, it takes perhaps two minutes for him to make the journey from the hut to the stream and back. On the fourth night, when the deprivation was considerable, it might take about thirty minutes. On the last, ninth night, it is an eternity: at least an hour of shuffled progress, in a greatly weakened, dehydrated and shrunken state, to make the journey, with the weight of the pole on his shoulders supported by helpers.

At the end of the initiatory period, the monk is the centre of a large celebratory and sacred feast, in which he is offered his first refreshment for nine days and nights: a bowl of tea. He takes a small sip, and the period of meditation comes to a conclusion. Two months after this remarkable ordeal the monks are back on their arduous ritual of nightly marathon walks for a further year or more until they have completed their task.

This ritual impressed me not only because of the awesome willpower and dedication of the monks, but also because the privation lasted for nine nights in literal time (it may have felt like nine years in phenomenological time!). So it may be the case after all that Odin's claim to have spent nine nights in his initiatory ritual may be a measure of 'mundane', everyday time, rather than being a symbolic or experiential calibration which differs in some way from this duration.

The number nine was held to be sacred not only by the people of the ancient European culture of Wyrd, and in contemporary Tibet, but also in recently surviving 'traditional' cultures all over the world. Shamanic rituals refer to nine heavens, nine gods, nine branches of the cosmic tree, and so on. Eliade describes, for example, how the Altaic shaman climbs a tree or post with nine notches, representing the nine celestial regions. And when people of the traditional Yakut culture make blood sacrifices, their shamans set up a tree with nine notches outdoors and climb it to carry the offering to the celestial god Ai Toyon. The initiation of shamans among the Siberian Sibo includes a small tree notched with nine steps. This highly significant number nine often delineates the levels, realms or obstacles that have to be negotiated and overcome when the shaman ascends to the sky in search of spirit powers.[16]

For our ancestors, the symbolic importance of the number nine was shared among many tribal groups. The Celtic parallel to the Anglo-Saxon, Germanic and Scandinavian shamanic archetype of Odin/Wotan/Woden is the god Lug who is, in Welsh mythology, wounded by a spear and hangs on a tree like Odin. The 'nine full nights' that Odin hangs in the World Tree are reflected by the fact that Lug's tree had sustained 'nine score fiercenesses'.[17]

It is remarkable the extent to which the number nine features generally in ancient Celtic ritual and symbolic tradition. Rees and Rees give instances of where it is stated, for example in the ancient Welsh laws, that the serf class should build nine houses for the king, while the serf's own house should also consist of a hall plus eight rooms.[18] Repeated allusions to houses comprising 'nine houses (or rooms) in one' in the fifteenth-century poems of Guto'r Glyn confirm the existence of a continuing Welsh tradition that a complete house should consist of nine component parts. Nine was thought to symbolise the whole, something complete. In Welsh medieval society the ninth generation was the recognised limit of kin relationship, and even the human body was thought of as comprising nine principal parts.

The number also appears in traditional British games such as Ninepins, in which the middle pin is called the 'king', and Nine Men's Morris, which was played on a square divided into eight sections around a central 'pound'. In Scotland the need-fire, built at ritual occasions, was kindled sometimes by nine men and sometimes by nine nines of 'first-begotten' sons. The number was also connected with the Beltaine fire in Scotland, and in Wales, as in parts of Scandinavia: the fire was made with nine sticks collected by nine men from nine different trees. Nines, and particularly the 'ninth', were very important in divinations and in folk cures. So in Welsh tradition the symbolism of 'nine' extended far beyond the special rituals of the shamans, and assumed a guiding importance in the structure of buildings, games, kin relationships and so on.

In ancient Irish literature 'companies of nine' feature prominently, often as a leader and eight others. Rees and Rees illustrate this by reference to descriptions of mythological kings, queens and heroes, including Medb's mode of travel in the story *Tain Bo Cuailnge*: 'and nine chariots with her alone; two of these chariots before her, and two behind, and two chariots at either side, and her own chariot in the middle between them'. King Loegaire, when setting out to arrest St Patrick, ordered nine chariots to be joined together, 'according to the tradition of the gods'. Eight swordsmen guarded Bricriu on his way to the feast he had prepared in his nine-chambered hall. Cu Chulainn had nine weapons of each kind, eight small ones and one large one. These examples concern the exploits of warriors and heroes, and lie at the centre of much of social custom and belief, as well as the cosmology practised and experienced by the shaman.

Of more direct significance in connection with Odin's nine nights on the World Tree is the calendar of the ancient Celtic peoples. In the Welsh laws the ninth day of the month often marks the end of the beginning of a period, and a period of nine days or nine nights figures in the literature as a significant unit of time. In Wales the period of bright moonlight during the harvest moon is called 'the nine light nights', and in Irish the terms 'nomad' and 'noinden' stand for units of nine time-spaces (either days or half days).

So in many ways the conceptual world of the Wyrd people was broken up into units of nine, sometimes with eight 'followers' and a leader, sometimes into nine equal parts.

Why nine? In the thinking of the people of early Europe, the connections, the doorways, the passages of contact between the inside and outside worlds, between body and world, are of primary importance. Today we more readily focus our attention on the dividing point between ourselves and the other. The skin is seen as a boundary, usually clothed and thus disguised, and we exist as separate entities, with an interior life largely divorced from those around us. We are truly alone, is the oft-staged assumption.

The body has nine major orifices or sense organs, which represent 'gateways' from the world of the interior to the outside world, connections between the organism and the external world of which it is a part: two eyes, two ears, two nostrils, one mouth, one anus and one sexual organ. For the people of Wyrd, these connecting points confirmed the integrity of the world of which they were a part. For them the body was a microcosm of the whole, and the bodily connecting points with the external were symbolic of the gateways to knowledge.[19] For these reasons, Odin's nine nights on the initiatory journey was not an arbitrary period of time. It reflected, rather, a deep-seated understanding of the significance of the connection between people, the environment, and the worlds of knowledge.

In contemporary culture, we pay little attention to the significance of numbers. In everyday parlance, we refer to the scoring of a century in cricket, or that someone who has accumulated a lot of money may be a 'millionaire'; these sort of numbers carry a symbolic significance somewhat beyond their relevance as a unit of counting. After all, 99 runs or 101 runs are very little different from the century in cricket, but are not remarked on in the same way. And 999,000 dollars is a lot of money, almost a millionaire, but does not bring into play the slightly 'numinous' quality of reaching that 'magical' target.

But perhaps more important than our ignorance of symbolic numbers per se is the element of meaning which lies behind the numbers, which also is missing and leaves a large hole in our cosmology. For we do not think any longer of the human body as having the gift of 'doorways' to the outer world, nor do we use such metaphors for connection with the environment, with 'other'. Instead we regard the body as a machine, which of course is an incestuous metaphor, for we are defining ourselves once again in terms of structures which we have built ourselves, rather than by recourse to naturally occurring phenomena. We lack any 'independent enquiry' into our nature.

If we are not to reinstate symbolic numbers, we nevertheless need to look urgently at reinstating concepts of enjoinment which the numbers represented for the early European tribespeople. The nine days and nine nights of Odin's sacrifice and meditational ritual represent in themselves knowledge we once had, but have long forgotten.

— Seeing Other Worlds —

In recent shamanic cultures, for people engaged in a vision quest, the ordinary, physical landscape transformed, as the mind-state changed, into a spirit landscape; a world of dreams in which it was possible to see things manifested which are invisible, unnoticed, brushed aside, and which simply do not exist in the experience of everyday consciousness. The visions which enrich these quests, and which are their primary aim, are sometimes of familiar features, say animals, which exist materially but which take on special and powerful significance in the mind's eye of the observer. Or they may be instead the appearance of creatures formed of the stuff of another world, spun into shape by the imagination, and manifested as convincingly as do objects in the everyday reality, which we support through the process of consensual validation.[20]

Odin's visions created, represented, illustrated, reflected the structure of the cosmos. He was not there at the beginning of creation, but rather discovered and articulated the structure of 'everything' as a result of the visions he achieved in his shamanic journeying. It is possible that this structure is a universal human one; that we are designed to be able to apprehend reality in a particular way, through certain dimensions and in specified forms, and that Odin articulated this. It is also possible that Odin was attuning to something that is outside human consciousness, and was 'seeing' a structure which has a reality in the language of the spirits. However one positions oneself on this dimension, the images Odin describes were to be at the root of much of Wyrd cosmology.

During his quest for visionary experience, Odin saw the cosmos as shaped like a vast tree, which encompassed all levels of existence. Connected and emanating from this vision is a complex and vivid system of worlds, realms, levels, each of which symbolically represents a particular kind of knowledge, power and dimension in the spiritual world.

The tree appeared in Odin's vision as a giant ash tree called Yggdrasil, so vast, says Sturluson, that 'its branches spread out over the whole world and reach up over heaven'.[21] This massive construction served as the axis of the cosmos, and everything else was constructed around it. Featured around the tree was the universe, visualised as a tricentric structure, like three gigantic discs set one above the other with a space in between each.[22] This is a vision which shamanic cultures all over the world have seen in the accounts from the intervening centuries. The top disc is usually called the Upperworld, the middle one is called Middle Earth or Middle World, and the bottom is the Lowerworld. Structured among these three realms were nine worlds: nine places or domains of knowledge, each with a particular ambience and energy. They were conceived of by the people of ancient Europe as locations, spaces, positions in a cosmic firmament.

There were various versions of this cosmic 'map', but the most developed was that of the northern Europeans as illustrated in the *Sagas*. This was an elaborated and literary expression of the ancient cosmology, and may be more developed than some earlier versions. But the parallels between the visions of manifold tribes are strong enough to render the Scandinavian descriptions of the cosmos appropriate as an extended, idealised model for that of the rest of ancient northwestern Europe.[23]

On the top level, in the Upperworld branches of the World Tree, was an image landscape in which lived gods and goddesses, represented in human form and subject to the powerful forces of Wyrd. These gods manifested human nature writ large in the cosmos. Their exploits represented the basic needs, desires, fears and achievements of humankind. The god belonged to two tribes, mirroring a distinctive feature of life on the human plane.

There was a tribe of gods known as the Aesir, living in great halls; they were warrior gods representing aspects of the old sky god called Allfather, who was eventually replaced by Odin. His powers, feats and foibles are manifested in the stories of the other gods surrounding him. Also in the Upperworld were the fertility gods known as the Vanir. Finally the Upperworld featured a third world of knowledge, the land of the light elves, magical, and unhumanlike creatures, who feature as enigmatic causes of illness.[24]

The second level, around the lower branches and trunk of the World Tree, contained further worlds. This realm was called Middle Earth. It is in this realm that human life unfolded. However, Middle Earth does not refer to the material world of everyday existence;

rather it is the spiritual world of humankind. It was surrounded by a vast ocean, and Jormungand, the terrifying world serpent, lay in this ocean; he was so long that he encircled Middle Earth and bit on his own tail. He 'bound', encircled, contained the energy of the realm; without him it would explode in a raging chaos.

Another world lay in this second level, at the outer edge of the disc 'over the ocean', called Jotunheim (home of the giants). The giants were the beings who established the Earth; huge elemental forces lie still at the centre of all earthly activity. They are brutishly strong but short on intellect. They are beginnings, not intellectual developments. The world of the giants is a realm in constant motion, seeking to oppose and give resistance to whatever it meets. It comprises a force of dissolution, the reactive power of destruction necessary to evolutionary change.

Also in this middle realm, in the north, lived the dwarfs. They dwelled underground in a world called Nidavellir (Dark Home), a 'subterranean' world of darkness where shapes are forged. And another world was called Svartalfheim (Land of the Dark Elves). No clear distinction, though, can be drawn between the dwarfs and dark elves; they appear to have been interchangeable.

The Upperworld and the Middle World were connected by a bridge of fire, a flaming rainbow bridge, called Bifrost (Trembling Way). This can sometimes be glimpsed from within everyday states of consciousness. Snorri Sturluson says: 'You will have seen it but maybe you call it the rainbow. It has three colours and is very strong, and made with more skill and cunning than other structures.'[25] The Trembling Way bridge transports the shaman from the world of mundane reality to the Otherworld, the transcended states of consciousness.

In the roots of the tree lay another realm, the Underworld or Lowerworld comprising Niflheim, the world of the dead, located nine days northwards and downwards from Middle Earth. Niflheim was a place of bitter cold and unending nights; its citadel was Hel, a place with towering walls and forbidding gates presided over by the hideous female monster, half white and half black, of the same name. However, the Lowerworld in ancient European cosmology is a realm which has to be completely re-visioned in order for us to understand

Vision Journey: *Riding the Tree of Knowledge*

its significance, for the word 'hel' carries negative connotations for Western culture of the Christian hell.

Certainly the Lowerworld of the European shaman was dark and potent. But this forbidding-sounding world was also the realm of knowledge and the wisdom of the dead. To journey to the Lowerworld was a great feat for shamans, full of danger but with great rewards in spiritual terms.

These three realms and nine worlds were arranged around Yggdrasil like a wondrously decorated Christmas tree; a sacred firmament. Yggdrasil had three mighty roots, one each for the three realms of Upperworld, Middle Earth and Lowerworld. One reached into Asgard, and nourishing this root was the Well of Wyrd, by the side of which lived the three Wyrd Sisters, makers of destiny. Each day the gods gathered here in council. The Wyrd Sisters (Norns in the Scandinavian versions) nurture the great tree. Snorri Sturluson writes: 'It is said further that the Norns who live near the spring of Urd draw water from the spring every day, and along with it the clay that lies around about the spring, and they besprinkle the ash so that its branches shall not wither or decay.'[26]

The second root spread to Jotenheim, and under this root was the Spring of Mimir, the great, wise giant who, as we shall see, played a central part in the shamanic initiation of Odin as his mentor and challenger. The waters of Mimir's well gave wisdom, and Odin sacrificed one eye to drink from it.

The third root plunged into the Lowerworld; under this root was the Spring of Hvergelmir, the source of eleven rivers and the lair of the dragon Nidhogg. The dragon, or serpent, Nidhogg sends challenges and riddles up the full length of the trunk of Yggdrasil, carried by a squirrel, to a great eagle whose claws grasp the highest branches.

This, then, is the wondrous vision that Odin experienced during his initiation; he saw it, and he created it. It was the 'sacred geography' of his spiritual journey.

Chapter Eleven

Giants:
Trusting Death and Rebirth

— Odin's Mentor —

*Nine lays of power I learned
from the famous son of Bolthor,
father of Bestla*

These few lines of sacred poetry allude to, in the sparest of shorthands, one of the central aspects of Odin's fantastic voyage of discovery to the Lowerworld: his journey to the Well of Wisdom, where he was taught the Nine Spells of Power. To understand the nature and significance of these spells we need to know the identity of his teacher, the mentor he refers to as 'the famous son of Bolthor, father of Bestla'.

At the beginning of time 'there was nothing but the Yawning Gap', says Snorri Sturluson. He describes a state of suspended power in which, before the cosmos was formed, there were two immense polarities of fire and frost.[1] Muspellheim was a region of pure heat and flame, raging, burning; Niflheim, freezing fog, was deep chill, locked, bound, creaking cold. These two mighty forces held each other in balance. The space between them was Ginnungagap, highly charged, explosive energy. This was the ancient European version of our Steady-State Universe.

And then came the Big Bang. In one fateful instant, the two mighty polarities intersected. Fire and frost exploded into each other's domain. In the yawning gulf between the formerly separate fire and frost realms, in Sturluson's words: 'where the freezing met the livid heat it melted and dripped away. From the fermenting drops fusing to life by virtue of the power which threw up the heat, there was shaped the likeness of a man. He is called Ymir.' But Ymir, though in the form of a man, was not human. He was huge, for the ice had melted

Giants: *Trusting Death and Rebirth*

into giants. Enormous giants, as big as mountains. Possibly they are ancestral memories of Ice Age glaciers; ice giants moving only a few feet each year, their immense footprints leaving tracks the size of valleys and gorges shaping the contours of the Earth's skin.

But the concept was even bigger than this. For out of the material being of this first giant was formed the entire world as we know it. Sturluson quotes from *Grimnismal*, one of the poems of the *Elder Edda*, which is in the form of a monologue by Odin:

> Out of Ymir's flesh was the earth fashioned
> and from his gushing gore the seas;
> mountain tops from his bones
> trees from his hair,
> heavenly sky from his skull.
>
> Then out of his brows the joyous gods built
> Midgard for the sons of men;
> and from his brains there burgeoned all
> the soul-encooping clouds.[2]

As the Earth was created other human forms appeared, some as people, others giant-sized. One of the humans was Buri, who had a son called Bor. A giant called Bolthor had a daughter named Bestla. Bor and Bestla had a child. This child was Odin.

These ancestral trees, important still as recently as in the Russian novels of Tolstoy, were central to the people of Wyrd. In ancient European life the awareness of generations within families established an identity, webs of influence, channels of life force and power, bonds biologically based and expressed through families, clans and tribes. In the fragment of Odin's family tree outlined above, the 'famous son of Bolthor, father of Bestla' was the brother of Bor, and so Odin's uncle. And the name of Odin's uncle, his mentor, the teacher of 'nine lays of power', the driving force behind his initiation, was the wise giant Mimir, a figure referred to in the most ancient of myths and sagas.[3]

For men, uncles were important in early European culture. The uncle, a related, older figure, who had known the young man since birth but had no direct hand in his upbringing, was considered to be ideally placed to introduce the adolescent into manhood. And in the case of Odin, where we are witnessing the transformation of manhood into shamanhood, his uncle presided over the transformation of qualified initiates.

The sequence of events for Odin comprises first of all, as we have seen, his climbing into a tree for a nine-night vision quest. But then, from all the stories available to him but lost to us, Snorri Sturluson tells us that 'Under the root that turns in the direction of the Frost Giants lies the Spring of Mimir.' The root to which he refers is one of the three great sources of the World Tree. The spring contains secrets, deep reservoirs of wisdom which form part of Odin's quest. Snorri tells us that in the spring is 'hidden wisdom and understanding; Mimir is the name of the owner of the spring. He is full of wisdom because he drinks from the spring out of the horn Gjoll.' Odin's initiatory quest is to obtain a drink of water from Mimir's well.[4]

Eliade says that shamanic ritual, timeless in its aim, form and content, always seeks to return the participant to Original Time, the sacred point at which man was in communication with all other beings, and before he became separated from the animals and plants. In his initiation, when Odin journeys from the tree to the Lowerworld, to the Well of Mimir, and asks Mimir for a drink from the spring, he is asking to taste the forces of the very creation of the cosmos. For Mimir's spring is formed from the mist of the cosmic realm of Ginnangagap – the charged, primeval creative energy that exploded into life as the Mist of Creation when the frost and the fire came together.

It is intriguing to imagine this wisdom residing within the primeval forces of the cosmos. Not in our minds. Not in our libraries, our scientific laboratories, or our computer banks. Truth not in our hands, but in the Earth's forces. Out there, in the dynamic energies of creation, condensed in deep pools of wisdom.

— Riding Sleipnir to the Otherworld —

Odin soared from the World Tree and flew on Sleipnir in initiatory ecstasy to encounter Mimir, the wisdom giant. We do not have a direct account of this ride, but there are several accounts of later journeys Odin took on Sleipnir; they give us a flavour of what this first journey must have been like.

One of the rides on Sleipnir was taken by the god Hermothr, whom some scholars think to be an alter ego of Odin. Since my purpose in telling you the details of Hermothr's ride is to afford a glimpse of the nature of Odin's journey to Mimir, I shall therefore refer to Sleipnir's rider here directly as Odin. He was on this occasion riding from Asgard, in the Upperworld, down to Hel, the deepest realm of the Lowerworld in search of information about his brother Balder. He mounted his shamanic spirit-horse Sleipnir, and galloped from Asgard.[5]

Odin surged and fell as the mighty World Tree bucked beneath him, and looking down he saw that it was now a horse: a magnificent, huge, white, eight-legged horse, its hooves kicking and sparking for the gallop through the heavens. He bent over the horse's neck – Sleipnir it was called, he knew – and gripped with both hands hanks of the flowing mane as they shot off into the night sky. The flash of stars soon turned to a twinkle of dew as Sleipnir's hooves struck rock and they rode towards a mountainside, and the dark, looming entrance of an enormous cave.

The sources describe how, to commence the journey, Odin had to get into a cave black as night, set among precipitous cliffs and ravines. This black cave, a magical entrance to the sacred geography of the Lowerworld, rather like the dark room of a journey into deep hypnosis, a state of mind of total, cocooned concentration, was the destination, but to get into the cave was an ordeal, because the entrance was guarded by a fearsome hound called Garmr. The huge dog had blood on his chest; if the dog Kerberos from Greek mythology is a parallel, then the blood is from the dead people who have tried to escape from Hel, the deepest level of the Lowerworld.

While the Lowerworld was a realm of wisdom, for it contained the collective knowledge of all people who have lived and died, it was important in the finely balance web of forces that these 'spirits of the dead' remained in the Lowerworld, only escaping into the world of the living at liminal points in the year: Hallowe'en, Midwinter's Eve and so on. And in the mythology of the people of ancient Europe, the end of the world would be marked by setting the hound free, leaving the way out of Hel unguarded – the dead come roaring back into the world of the living: entropy exploding.[6] So Odin has to get past Garmr by the use of charms, or runic spells; presumably bonding spells such as I introduced in the earlier discussion about the threads of Wyrd being tied into ethereal knots; the dog is thus bound by magical forces (as was Fenrir the wolf), and Odin can slip inside.

Odin reined in Sleipnir by pulling at the mane, but the horse was already hopping sideways and slithering on the rocks to give Garmr a wide berth. Odin knew some binding charms, which he chanted over the baying hound, and the dog became constricted in its movements. It tried to bite at invisible bonds, then lost its footing, and was soon trussed up and helpless. Odin urged Sleipnir into the cave before the spell wore off and the dog could chase after them.

The high-roofed cave went deep into the mountain, and as they rode into the darkness even the glow of Sleipnir's coat faded like a dying candle. On they rode, until finally the cave opened out on the other side, a mere pinprick of light at first, getting larger, and then out into moonlight. The air smelled different: cooler, wetter; they were on their way to the Lowerworld.

'He rode nine days and nights down ravines ever darker and deeper, meeting no one,'[7] say the lines of sacred poetry; he is travelling the same magical time as he stayed in the World Tree; perhaps his journey began the moment his initiatory fast began. Descending trails along the floor of deeper and darker ravines, he was now entering the Lowerworld proper, the Realm of Shadows.

'Until he came to the banks of the river called Echoing.' The river is an important boundary, a great, open, echoing space blocking progress, testing one's will to cross. And there is only one way for Odin to cross the surging flow of Echoing space – over a bridge: 'this bridge is roofed with burning gold.'[8] The bridge of burning gold is like other references to a magical bridge which links the realm called Bifrost, which is also a bridge of fire and gold.

At the entrance to Echoing Bridge there is a mysterious maiden called Mothguthr who guards the bridge. She asks him his name or lineage, saying only the day before five droves of dead men had padded over the bridge, 'but the bridge echoed less under them than under thee'. 'Anyway,' she said, realising he was not dead but some sort of a shaman journeying in the realms of the dead, 'you haven't the pallor of a dead man; why are you riding down Helway?'

Odin tells her the reason for his trance journey, explaining that he was seeking the soul of a god called Balder. 'You don't happen to have set eyes on Balder on the road to Hel?' He was in luck. She replied that Balder had already ridden over the Echoing Bridge, and 'the road to Hel lies down still and to the north.'

Odin urged Sleipnir past the woman and thundered over the bridge to the other side, the horse's eight hooves drumming on the path Helway, and galloped on until they came to Hel Gate, an enormous barrier. Odin slid off his shamanic horse and tightened the girth. 'He mounted again and raked his spurs along the animal's ribs. The stallion leapt so high there was plenty of twilight between him and the bars.'[9]

From here the shaman rode on to the hall where resided the Queen of Hel. At the Hall of Hel he dismounted and went in to see 'his brother Balder sitting on a throne'. He had completed his journey.

Of course, in exploring Odin's journey to his initiation, he had a different destination: he was heading for an encounter with Mimir. The journey may have been slightly different, because Mimir lived next to a Well of Wisdom by one of the three roots of the World Tree. But since the roots sink to depths beyond anyone's understanding, they must be deep. I imagine the atmosphere, the obstacles, the time frame (nine nights and nine days) to be similar to Odin's journey into the Lowerworld.

While we may explore Odin's visions for their own sake, in the sacred stories of the ancient tribespeople of Europe his initiation was considered primary: it set the pattern for all initiations to follow. And it is remarkable that a description by Eliade of a recent shamanic ritual in Siberia has such strong parallels to that established in the story of Odin.[10]

Here the shaman is searching for the lost soul of a sick client; his task is to find and recover it, returning it to its owner: 'At the end of such a seance the shaman gave Jochelson the particulars of his ecstatic journey,' writes Eliade. Accompanied by his helping spirits, he had followed the road that leads to the Kingdom of Shadows. He came to a little house and found a dog that began to bark. An old woman, who guarded the road, came out of the house and asked him if he had come for ever or for a short time. The shaman did not answer her; instead, he addressed his spirits: 'Do not listen to the old woman's words, walk on without stopping.'

Soon they came to a stream. There was a boat, and on the other bank the shaman saw tents and men. Still accompanied by his spirits, he entered the boat and crossed the stream. He met the souls of the patient's dead relatives, and, entering their tent, found the patient's soul there too. 'As the relatives refused to give it to him, he had to take it by force. To carry it safely back to earth, he inhaled the patient's soul and stuffed his ears to prevent it from escaping.'

The road leading into darkness, the 'Kingdom of Shadows', the little house (cave) where he encountered a dog which barked at him, the woman who guarded the route who challenged him, the crossing of a stream (this time in a boat rather than over a bridge), and finally arriving at the land of the spirits of the dead: the similarities demonstrate remarkable parallels between the details of journeys separated by so many centuries, and the timeless quality of these rituals.

— The Giants —

The land of the giants was called Jotunheim, one of the nine worlds of knowledge in the World Tree. It was a world on an enormous scale, as befits its residents, a landscape of towering forests, strong rivers, vast caverns, mighty mountains and tremendous distances. When the god Thor went to Jotunheim: 'Thor and his companions saw soaring high above them a castle set in the middle of an open plain. Even though they pressed back the crowns of their heads on to the napes of their necks they still couldn't see its battlements.'

The giants were the first forms of life which were shaped from the coming together of fire and frost, at the creation of the cosmos. They were then possessed of huge elemental powers. Cleverer beings, like dwarfs and humans, have come along since and elaborated the world, but the basic structure, dynamics, bases of life were in the hands of the giants. This is a kind of brute wisdom. Knowledge from the beginning.[11]

Both good and evil giants are depicted in myth all over ancient Europe, ranging from helpful, relatively harmless creatures like larger versions of household and farmyard elves to hideous ogres, eaters of human flesh. 'Ent' is an Old English word meaning 'giant', and usually referring to an ancient fallen race of wise and faithful giants whose passing was spoken of regretfully in the *Prose Edda*. On the other hand, in ancient Teutonic myth, giants and trolls were often personifications of natural elements in their most terrifying forms. Aegir and his wife Ran, for example, were Scandinavian giants who represented the violence of the sea. Other giants were responsible for the growls and roars in river chasms, for earthquakes and for thunderstorms. The elemental forces they embodied constituted the very fabric of the world we inhabit.

In northern mythology the giants are images which embody complex nuances of significance within an animistic interpretation of natural phenomena. Rockfalls, landslips and earthquakes were the work of rock giants; flaring volcanoes, destructive lightning, and the frightening northern lights were caused by fire giants; and avalanches, glaciers, ice-caps, freezing seas and rivers by ice or frost giants.

The wisdom of the giants emanated from their intimate connections with the elements of nature. The god Thor (called Thunor in England),[12] who was as prominent as Odin in some areas of western Europe and Scandinavia, was a large, bluff, farmer's god. The god of thunder, he wielded a big hammer as weapon, and his main role in the delicate web of forces which held together the cosmos was to fight the giants, to keep them penned in their kingdom, and dissuade them from invading the realm of the gods; to keep the elements under control.

On one of his sojourns into the land of the giants, he came upon the mead hall of the mightiest giant of all, banged on the doors, and asked for hospitality.[13] The Thunderer was not shy. 'I admit to my hall only those who are masters of some trial,' boomed the giant, his lips curling into a sneer. 'What can a puny individual like you hope to achieve against my giant warriors?'

Thor could not resist such a challenge, though he knew he would be up against it. These were seriously big giants. His brow furrowed in thought for a moment. 'There is no one in your hall can eat faster than I!' he retorted, pulling himself up to his full height and almost reaching the kneecap of the giant.

The giant admitted Thor to his hall, and called for an enormous trencher of meat to be brought in. Thor sat down at one end and a giant warrior at the other, and they both ate as fast as they could. Thor crammed the meat into his mouth and swallowed without chewing (he was not a very elegant god); they met in the middle of the trencher and Thor thought he had at least matched the giant for speed of eating. But then he saw that while he had left only the bones of his meat, the giant had eaten all his meat, bones and his side of the trencher as well. Thor had lost the contest.

But Thor was not finished. He valiantly challenged any giant in the hall to a drinking contest. The giants stopped laughing long enough to drag out an enormous ale-horn, fill it, and challenged the Thunderer to empty it. Thor's eyes popped as he took three immense draughts, until he thought he would explode, but the horn was not emptied. The giants were helpless with mirth at Thor's efforts.

Our hero stood up to them, his eyes blazing, feet astride: 'Now I am really angry!' he shouted. 'I will show you how strong I am. I challenge any of you to a wrestling match.' When he heard himself say this, Thor felt a slight twinge of doubt, but he quickly conquered it. He had a mighty heart, full of optimism and self-belief. He would try to his utmost. As he pumped himself up as big as possible, the giants seemed to be dithering over who should wrestle with him.

But then an old crone shuffled into the arena, and the giants roared their approval; Thor would wrestle with her. He tried to object, furious that the ignorant huge ones would impugn his dignity so, but as he was remonstrating with them, the crone suddenly started grappling with him. She was surprisingly strong, and although Thor tried with all his strength, he could struggle only evenly with the old woman and eventually she threw him to the ground.

The Thunderer felt humiliated. Slowly he climbed to his feet, and crept towards the door, his head hung in shame. But as he reached for the latch, the mighty giant called him back.

'Wait! Noble One, had I known you were so powerful I would have never admitted you to my hall, for I would have been afraid of you.'

Thor thought the giant was mocking him, but when he turned he saw that all the giants were regarding him with respect. 'How can that be?' he asked. 'I lost all three contests.'

'Yes,' said the giant, 'but you did not realise who it was you were contesting. You first competed for eating speed with Wildfire itself, which can consume entire forests at one sitting.' Thor took a step back into the hall. 'And the enormous drinking horn had been connected to the oceans, and in each of your three draughts, you lowered the level of the sea by one inch.' The giants were nodding and smiling in approval.

'But the old crone?' said Thor. 'She threw me to the ground.'

The Mighty Giant laughed. 'She was your most formidable opponent, for she who threw you to the ground was Old Age herself. She defeats us all eventually!'

Most of us are, at times, too hard on ourselves. We take on too much, expect too much. It is easy when we succeed, because the rewards are self-evident. But when we attempt something ambitious and feel that we have failed, it is good to be sure to give ourselves credit for at least making the challenge. Sometimes our failures are more impressive than our successes; it all depends with what we were competing.

So when Odin arrived at the Well of Mimir the Giant, at the root of the World Tree, he was dealing with an old, huge and *wise* being.

— What Odin Wanted From Mimir —

Odin's ultimate quest was to obtain a drink of 'magic mead', but first he needed to gain some powers, 'nine lays of power', from Mimir. However, this was not being offered to him on a plate (or in a drinking horn); Odin was engaged on an initiatory path, and he had tasks to complete, obstacles to overcome, tricks and talents he needed to display. And they started with his encounter with Mimir.

Mimir's well was under the root of the World Tree, a setting so ancient as to be timeless.[14] Sometimes it is referred to as a spring, so the soft, trickling sound of water pouring from the depths might be all that one could hear of it: melodious and peaceful. But Mimir conjures a more noisy image. As a giant he must have been huge, much larger than Odin: giants were tall as huge oaks, feet splaying yards across the ground, heads sometimes ethereal-looking as they stuck up into the clouds.

Some of the giants were good-natured, but if provoked, the giants of legend could be very dangerous. In rage they uprooted trees, hurled rocks, and squeezed water out of stones. Mimir would have had no trouble crushing Odin in his fist if he wished. So when Odin arrived at Mimir's well, he must have had to gather all his courage even to begin negotiations. His ultimate quest was to obtain a drink of the mead of inspiration, the drink that enabled the drinker to speak the poetry of ultimate truth, to be the knower of Wyrd.

But in describing what happens next, I also need to provide a bit of a plot summary.

Odin 'knew' that if he asked for a drink of mead, in his identity as Odin, then he would not get any. He was expected to earn it, and to use his wits to obtain the drink.[15] So he decided that he had to appear to Mimir not as someone who was seeking knowledge, but as an amiable traveller, a guileless companion. In a piece of sacred text called *Grimnismal*, Odin says: 'I was called Svithurr and Svithrir at Mimir's, when I fooled the old giant and single-handed became the death of that famous son of Meadwolf' (i.e. Mimir).

Odin's 'disguise' names of Svithurr and Svithrir are etymologically the same as a character in one of the sagas who was a noted heavy drinker. So the lines tell us that Odin lurched into the vicinity of Mimir's well pretending to be a drinker who merely and innocently wanted a swig of mead, rather than an initiate intending to drink it in pursuit of shamanic inspiration.

But it turned out that Mimir does not, after all, have the magic mead. Other sources explain that the mead was originally in the hands of Mimir's father (the Meadwolf), but is now kept under guard in a place called Okolnir, a region of fire and flame where the Fire Giant Surt lives. Surer, and his fiery comrades, now have possession of the magic mead. But although Mimir does not have the mead, he does have the magic spells by which Odin might journey in search of it. And before Odin could journey in quest of a drink of the mead he had to obtain the 'nine lays' from Mimir.

So what happened between them?

— Odin Pledges an Eye —

Snorri Sturluson quotes the lines of the ancient poem called *Sybil's Vision*:

> I know it all, Odin,
> where you hid your eye
> deep in the wide-famed
> well of Mimir;
> every morning does Mimir drink
> mead from Allfather's pledge . . .[16]

And Snorri tells us that, 'All-father [Odin] came there and asked for a single drink from the spring, but he did not get it until he had given of his eye as a pledge.' So Odin pledges to the giant Mimir one of his eyes, which is to be put in Mimir's well, and forms some sort of deal which allows Mimir to drink the mead every morning and, in return, enables Odin to learn the 'nine lays of power'.

Odin's giving up of an eye is a gravely serious pledge, of course, horrifying and gruesome in its literal sense. What is he gaining? Giving up an eye is an intriguing pledge. Our two eyes, used together, provide perspective. The Vikings would have been well aware of this. There were plenty of eye injuries in those times – farming, hunting accidents, as well as combat injuries, and in a practical craft society, it would have been noted that people with only one eye have an impaired sense of perspective. Odin, embarking on a dangerous quest, is nevertheless prepared to give up an eye, and is thereby handicapping himself in his ability to accomplish certain practical tasks.

Why should he accept the loss, unless he is aware of the advantages? Certainly in modern Western society, sight is the primary mode of sense that we employ in maintaining our everyday sense of 'reality' –

the waking state of consciousness. Under altered states such as meditation or hypnosis, drug-induced, other senses come into more prominence, and sight of the material world may be a minor or even absent factor. So one way of regarding Odin's sacrifice, his pledge, is that in giving up an eye on his way to initiation, Odin is making an investment in altered reality.

Odin's act of sacrifice has survived in the practices of more recent shamanic cultures where the pledging of body parts is in the service of a death-and-rebirth initiatory remaking into a shaman's body. However these pledges, while marked by physical ordeals, are metaphorical and have a psychological rather than physical grounding.

Eliade quotes fieldwork observations which testify that during the Araucanian shaman's consecration festival the shamans were seen to tear off their noses or tear out their eyes. He makes it clear that he considers this to have been an act of illusion: 'The initiator made the profane audience believe that he tore out his tongue and eyes and exchanged them with those of the initiate.'[17] So the initiator, the shaman with the knowledge, exchanges his eyes with those of the neophyte, so that the apprentice will have the ability to see as a shaman sees, in the spirit world. We have no indication that Mimir exchanged eyes with Odin, but he did something even more dramatic, and of greater import: Mimir gave Odin his head. Or rather, Odin won Mimir's head in a bizarre ritual.

— The Beheading Game —

In the *Verse Edda*, the seeress says:

> Shrilly shrieked Heimdall's
> horn across the sky;
> Odin whispers
> with the head of Mimir . . .[18]

And we know from other sources that these lines refer to an astounding ritual whereby Odin cuts off Mimir's head. So how did the beheading come about? And how could it be that Odin cut off Mimir's head and 'become the death of him' against an opponent so

Giants: *Trusting Death and Rebirth* 225

many times his size? We have no more details about the actual incident, but a story from the Celtic tribespeople of ancient Ireland sets the scene for understanding the beheading of Mimir.

In the Irish tale of the *Feast of Bricriu*, there is described the 'game of the beheaded man'.[19] Three mighty Irish warriors, called Cu Chulainn, Loegaire and Conall, were quarrelling over which of them should be accorded the title of 'hero', an accolade to be given to the bravest of the three. Finally the warriors went for a judgement from Uath Mac Immonain (the 'Terrible Son of Great Fear'), a wild and formidable giant, who said to them, 'I have an axe. Let one of you take it in your hand and cut off my head today, and I shall cut off his head tomorrow.' Horrified, Conall and Loegaire refused to accept this deal. But Cu Chulainn agreed.

'After pronouncing an incantation over the blade of his axe, Uath laid his head on the stone before Cu Chulainn, who took the weapon and cut off his head. Then Uath left and dived into the lake, holding his axe in one hand and his head against his chest with the other.' When, the following day, Cu Chulainn came as arranged and laid his head on the stone, Uath, who appeared to be as well as ever, was content to brandish his axe three times over the neck and back of the hero, declaring him worthy of the honour he claimed.

This beheading 'game', a test of bravery, is testimony to the fact that the heroes believe that they will not die from the beheading. Uath was able to walk and be alive even after losing his head. Losing his head did not literally kill him, though it might have been formally called a 'death'. He was able to return the next day with his head fixed back on to his body, 'reborn'. There is a kind of mutual sacrifice, but it ends in a symbolic gesture rather than a literal beheading.

In this story, the giant Uath was dealing with warriors competing for bravery, rather than a shaman looking for a drink of magic mead. But it seems likely that Odin would have to prove himself in his Otherworld quest, and since he was a warrior before entering this quest, he is well equipped. In a line of poetry Odin is referred to in the following terms: 'He stood on the cliff with Brimir's sword . . . then Mimir's head spoke.'[20] I shall explain shortly how this refers to the moment at which Odin had cut off Mimir's head. 'Brimir' refers to a sword with special powers: another manuscript tells us of 'Brimir best of swords'.

So Odin has a special sword, the 'best of swords', which he has obtained from the fire giants, and it seems likely that in beheading Mimir he cheated the giant: 'I fooled that giant and killed him.' If the giant Mimir played the beheading game with Odin, as a test of his bravery, and allowed Odin to strike the first blow as in the Irish story above, perhaps Odin's use of the special sword meant that the giant could not put his head back on. As I describe below, Odin kept the head, and it spoke to him, telling him nine lays of power and many secrets.

If we turn to another Celtic story, from the ancient Welsh narratives, representing the British tradition before the separation of the Bretons, we see that the second section of the document called the *Mabinogion* is about a severed head. The story concerns the prominent mythological figure called Bran the Blessed.

The French scholar of Celtic mythology, Jean Markale, relates a story[21] which concerns an expedition mounted to Ireland by Bran and the British to avenge an injury to his sister Branwen and to recover a magic cauldron that brings the dead back to life. The expedition struck disaster, as in battle Bran was wounded in the foot by a poisoned spear. He asked the seven surviving Britons to cut off his head and carry it with them, which they did. Together with Branwen, they reached Harddleck, where they settled. 'They began to lay in a wealth of food and drink and consume it. Three birds came to sing them a song, which made other birds they had heard seem dull. This meal lasted for seven years, at the end of which they left for Gwales in Penvro.'

There they stayed in a great hall with the head of Bran fully displayed. 'They remembered nothing of all the suffering they had seen and all they had experienced, nor of any pain in the world; they stayed for twenty-four years and it seemed to them the best and most agreeable time in all their lives. They felt no more tiredness and none of them could see that the others had aged at all since the time they had arrived.'

After the twenty-four years had elapsed, they opened a door and immediately their memories returned along with their tiredness and sufferings, and they went to carry out Bran's last wish that his head should be buried in the White Hill in London.

In this story, the Britons have failed to recover the magic cauldron which brings the dead back to life, and Bran's head, offered to the men, provides a stopping of time. The men do not age. They experience good cheer and food and no pain. So the head brought healing. And peace and plenty. But primarily, the stopping of time.

But beyond this, we need to consider how it was that the head could bring eternal life. To understand the significance of this act about the head, we need to consider first the concept of the soul among the peoples of Wyrd; as I explained earlier, among the tribespeople of ancient Europe the head was considered to be the seat of procreation, of life force.

Connecting the head and life-soul with procreation also explains the custom constantly alluded to in *Beowulf*: the head contained the life and life-soul, so that men who defended themselves were said to 'guard their heads'. The helmet or 'head-protector' is referred to simply as 'the boar'. It is 'the boar, the head-sign'. 'The boar kept ward.' This seems to mean that the head was committed uniquely to the protection of the god of procreation and fertility, Freyr, whose emblem the boar was.[22]

Also it is the head that matters in battle. Wiglaf 'bears his war-head to help his lord'. When Beowulf and the dragon have slain each other and are lying dead, Wiglaf 'keepeth guard over the heads of friend and foe'. It is the head that goes to the Norse Realm of Death. So in old Germanic belief the soul which survives death was located in the head.[23] This was the seat of death and rebirth, for it was the fertile, vital aspect which survived physical death.

For many tribal groupings, such as the Angles, Saxons, and Norsemen, freedom was a condition of the procreative element, and explains why Angles and Saxons used the expression 'heofod ninam', 'to take [his] head'. While one who surrendered himself thus into the power of another was said by the Norsemen 'to bring his head to one'.

From this we might adduce that the beheading game was one in which the two protagonists 'surrendered their heads' to the other, gave themselves into each other's power, absolutely, in a form of bonding. To make oneself so vulnerable as to have one's head chopped off by an 'adversary', on the understanding that it can be put back on again, is a truly remarkable level of trust. It must be akin to the notion of 'blood brothers' which has survived into modern culture. This latter contains no hint of rebirth, but rather the notion that self-inflicted wounds can lead to a sharing of blood in a bonding ritual. In more recent times it refers to a very close 'brother' relationship between men, without necessarily having the physical ritual played out.

But this is not the same thing as having the brain, or even the mind, in the head. Rather it is a function of the person's very identity. Who he or she is. The personal presence. When we 'capture' someone for a position in business, a position for which the person is highly prized, they have been 'head-hunted'. Not for their brain only, but for their very being. When a person is fired from a job, they 'get the chop'. And when our sense of our life force is exaggerated, blown up, we have become 'big-headed'. And the leader of an organisation, the person who represents it, runs it, expresses its life force, is its 'head'.

If we follow the points above about the head being the seat of the soul, the focus of the procreative juices that guarantee fertility, rebirth, then to take one's head is to take that element of a person which will be reborn. And so to play a game in which one allows one's 'antagonist' to take one's head and then to do the reverse is to pledge oneself to another for ever. Literally. And this is what Odin did with Mimir.

Finally, one more perspective rounds out the picture. For if the life force of a person resides in the head, then the taking of that head adduces the power of the person to the taker. In the Native American tradition of 'scalping' slain enemies, and the hunting tradition of keeping tails and so on as trophies, there is a strong element of this belief. It is not just a count of success, it is a taking of that power for oneself. And if the Anglo-Saxons believed in a spiritual soul-matter which pervades the whole body but is concentrated in the head, a soul-matter which maintains all life, 'then the taking of a head brings also the effectiveness of the soul-matter to the taker and his people. This is in effect what happens when Odin takes Mimir's head and uses its wisdom for his and the Aesirs' good.'[24]

Odin 'captured' Mimir's head; this was an act of sabotage, but an act expected of him, for he was engaged in a quest for knowledge. For this he had to fight. And in fooling Mimir, he gained for himself the wisdom of Mimir (as we shall see shortly).

This is a rather complex analysis, necessarily so, for we are dealing here with aspects of the beliefs of our ancestors which are embedded in many threads of the web of Wyrd. A lot of it seems to me to be about risk, commitment, and the juices of life. The most satisfying forces in one's life are self-rewarding; they increase vitality, life force, energy.

Indeed a much more common term that has survived in modern Western parlance refers to the taking of a risk as 'sticking one's neck out'. Often it refers to the making of a risky statement, or judgement; the declaring of a viewpoint which might be proven wrong or unpopular, and therefore leaves one's neck vulnerable to 'the chop'. And yet in the making of these statements, we are expressing our selves, our true beliefs; it is saying what we think even if to do so involves risk. So the sticking out of one's neck is an act of self-validation.

It is the truest way to fulfil our personal destiny. The shaman underwent physical death and rebirth, and here, in the ritual of Odin and Mimir, we can see that death and rebirth involved cutting off the head, the point of vital flow of life force, and then putting it back on again.

But the important point for us today is that the principle is provocative: to live 'near the edge', to be aware of the boundaries of experience, of sticking one's neck out, encourages the person to live to the full. We do not need to go beyond the boundaries, but to test them was, and is, a test of one's commitment. Awareness of death introduces one to the fullness of life.

But in holding back in safe areas, of being cautious so as not to invite the 'chop', we miss out. For then we have not affirmed what Odin and Mimir and Bran were affirming in their game: that psychologically and spiritually at least, and physically if we are a god, we can die and be reborn – a psychological death is not the end of life. It is an opportunity for rebirth. At the end of a bloodthirsty chapter, I find that a comforting and encouraging message.

— How the Head Spoke —

Let us return to the story briefly and consider how Odin deals with Mimir's head, the head he has cut off. First we are told that he carefully preserves it with the use of herbs and incantations. So if Odin consulted Mimir's head at the time of his initiation, what did it say? And how did the ritual work?

Odin's consulting of the preserved head of Mimir suggests the Yukagir method of divination by the skulls of ancestral shamans.[25] Until the last century in this culture the skulls of dead shamans were still venerated; each was set in a wooden figurine, which was kept in a box. Nothing was undertaken without recourse to divination by these skulls. The method most usual in the Arctic was employed: if the skull seems light to the diviner when he questions it, the answer is 'yes', if heavy, 'no'. And the oracle's answer must be obeyed to the letter.

But there is evidence in the sacred poetry that Odin did something rather different with Mimir's head in the following lines: 'Hroptr read them [the runes of wisdom], cut them and thought them out from the lees which had leaked out of Hethdraupnir's skull and out of Hoddrofnir's horn.' Hroptr means 'the sage', and refers to Odin. Brian Branston identifies the names Hethdraupnir (Clear-Dripper) and Hoddrofnir (Treasurer-Opener) as nicknames referring to Mimir.[26]

So this piece of poetry says that Odin, in his sage guise, reads the runes of wisdom, carves them into wood staves, and thinks them through so he understands them, and obtains these patterns from the clear-dripping, treasure-opening shape and quality of the water (lees?) which drips from Mimir's skull and out of his horn.

The head leaks and tells Odin the shape of runes, in the form of nine mighty lays, or spells. These are the spells he must use to obtain a drink of the mead as inspiration which will transform him into a spell-singing shaman.

— The Significance of Mimir —

The name Mimir means 'memory, remembrance, mindfulness'. The stories of ancient sacred literature refer not only to universal scenarios, but can also be read as referring to individual ones which are a microcosm of the whole. As when we consider the significance of a dream, the various 'characters' in the drama represent aspects of the protagonist. In this case, Mimir is an aspect of Odin. What does this tell us?

Clearly in terms of individual sacred psychology, Odin's encounters with Mimir are direct dealings with the collective unconscious. He is negotiating with material which is 'memory' and 'remembrance' of the human species, shared among all peoples and preserved in all subtleties of cultural forms. In psychological terms, the memory is 'inside us', but so deep that it is inaccessible to the conscious mind. These ancient and deep images come to us only in deep dreams (not everyday wish-fulfilment dreams, or those night images playing out the psychological dynamics of our social relationships and personal obsessions and insecurities). Messages from the collective unconscious cannot be recalled at will. Unless, that is, a deal is done, a ritual performed, a kind of inner journey undergone as in Odin's dropping down to the hidden roots of the World Tree to encounter a giant from the primeval past.

Odin's initiatory ordeal on the World Tree, in which he fasted for nine days and nine nights, was such a ritual; it enabled him to reach those secret primeval layers of psychic experience which are the reward of such deep voyages. In claiming archetypal memories in coded runic form (Mimir's head speaking), Odin has had to let go of some of the connection with everyday consensual reality. He will never again see things in a 'normal', socially sanctioned framework. The ritual encounters with Mimir are a transcending of the gulf between everyday reality and the deepest of inner knowledge. To maintain that bridge, Odin braved possible psychological death: the severing of his 'head'. Today, someone dipping into temporary insanity is sometimes spoken of as having 'lost his head'.

Odin did not get away with Mimir's head without having to make the compensatory gesture where he pledged to Mimir one of his own eyes, the eye of 'normal perspective'. The eye was to be submerged in Mimir's well and left there. So that while Mimir's head was helping Odin to see, so Odin's eye was helping the headless Mimir to see. It is a ritualistic bonding, a way of exchanging virtue, of balancing the powers, and of maintaining a deeply imaginative vision even as one lives partly in the 'normal world'.

Shamans, mystics, archetypal psychic voyagers such as Odin go further than the rest of us. We are not meant to take such drastic steps; nine-day fasts are not advisable psychologically and certainly not physically, even with a doctor's certificate for vigorous sporting activity. But just as Olympic athletes can run faster than the rest of us, we can all run, nevertheless. Understanding the point and appreciating the sacrifice of Odin's encounters with Mimir can provide us with a glimpse of the sacred potential for gaining inner knowledge; even if we cannot get to that level, we can all go part of the way. But this shamanic journeying into the mysteries of Wyrd is for supervised experience only.

— Our Own 'Talking Heads' Ritual —

The image of a severed head being used as an oracle of wisdom is a deep and somewhat disturbing one to us, a ritual form from the ancient culture of our ancestors; one that we may learn something from, but perhaps not one that we would wish to emulate literally. Except that it is amusing and instructive to acknowledge the ways in which we do something similar. In the Western world the television news as a source of information delivered from 'severed', or at least disembodied heads, is very widespread. And frequently politicians or other opinion-makers are interviewed with just their head, or head and shoulders, showing.

The people to whom the heads belong are often famous, and listened to regularly but are not known personally to the people watching the set. Their opinions have influence, and often more so *because* they are on television. And when politicians, in particular, are preparing speeches that they know will be transmitted from their disembodied heads oracular-style on television, they often prepare their words in 'sound-bites', a special language of significance for the disembodied head ritual that millions of people participate in each evening. Television producers even refer to these sort of broadcasts as 'talking heads' programmes. An anthropologist from another planet observing the flickering image of the disembodied heads on television sets in the West might speculate on the occult significance of the talking head in contemporary society!

Chapter Twelve

Love Magic:
Creating the Elixir of Life

— The Magic Mead —

Spellcasting, the ability to conjure words and runes to ripple the flow of Wyrd, to make tiny interventions in the forces of fate, was the glittering prize at the centre of Odin's initiatory quest. He wanted it, needed it, not for his self-glorification, even though Odin never shrank from claiming the brightest firelight in the world of the gods. No. He sought it for the Aesir, the warrior gods, and for Middle Earth, the ecstatically inspired shamans, the people who could turn such knowledge to advantage in healing, fortune-telling, sacred ceremony.

The story from the ancient manuscripts which best captures Odin's battles of wit and strength, love and 'powers' from Mimir, in search of wisdom is his journey to the stronghold of the giants.[1] He goes to the mountain castles of Suttung the fire giant to obtain, by any means necessary, three draughts of a special drink, the mead of 'poetic inspiration', the drink which confers the knowledge to use word-magic.

Hanging on the World Tree, undergoing his ritual initiation, Odin says, when 'Nine lays of power I learned from the famous Bolthor, father of Bestla: I got a draught of precious mead, Mixed with magic Odrerir . . . Learned I grew then, lore-wise, Waxed and throve well.' What exactly was the nature of this mead? Why did it render him learned, lore-wise and thriving? And how did Odin get it? The answers to these questions open another doorway to the hidden world of wisdom of the people of Wyrd.

According to Snorri Sturluson, the special mead which was to become the target of Odin's most dangerous quest was created originally as part of a pact between the two warring tribal groups of gods, the warrior gods and the fertility gods, near the beginning of time.

Snorri Sturluson records a question and answer session between the gods. 'Where did the accomplishment known as poetry come from?' said one god. This was a deep question, of course, for as we have already seen earlier, poetry was considered to be of great import. It was not, as today, regarded as a minor and specialised form of literature. Rather, poets were lauded for their skills in 'capturing' life in the magic of words. And for shamans the power of poetry was the forming of spells and charms.

As we have seen, when the gods made peace, from their joint saliva was conjured a man called Kvasir, who was original knowledge. But at this point, competition for possession of Kvasir's knowledge began. The polarities, the forces pulling this way and that for the balance of the cosmos, begin to wrest the knowledge from the human figure of Kvasir. The story goes that he came once to feast with some dwarfs. Two of them, Fjalar and Galar, 'called him aside for a word in private and killed him, letting his blood run into two crocks and one kettle'. These were no ordinary containers, for the dwarfs were figures of transformation. The crocks were known as Son and Bothn; the kettle was called Odrorir. The dwarfs mixed Kvasir's blood with honey, and from it brewed the mead which makes whoever drinks it a wise person with the inspiration of poetry. The warrior gods heard that Kvasir had died. They demanded to know from the dwarfs what had happened. 'The dwarfs told the Aesir that Kvasir had choked with learning, because there was no one sufficiently well-informed to compete with him in knowledge.'

But the two dwarfs, though possessing the mead of inspiration, obviously did not profit from it directly. They continued their blood-thirsty ways. They killed a giant in an accident at sea, and then his wife. This was a big mistake, for when the giant's son, called Suttung, heard of the murders, he went to the dwarfs, seized them and took them out to sea, where he chained them on to a skerry covered by the tide. The dwarfs begged Suttung to spare their lives, offering him as compensation for the death of his father the precious magic mead of knowledge. Suttung accepted the deal, took the mead home and hid it in the inner recesses of his mountain dwelling, which was known as

Knit Mountain. He appointed his daughter Gunnloth as its guardian.

'This is why we call poetry Kvasir's blood,' says Snorri, 'or dwarfs' drink or intoxication, or some sort of liquid of Odrorir or Bothn or Son, or dwarfs' ship, because it was that mead which ransomed them from death on the skerry, or Suttung's mead . . .' It was Suttung's mead which was the object of Odin's vision quest to the land of the giants.

— The Story of the Journey to Knit Mountain —

We are told the story of Odin's quest for the sacred mead in Snorri's *Prose Edda*, and in a section of the famous poem from the *Havamal* which I introduced in the chapter on the World Tree. In order to gain access to the mead, Odin has to journey to the land of the giants, the mythical landscape on the edge of Middle Earth. It is a quest which tests all Odin's nine lays of power, and involves him in attempting to win the mead through the shamanic arts of love. It also leaves him in a crisis of choice between the ultimate concerns of his quest and personal love.

Odin set out on his journey to Jotunheim, the land of the giants, a journey in mythical time where hours in the imaginal can be experienced as days, weeks, or even months.

His long trek was finally rewarded with a sight of the giants' Otherworld, a bucolic scene of nine giant men in a line, slowly advancing across a vast field, cutting hay. Odin's eye (he now had only one) took in the situation in a flash. Without breaking stride, but with all his senses alert, he strode up to them. They regarded him suspiciously, but continued their work. Odin hooked his hands in his belt and watched them for a few moments, his head cocked on one side critically. He saw his opportunity. A plan formed in his mind.

He stepped closer. The giants stopped scything, the sweat of hard labour dripping from their noses, and glared at him. Quickly, while he was still alive, Odin asked if they would like him to sharpen their scythes. Eagerly they agreed that they would. They laid their scythes down and gratefully sprawled about, resting. Odin took a sharpening hone from his belt and deftly put an edge on their tools. The giants reformed their line, tried cutting again, and were mightily impressed. With grunts and murmurs of approval, they all agreed they could cut much better and easier with the sharpened scythes. Odin asked whether one of them would like to buy his sharpening tool. Not surprisingly, they all wanted it.

Odin said that the price of the hone for whoever purchased it should be paid by his giving a banquet. The giants, who were not very bright, did not recognise this as a strange bargain. They were no longer suspicious, just keen to make their work easier. And whichever one of them owned the sharpening tool would have the sharpest scythe and the easiest work of all. The giants put their scythes over their shoulders and crowded round, all demanding that they should be the one given the hone. Odin suddenly flung the hone high up into the air, and as they all scrambled to catch it the sharpened scythes whirled around in their hands, cutting one another's throats. They fell dead. Odin smiled at the 'sharpness' of his wit. Mimir would be pleased.

Having successfully accomplished the first step of his quest, Odin now pressed on in search of the employer of the nine dead giants. He already knew who it was, for Mimir had 'told' him. He was a giant called Baugi, and Odin knew also that he was the brother of Suttung, who had the mead.

As the sun set over the land of the giants, Odin strode up to the huge door of Baugi's house, knocked on it nine times, and when the giant appeared Odin sought lodgings for the night. Later that evening, as they sat talking, Baugi confessed that his affairs had taken a turn for the worse: his nine workers had all killed one another and, he complained, he would now have no hope of finding any other labourers at this time of the summer, when crops were being harvested. Odin, giving his name as Baleworker, proposed an unusual deal. He offered to do the work of nine men for Baugi, and asked as wages at the end of the harvest one drink of Suttung's mead.

Surprised, Baugi protested that he had nothing to do with the mead, adding that Suttung was anxious to keep it under his exclusive control. Odin/Baleworker insisted that was his price for the work in the fields. Baugi was desperate. He agreed to go along with the spirit of Odin's proposal at least. He could not guarantee a drink of the mead but he promised that he would, at the end of the harvesting season, take him to see Suttung to make his request.

That summer Odin did the work of nine men for Baugi, and when winter came he asked Baugi for his payment. They both went to see Suttung. Baugi told his brother of his bargain with Odin, but Suttung flatly refused them a single drop of mead. Baugi smiled to himself. He had known all along that this would be Suttung's response.

As soon as they left Suttung's presence, Odin remonstrated with Baugi, saying that he had not yet fulfilled his bargain to help him get some of the mead; that they must try to get hold of the mead by some kind of trick.

Baugi pretended that he thought this was a good idea, although he never really had the intention of helping Odin to get some of his brother's mead. Odin produced a hand drill, the auger called Rati, and said that Baugi was to use his giant strength to bore a hole right through the centre of the mountain where Suttung kept the mead hidden under the guard of Gunnloth. Baugi, putting his giant's strength behind the drilling, bored into the rock. Finally he stepped back, said that he had now fulfilled his pledge to help Odin, and that he was going to leave.

But Odin did not trust the giant, and to test it he blew into the hole left by the auger; chips of stone flew back into his face, and he knew that Baugi had not pierced right through as he had promised to do. He realised then that Baugi wanted to cheat him, and angrily told him to try harder. Baugi bored again, and when Odin blew into the hole for the second time the chips were blown through. Instantly Odin shapeshifted into a snake (one of his 'lays of power') and crawled into the auger hole, Baugi stabbing wildly at him with the auger but just missing. Odin slithered towards the centre of the mountain.

The detail of what happened in the centre of the mountain is frustratingly vague. Snorri tells us only that Odin, in the guise of Baleworker, 'came to where Gunnloth was, and slept with her for three nights, and then she promised him three drinks of the mead. At his first drink he drank up all that was in Odrorir, at his second, Bothn, and at his third, Son – and then he had finished all the mead. Then he changed himself into an eagle and flew away at top speed.'

The last part of the story depicts Odin as having to run from Suttung the giant. Snorri tells us that

> When Suttung saw the eagle in flight, however, he also took on eagle shape and flew after him. Now when the Aesir saw where Odin was flying, they put their crocks out in the courtyard, and when Odin came inside Asgard he spat the mead into the crocks. It was such a close shave that Suttung did not catch him, however, that he let some fall, but no one bothered about that. Anyone who wants could have it; we call it poetasters share. Odin gave Suttung's mead to the Aesir and those men who can compose poetry. So we call poetry Odin's catch, Odin's discovery, his drink and his gift, and the drink of the Aesir.

But we need to build a closer picture of Odin's encounter with Gunnloth. How did he get her to promise him three drinks of the sacred mead?

— What Happened in the Mountain? —

The crux of our understanding of Odin's quest for the mead is the events in the mountain, especially the relationship between Odin and Gunnloth. Snorri's outline of the story leaves us starved of the main details, but fortunately we are able to develop a fuller picture by reference to other fragmentary accounts which have survived over the past thousand years.

For example, Odin says in *Havamal*:[2] 'The heron of forgetfulness hovers over banquets and steals away men's wits: I myself was fettered with that bird's feathers when I lay in Gunnloth's house. I was drunk – I was dead drunk at the wise Fjalar's: and the only comfort is that a drunkard's wits do come home when he's sober.' In addition to the accurate observations on the effects of heavy drinking on one's faculties, these lines are revealing. It is clear that Odin was drunk in the mountain stronghold, 'in Gunnloth's house'. And when he is dead drunk 'at the wise Fjalar's' he is referring to one of the dwarfs who was responsible for creating the mead in the first place by killing Kvasir, and mixing his blood with honey to create the inspirational drink.[3]

Odin's statement could mean a number of things. In the literal progression of the story, it could mean that Odin was referring to Fjalar sarcastically as 'wise', for it is possible to see him as not wise, in that he won the right to make the mead, and then had to bargain it away to save his life. But while he had possession of the magic mead, Fjalar had access to wisdom, and it seems more likely that Odin was thinking of him in these terms. Another possibility is that during his sojourn in the mountain with Gunnloth the two of them journeyed to Otherworlds. If so, then it is possible that they went to the Lowerworld abode of Fjalar, where they got drunk on the mead. Or drunk on other alcoholic drink, like ale, *talking* about the mead!

Odin might also be making the reference to Fjalar in mythological terms, in which he adopts the identity of Fjalar as a drinker, or at least seeker after the mead. Draughts of the mead might even be referred to as being 'at the wise Fjalar's' in that the dwarf's name could refer to the mead itself. In this case, Odin is telling us that he became 'dead drunk' drinking from the magic mead.

It does not seem likely that Odin was drunk with knowledge, for he refers to his state as being witless. Becoming drunk, and forgetting his wits, does not seem like the behaviour that Odin would have liked to have seen in himself. Obviously something went wrong. Was it the power of the mead? That he simply could not handle it?

In one of the poetic texts he refers to Gunnloth as 'that best of women within whose arms I had lain'.[4] It is possible that the fact that he is drunk and forgets his wits is due not only to the inebriating effect of the mead, but also his feelings towards Gunnloth. So it is conceivable that when Odin says he forgot his wits, he might have been forgetting the purpose of his quest.

A few very important lines of poetry are from *The Words of the High One*:

> Gunnlod sat in the golden seat,
> poured me precious mead:
> Ill-reward she had from me for that,
> For her proud and passionate heart,
> Her brooding foreseeing spirit.

> What I won from her I have well used:
> I have waxed in wisdom since I came back,
>   bringing to Asgard Odrerir,
>   the sacred draught.[5]

The poet then permits himself this comment: 'Odin, I am sure, had taken the oath on the ring; who shall ever believe his word again? He swindled Suttung out of his mead and left Gunnlod to weep.' There are many different kinds of pledges that Odin could have taken. But one possibility is that he had pledged his love – and perhaps marriage – to Gunnloth in return for three drinks of the mead. The implication of the poet is that Odin was duplicitous, and pledged to Gunnloth simply in order to gain drinks of the mead. He says, in another line of poetry: 'I let her have ill repayment for her loyal heart and faithful love.' It appears that he violated warrior honour by pledging to Gunnloth and then breaking the pledge.

But there is another possibility: Odin has admitted that he was drunk in Gunnloth's house, and as a consequence had 'lost his wits', but that fortunately they came back to him when he sobered up. I think that Odin returned Gunnloth's love, became drunk on the mead and forgot the purpose of his mission. And it was only after he got his 'mind back in order' that he had to face up to the reality of his impossibly hard choice: the choice between staying with Gunnloth, whom he loves, or having to break his pledge and her heart to serve the purpose of his quest.

Gunnloth must have supported him, however sadly, when he made his decision, for he says that it is down to her that he escaped by the skin of his teeth from Suttung's kingdom: 'I doubt whether I should ever have escaped from the giants' garth if Gunnloth had not helped me – that best of women within whose arms I had lain. Next day, the frost giants came . . . asking after Baleworker, whether he was back with the gods or had Suttung managed to kill him?'[6] Drunk on all the mead and Gunnlod has to help him with his spells to turn into an eagle?

But Odin was on a quest; he had to fight the wish to indulge his love for Gunnloth, and so to leave her. And he knows that his personal sacrifice, if that was what it was, worked well, for he says: 'The fraud-got mead has profited me well and the wise man lacks nothing now that Odrerir is come up into the midst of men on earth.'[7] This is his pride in that he opted for service rather than indulgence, but fraud-got – obviously in getting this knowledge he was not following the accepted rules of social etiquette and warrior courtesy. Indeed by this he seems to have accepted that he had to make a compromise and that his quest transcended personal feelings.

— The Parallels Between the Mead Love Ritual and Tantra —

The ancient sources do not explain exactly what went on in the mountain. Scholars agree that Odin and Gunnloth engaged in some sort of 'love magic'; perhaps the details were in the original stories, but Christian censorship has led to them being dropped, just as the 'outrageous' sexual elements of Freya's ceremonies (which Snorri called 'turpitude' or 'base wickedness') for women have been lost.[8]

But this leaves us with only the manifest content of the myth. I think that if we knew more about the 'love magic', we would understand more deeply the nature and significance of the 'mead of knowledge'. And I believe that we can reconstruct the details of the encounter between Odin and Gunnloth if we tease out the meaning of the clues in the ancient manuscripts by comparative analysis, in which the information is considered in relation to the elaborated rituals of other, related traditions.

Many scholars of European mythology and religion propose that an infusion of some of the beliefs, practices and stories from Asia came into ancient Europe and Scandinavia early in the first millennium.[9] Whether there was an actual importing of these traditions into Europe from the East, or whether the obvious parallels are due rather to separate cultural traditions expressing the same universal human truths in similar ways does not really matter here. Either way, the important thing is that there are striking parallels which might indicate a common tradition, and which provide a basis from which we might explore what Odin and Gunnloth got up to behind the locked doors of a sacred cavern deep in the heart of Knit Mountain. It is a bit

Love Magic: *Creating the Elixir of Life*

involved, but I think it is worth it, for the insights the analysis affords locate the secrets of Wyrd, the inspiration of the 'magic mead', within the meditational compass of men and women. More than this, it is composed of the essence of love.

The Eastern traditions which eventually elaborated into Hinduism and Buddhism had their ancient origins, going back at least two thousand years, in the shamanic culture called Bon Po.[10] This was based upon a cosmology expressed partly through practices of 'love magic' which, over the centuries, became evolved into a practice called Tantra. So the Eastern tradition of Bon Po may share Tantric practices with the early European techniques referred to by scholars (but never elaborated) as 'love magic'. Tantric scholar Philip Rawson says there are 'symbols in the vast natural caverns of Palaeolithic Europe', dating from about 20,000 BC, which can be 'accurately matched with symbols still used today by Tantrikas'.[11] And in the story, Odin shapeshifts into the form of a snake in order to gain entry into the mountain, and perhaps he is still in snake form when he first appears to Gunnloth. One of the most ancient and powerful symbols for cosmically creative and sexual energy, which figures in many Tantric works of art, is the snake.

We know that Odin practised some kind of 'love magic' with Gunnloth, who held the power to gain access to the mead of knowledge. Similarly, Rawson confirms that in the Tantric tradition, innumerable legends are recorded about the way its most famous male adepts were initiated, and that in these stories the central episode is usually a ritual sexual intercourse with a female 'power-holder', whose favours the initiate has to win.[12]

In the ancient European shamanic view, as we have seen in earlier chapters, organisms and the cosmos were considered as microcosm and macrocosm. The human organism was imaged as being constructed on the model of the cosmos,[13] with the nine orifices in the body representing gateways to knowledge, and forming the basis of the 'sacred number nine'. As Philip Rawson explains, in the Eastern tradition of Tantra, knowledge of the cosmos is similarly considered to be contained, metaphorically, in the human body, and approached through our senses and worlds of experience.[14]

Odin has an intimate identification with the World Tree,

Yggdrasil, during his initiation and the tree embodies his psychological journey into the sacred worlds. He says of the tree that 'no one knows from whence those roots spring'. In the Tantric view also the human body grows as the World Tree, a plant from the 'ground' of the Beyond: 'just as the vital juices of a plant are carried up and outwards from the root through channels and veins, so are the creative energies in the human body.' This parallels the Wyrd concept we explored earlier of life force flowing through the body.

In Tantra, the life force flows in from the Beyond at the top of the skull. After spreading along through the body's channels it flows to the outermost tips of the senses, and even further out, to project the space around it. In Wyrd too this is the flow of life force, generated in the head and flowing outwards to the bodily extremities. In Eastern systems 'the pattern of vein and channels which comprise this system is called the "subtle body", and is the domain of ritual activity and symbolic practice.'

In the mythology of our European ancestors, the original wisdom of Kvasir – the human created by the declaration of peace between the warrior and fertility tribes of gods – represented conscious and unconscious forces which were concentrated and converted into the mead of inspiration. In Tantric ritual the emotions and the intellect are concentrated and aroused to their highest pitch so that 'the person's store of memories and responses can be awakened and re-converted into the pure energy from which they all originated'; an interesting echo of the creation of Kvasir.

We are told in the ancient manuscripts that Odin and Gunnloth spent three nights together, and they practised some kind of 'love magic'. Let us consider how this is practised in the Tantric tradition; the various parallels drawn above lead me to think there may be similarities to that enigmatic love magic of our European ancestors. In Tantra sexual intercourse is regarded as a metaphorical and spiritual union in which the sexual partners represent, identify with, and in spiritual terms *become* the macrocosm, 'the polarities of the cosmos transcended and unified'. A sacred ritual first identifies the 'ordinary man and woman' into personifications of male and female forces/gods; and then their union is consummated in sexual intercourse.

Through Tantric sexual intercourse, 'enormously prolonged' (the three days and nights Odin and Gunnloth spent together ought to satisfy this requirement), arousing and controlling extraordinary energies, the man and woman are both led to experience the condition of the cosmos before the separation of polarities: 'It is an unparalleled joy, the joy of Being before and beyond Genesis.' Much of shamanic ritual is geared for returning to the source, the original human state of being, when all forces were united, and before humans were split off from original creative wisdom.

So if the parallels between the shamanic traditions underlying Tantra and those of the ancient European shamans hold true, we may now go one step further, and reconstruct the meditation ritual which sets up the sexual union, and the cosmological basis which informed Odin and Gunnloth's love-making, and which led to the three drinks of mead.

— Meditation on the Worlds of Knowledge —

Philip Rawson explains that the ritual begins with the man settling himself at the centre of his own world. He first visualised the Earth, with its continents and seas, as an immense plane disc spread out around a colossal central mountain pinnacle, like a high peak of the Himalaya. Around this disc he sets out the circling orbits of the planets and the apparently revolving constellations, perhaps visualising them in the form of anthropomorphic deities. According to this meditation, Odin would have visualised himself in the mountain, where he was with Gunnloth, surrounded by the nine worlds of knowledge and the three realms of Upperworld, Middle World, and Lowerworld. (This ritual is being described from the perspective of the male participant; Gunnloth would be developing a complementary meditational vision.)

In the next phase of Tantric ritual he identifies the inner central column of his spine as the centre around which the whole circuit of his world revolves. Cosmos and man are identified, all individual's centres are intrinsically the same. So Odin is the World Tree visualised, along with the nine worlds of knowledge, all connected to, flowing from, revolving around his position at its centre.

In Tantric meditation the component energies of the world are imagined as flowing out into the world from the meditator's own sensuous and mental structure. He focuses them upon the lowest of the chakras or 'lotuses' which he imagines strung vertically up the shining filament of the central column. The usual number is six, plus a seventh at the top of the skull. Some traditions visualise more, towering beyond the head into different levels of the Beyond.

It is a fascinating parallel to consider the three realms and the nine worlds of knowledge of early European shamanism ordered as this Tantric structure. In Tantra the mandalas are usually imaged as circular symbolic designs of energy set like saucers at intervals up the spine. The ancient Europeans depicted the three realms as such, as three concentric circular arrangements, one on top of the other. Since macrocosm/microcosm was a fundamental aspect of their world view, it seems possible that they too could have an 'inner' structure akin to the chakras of Tantra, in which the three realms and associated worlds of knowledge were arranged in ascending order for meditational and ritual purposes. So we may surmise that if Odin engaged in Tantric ritual with Gunnloth, he may have first set out a meditational image like the one above.

In Tantra, another pair of subtle energy channels, male and female, twine in a spiral around these lotuses, circulating energy. The Wyrd cultural image which corresponds with this is the world serpent which encircles Middle Earth, and then Bifrost, the flaming bridge, which connects the levels of the cosmos together. In a Tantric-like ritual, these images would symbolise circulating energy, connecting the levels. In Tantra, the subtle energy channels are controlled by the breath. Odin is known as the 'wind god', the god of breath and ecstasy, and here we have something close to an alchemical transformation through breathing of inner energies 'up through mountains'.

— The Three Crucibles —

The lowest lotus in Tantra is at the base of the pelvis, in the perineum just in front of the anus, located there as the subtle energy snake Kundalini who is each man's own goddess-world-projecting function. In building the energy to bring Kundalini to life in Taoist tradition, Rawson explains, 'the transformation takes place in three chief stages, in three "crucibles", each of which is itself a transformation, and is located at a place on a central column within the body. The lowest is inside the belly, just below the naval. The second is behind the solar plexus; the third is in the head, behind and between the eyes.'

They are called 'elixir-fields'. The lowest is contained in a 'cauldron' or 'furnace' with three feet, which is kept stoked up with an inner fire at the lowest point, almost to the end of meditation. This process has a remarkable similarity to the three containers of mead from which Odin seeks to drink: the cauldron called Odrerir (the exciter of inspiration, which is also a name of the mead itself), and the smaller kettles called Son (atonement) and Bohn (container). Odin proclaims in his sacred *Havamal* poetry that he obtained power from the magic Odrerir.[15] But in comparing these elements of the ancient European story with Tantric traditions, the three containers of the mead symbolise aspects of Odin and Gunnloth's spiritual psyches.

In Tantra, what is transformed in the crucibles, the 'substance', is the sexual energy, called 'ching'. True Taoist ching was 'an intimate accumulation of the energies of both sexes, nourished by elaborate sexual exchange.' This was the 'alchemical substance', the essence around which the whole inner transformation revolved.

In Tantric tradition, the sacred sexual ritual, mindful of the world-disc within the circle of the lotus, awakens Kundalini, who begins her ascent. 'The initial sensation is violent and quite indescribable.' Thereafter Kundalini enters each higher lotus in turn as the practitioner focuses his mind on its structure and meaning. In the tradition of Wyrd, the Kundalini would be symbolised by the serpent-dragon called Nidhogg,[16] who resides at the very bottom of the lowest world in the Lowerworld, climbing up the trunk of the World Tree.

— The Mead of Inspiration and the Supernatural Nectar —

Tantra traditions describe how, near the summit, the 'female energy encounters the male seed of Being, uniting with it sexually . . . From this union a supernatural nectar flows down to flood the body, while the whole man or woman becomes identified with the source of self and world which lies beyond the crown of the head.'

It is intriguing that the climax of this Tantric ritual is a supernatural nectar flowing down to flood the body. The World Tree on which Odin underwent his initiation and which is created by him through his ecstatic meditation, is described as 'dripping dew so sweet that bees use it for the making of honey'. It is nectar. And honey is what mead is made from.

In Tantra, finally, the achievement of the ascent, the flow of Kundalini through sexual union ritualised, is sometimes symbolised by a great bird. The World Tree of Wyrd has at its very summit a great eagle. Odin tells us that after he had drunk the mead of knowledge, the supernatural nectar, he transformed into an eagle and flew away from the mountain. And he says that he thinks he could never have achieved this if Gunnloth had not helped him, 'that best of women in whose arms I had lain'.

In this speculative analysis I have regarded the World Tree, the three realms and the nine worlds of knowledge as aspects of a vision, a meditative ritual vision which accompanies initiation. It is reasonable surmise, for it is clear that in addition to the World Tree featuring centrally in the cosmology of Wyrd, it is also regarded as being formed by the meditator, the shamanic vision. The World Tree and associated images are a representation of the human subtle body and the flow pattern of subtle energies, to be apprehended through ritual.

And since the acquisition of the mead of knowledge, resulting in Odin transforming from a serpent into an eagle, is cast so clearly in sexual terms with his winning the love of Gunnloth, the possibility of a ritual of love seems plausible. If in some of the details above I may have forced the parallels a little too far, I believe nevertheless that the essence is right. The seat of Odin's wisdom is love. When Gunnloth, in Odin's words, 'Sat in the golden seat, and poured me precious mead,' the mead may well have been poured from pre-existing material pots. But a much richer and I believe truthful image is that the mead was formed from their sex together. The golden seat was the sexual position during intercourse, and the precious mead was the nectar of their subtle energies produced by their union.

So in this final perspective on the wisdom of our ancestors, the pinnacle of Odin's initiatory quest, the three drinks of the 'mead of poetic inspiration', was made available to him by Gunnloth through their mutual love. So much of what I have described in this book has hinged on an understanding of the polarity of masculine and feminine forces that it is perhaps fitting that we should conclude with this celebration of the nectar, the mead of wisdom, which is generated by their coming together in the ecstasy of sacred sexuality.

I am not going to attempt to draw pragmatic lessons from this story for our lives today, for I think that as an inspirational image it serves us best as a narrative for our own meditation. We can think of the feminine and masculine as polarities within our own inner psyche, each representing crucial elements of our life, but also with the potential for integration. Or we might view the two forces as the coming together of lovers, metaphorically and physically, making more than the sum of our separate presences. And also the feminine and masculine polarities in the forces of nature itself, encompassing and enchanting the tragedy and the beauty of our species.

CHAPTER THIRTEEN

Reflections

The way of being, of life, of our ancestors was grounded in the sacred. They called it Wyrd. I believe that the way of Wyrd holds lessons for us still, touching as it does upon many of those aspects of our contemporary world for which we are today seeking inspiration. Throughout the book I have sought to address some of the implications of the wisdom of our ancestors for our lives in the modern world, and how we might go about learning from them. In this final chapter, as a kind of pulling together of threads, I have picked out some of the more significant ideas from the culture of our ancestors of ancient Europe in the context of our current concerns. Identifying and articulating the important questions is an urgent requirement for us today; I offer the following thoughts as a contribution to this process rather than as a catalogue of my own 'answers'.

— The Natural Connection —

The tribespeople of early Europe sustained a close harmony, an empathy, a deep spirit of cooperation between their lives and the natural landscape of which they were a part. In contemporary Western culture we have become separated from our environment and this has reaped some unpleasant ecological rewards. We are now scrambling to reconnect with nature. Our ancestors had rituals of some sophistication, meditations, celebrations, dynamic connecting processes between themselves and the landscape. They sustained a kind of spiritual and psychological umbilical cord with the land.

Their example leads me to feel that we should reconsider very carefully the kind of psychological relationship we have with our environment, and how it may be modified, corrected, inspired towards a view which heals the wounds we have wrought on ourselves and the land. Complementing our ongoing biological and economic analyses of ecological systems, we need to establish once again a sacred grounding as a fundamental prerequisite for the development of a deep ecology. One of the attractions of the sacred ways of Wyrd is the acceptance of the simple givens, the energy parameters of nature, a placing of oneself spiritually in harmony with the environment. We need to rebalance our view, to intervene within the natural parameters, rather than violating them chronically as we do now.

One benefit for us in reaching out to the sacred in this way is that it might help us to acknowledge the complexity, the magnificent multiplicity of factors which dazzle and delight when we experience our environment aesthetically, but which we necessarily disregard when we try to deal with it scientifically. It is as if the two are entirely separate.

But we now know, towards the end of the second millennium, that science cannot answer all our questions. There are many aspects of life which fall outside the empirical frame. Attunement entails a recognition that the multiplicity of variables in any natural setting are far too complex ever to be completely controlled by a scientifically based engineering process. This acceptance is a crucial first step towards a sacred dimension in a new ecological psychology. It is a dangerous and unsettling step, for it means that we give up the illusion of control. We settle instead for our place in the large whole. We cannot control it, but we can live within it.

Perhaps this, then, is a fundamental lesson from our ancestors: to have an open mind and an open heart about the unknown, and to turn outward into the complexity of our environment to find ways of embracing and attuning to it.

— Power of Imagery —

Today, in some ways and rather surprisingly, we seem to be less sophisticated and aware than were our ancestors in appreciating the deep impact on the way we understand ourselves of the images which permeate our lives. The tribespeople of ancient Europe used prominent images to focus their lives in many ways, because images can embody so much information and at the same time carry the psychological and the sacred in the same image. Today our environment is image-rich, but mainly for the purposes of selling goods or providing entertainment. Increasingly we rely for models of how we function, communicate and relate with one another on machine-models – especially that of the computer.

We need to be aware and cautious of the ramifications of such a model for our general self-understanding. Computational language is far better, for example, at modelling human thinking than human feeling, and our increasing use of such machine languages to attempt to describe organic and complex social processes reveals just how seductive such images can be.

One central image, among many, used by the tribespeople of early Europe featured the World Tree. This image differed crucially from the computer metaphors we use now in that it occurs naturally outside human creation. And like other organic images in the culture of the early Europeans it gave a sense of life which transcends our anthropomorphism, the human-centred world view which leaves us feeling separated and alienated from our environment. The tree linked the early Europeans to the world of which they were a part, the organic environment. Such a world view, which so centrally connects humans and the environment, means that to be alienated from nature is to be alienated from a part of ourselves. I suspect that deep within us we realise this; and the loss is profound.

Where our modern outlook differs crucially and, ultimately, tragically from that of the indigenous cultures of today and the tribespeople of early Europe is in assuming that the 'everyday waking state' sees reality more accurately than do imaginal states of mind. If we take seriously the emotional as well as the physical experience of landscape, for example, then the internal and external are virtually indistinguishable. There are no hard and fast dividing lines between what is us and what is our environment. Since the actual 'creation' of our sense-world is an interaction between the 'external' of the material world and the 'internal' of our nervous system, the cognitive and the emotional, we need languages which fully reflect this complexity.

The pragmatic mind-set is fundamental to conducting the business of everyday life, but what we are missing, and chronically searching for in healing our split from the environment, is that magically charged crack between the physical and mythological, the observable and unobservable, the pragmatic and the sacred.

— The Night —

Night came first. The rhythm of time was marked by moon phases, and in the lives of the Wyrd people the hours of the night were primary, the most important phase of the inner rhythm in which external images are no longer visible, and internal images come to the fore. The secondary realm of day was for the more prosaic mental functions, the analytical considerations of the material world.

In contemporary society, we are visually oriented, and the daytime hours seem to us to be reality, the time where we can see everything, anticipate events, and control our lives. The night time, darkness, is danger, lack of control, presence of the unseen. We have relegated our night hours to 'entertainment' time, whereas daytime is for real work. And yet what we think of as entertainment is often the setting for the most significant business we do in terms of the psychological transactions of our lives, social and personal relationships.

One of the outcomes of today's human-centred viewpoint, in which our 'home range' has become limited to the parameters of the territories we have constructed (towns and cities, television and radio, telephones and faxes, offices and factories, cars and trains, pubs and restaurants, cinemas and theatres: the territories of *homo sapiens urbanis*) is that we tend to ignore, or even dismiss, influences on our lives, external forces, that we have not created. We are relatively sheltered from the extremes of weather which must have been a prominent feature of the lives of our tribal forebears, for example (apart from the occasional but devastating 'reminders' of tornadoes, hurricanes and earthquakes). Quite understandably, we no longer feel the need to attend to the external natural factors, for they no longer play a significant part in the everyday unfolding of our lives.

Or do they? Are we still aware, at a dimly recognised level, of myriad outside influences filtering in, under, through our cocoon of civilisation?

We know that the moon moves the ocean into tides, but for the people of Wyrd the moon's cycle of power was finely calibrated, and studied in detail. Is their attention to such forces a naïve, romantic notion which intrigues us but which we cannot believe, or is there something in it? A subtle influence does not have to be dramatic and immediate to have substantial impact over the course of a lifetime, and an open-minded, open-hearted, holistic enquiry might yield some surprising findings. Waves beating on a shore do not appear to have immediate impact until one understands how the massive erosional forces of the water have over time dramatically transformed the shape of the coastline. And so, perhaps, the same forces occur over time between the pull of the moon's rhythm and the conduct of our lives. More research into these subtle factors might play an important part in reconnecting us to the environment from which we feel separated and alien.

— Liminal Moments —

For the peoples of ancient Europe, the alternation of night and day, of darkness and light, went well beyond the imprecise and seasonally variable indicators of time that we use now, and carried a highly charged and significant manifesting of a fundamental duality which permeated every sector of life. Daily, monthly, seasonal, annual divisions of experience, which we calibrate in terms of passage of time, were for the early Europeans demarcations of liminal times, those moments at which the turning of events moved from one state to the other, whether it be night and day, one month or another, summer and winter. These moments of change were experienced as being highly charged, emotional, dangerous, and suffused with sacred power. They were entered with awareness and ritual.

Today, in a Western culture in which Christian observance has been dominant, the rhythm of prayer and observance became weekly, each Sunday. In comparison, the sacred rhythm of the people of Wyrd was more complex and frequent. This is not unusual in itself, of course: in many contemporary religious traditions around the world prayer and meditation are carried out at frequent intervals, at times during the day which have sacred significance.

But the belief and practices of the Wyrd people throw into relief our current behaviour, and it seems to me that most people develop a subconscious 'liminal points' calendar within themselves; not necessarily publicly shared, but nevertheless quite potent. Liminal times would include one's own birthday, and those of family and friends, high points in the year to be marked out in some way. There is in our secular society no particular reason for celebrating the date of one's birth each year; it survives from the customs of the tribespeoples of early Europe, in pre-Christian culture, and is perhaps an indication of just how important are these punctuation points in the flow of psychic time

— Cycles of Time —

Another dimension of the world view of the tribespeople of ancient Europe is their conception of the passage of time. Today we maintain an idea of time as a linear unfolding from the past, through the present and into the future. The people of Wyrd also used this model of time, for it is fundamental to the cause-and-effect sequencing of behaviour in everyday life. However, they regarded it as inadequate for other, more important purposes, like the unfolding of individual lives, or the development of communities. They complemented it with another view: the experiencing of the passage of time as cyclical.

In linear time events from the past are repeated in the future, although of course we can only experience them in the present, whether through memory, recognition, or anticipation. We exist in the present. In cyclical time this is taken as the starting point.

In contemporary culture, our idea of progress is firmly anchored in our conception of linear time: of things improving from historical time to future time, with us in the middle, in the present, struggling to bring that about. This idea has value, of course, but where we limit our views of the unfolding of life is when we become wedded to one exclusively held perspective. In terms of individual lives, for example, the notion of perpetual self-improvement, a perennial and understandable aim, is probably not best served by viewing one's life as a linear progression. It engenders a way of being in which we are living in the past, regretting mistakes, and anticipating the future, worrying about what might go wrong. It is quite exhausting as a psychological way of experiencing the daily, annual passage of one's life.

The cyclic conception of time, with liminal points of significance and success, searching and failure, often matches a person's life experience more accurately, more sympathetically, more in keeping with the language of experience, which is like a piece of music with repeated chords and movements.

Also, thinking of life in terms of cyclical time encompasses the understanding that themes are repeated, scripts play themselves out, experience is overlapping, and especially that there is to most events and actions a natural lifespan, a season of flowering and dying away, so that everything we do needs rest and renewal, rather than a kind of continuous production of energy like a machine. The articulation of life experience in cyclic rather than linear time might well be of benefit for us in models of counselling and psychotherapy, especially where the deepening of positive experience rather than the progression from bad to good is a main theme of the work. Some of the examples of practical work that I gave earlier in the book addressed these issues.

— The Feminine Principle —

The imagery of the way of Wyrd was a balance between the feminine and masculine principles, the former experienced particularly through its concentration on the fertile powers of the Earth, the healing qualities of the Earth's surface and sources, the prominence of the goddesses. In considering the implications of this view for contemporary psychology, we need to be aware that archetypal polarities do not translate into gender imperatives in a simple and straightforward way. The feminine and the masculine are principles which impinge on the lives of both men and women.

Nevertheless, having recognised this caveat, it is undeniable that today the forces of the masculine dominate the Western world and a good deal beyond. In the early European culture of the Wyrd people, feminine principles played a more prominent part in their balanced view of life. The Wyrd Sisters, for example, those spinners and arbiters of life to whom even the gods were subject, were represented clearly as sisters, with the biological and bonding implications of this designation. I find it fascinating that this was a primary link between what were arguably the most powerful beings in the cosmos.

Today, in recent times, sisterhood has been rediscovered by some women. It is a bond born of common purpose, shared experience, mutual support and obligation. Sisters speak from the domain of the deep unconscious, and the power and potency of sisterhood is confirmed from the ancient cosmology of the Wyrd people.

— Motherhood —

The Wyrd view of birth reminds us that motherhood is an expression, from within our own species, of a cosmological principle, in which birth of everything is a never-ending process. The welcome advances of scientific medicine which enable us to enhance the safety of mother and child at birth also have the unfortunate effect of anaesthetising us to the miracle of the creation of life. In birthing all creation, the three sisters underscore the state of motherhood as powerful. Motherhood, while having its many prosaic and practical aspects, nevertheless was attuned to in Wyrd culture as being in many ways both the basis and the pinnacle of life.

Today, in a male-dominated obstetric and gynaecological environment in which midwives struggle for recognition, and for permission to carry out their uniquely suited combination of medical and psychological (sisterly and motherly) support for women giving birth, the way of Wyrd suggests that we need urgently to reconsider our options in how we provide a balance of medical services. It would be naïve and foolish to deny the importance of scientific medicine in offering a safety net both for mother and baby, but our psychological, let alone spiritual, awareness of childbirth is poverty-stricken compared with the awareness of a thousand years ago.

The lesson I draw from our indigenous heritage is that childbirth should be returned to women; midwives ought to be the central figures in the support of the birthing process; scientific medicine should be available as a back-up in medical emergency in the most effective manner possible. Perhaps then we would begin to return some of the power and magnificence, without embarrassment, to the women's secret processes of life creation.

— Female Intuition —

The ancient Europeans had an established tradition of seeresses, generally approved for and practised by women only, and presided over by the goddesses Frigg and especially Freya. Both appear at times as the beneficent goddess helping women and girls at times of marriage and childbirth, as well as shaping the destiny of children. The seeresses were really spirit mediums on missions from the goddess Freya.

In sacred ceremonies in which the spirits revealed mysteries to the seeresses, the women mediated the power that created new life and brought increase into the fields, among the animals, and in the home. They brought also the power to link people with the unseen world, and offered wise counsel granted through divination concerning worldly events.

The seeresses who practised divination were treated with great respect, but men who tried to learn or practise it were castigated. The indigenous peoples of ancient Europe believed that there are secret wisdoms that only men can know, and secrets and wisdoms that reveal themselves only to women. But also, on the path to initiation, there are paths which transcend this divide, where men are led by women and women by men. The greatest shamans, like Odin, were individuals who transcended the divide, who were initiated into some of the secrets of the opposite gender.

In contemporary society we have at last recognised that the options for women have been restricted and they have been for some time the repressed gender in Western society. In attempting to alleviate this we have sometimes suppressed distinctions between the genders, in psychological, physical, spiritual terms, with the right motives but occasionally, in the view of our ancestors, misguided outcomes. Their perspective on the relationship between the genders was equality in some matters (right to own property, for example) and equal but separate traditions in other areas which deal with, for example, childbirth, and women's mysteries in the realm of sacred psychology.

— The Masculine Principle —

In recent years we have, in contemporary debate, begun to look more closely at the damaging qualities of our over-emphasis on the forces of the masculine. These principles are polarities, operating at the archetypal level of myth. But in making a translation into gender roles, we have also realised that we have lost a sense of how the masculine principle can best be unfolded in the life patterns of men. The tribespeople of ancient Europe offer some provocative models, especially in the figure of Odin and his English (Woden) and German (Wotan) counterparts. Odin was a seeker of truth, and underwent deep psychological and spiritual explorations to achieve the insights that he gained. Much of the interest in rediscovering ways of masculine maturity seem to be inspired by tribal values: drumming, initiation and myth enactment. Our heritage of experience from the times when we were indigenous peoples is a resource yet to be tapped.

— The Pattern of Life —

The world view of the Wyrd tribespeople encompassed an image of supreme interconnectedness. Everything involved and implied everything else in an ecological, holistic vision. They believed that created for each individual in our inner nature at birth was the frame of a pattern that set our course, and which reflected the interconnectedness of everything. In this view, as individual life patterns are changed, altered, invaded, the emerging new pattern acknowledged the integrity of the existing pattern. It was an organic image of psychological change rather than a mechanistic one.

Today our lives are conceived of as the action of free will to achieve goals which are within our compass. But we also know that the division of life into free will or determinism is a black and white, yes and no, artificially constrained mind-map of immeasurably complex and interacting forces. Wyrd went beyond a simple view of fate. For the tribespeople of ancient Europe, life was a highly charged negotiation between what is free and what is ordained.

The concept of being 'bound' is central to this vision. Today we say that something was 'bound to happen' without awareness of the image we are conjuring up. By this phrase, we mean that the weight of the factors impinging on an event lead almost inevitably to a particular outcome. But the phrase has ancient roots, and in the time of Wyrd it was used with more precise intent. At every moment of our lives we are constrained and limited by the many, unseen 'bonds' we place on ourselves, which have settled into place, twisting and tightening, during our lifetime. They restrict us, handicapping our ability to deal with issues which face us. It is a way of imaging psychodynamics, a way which focuses attention on the restricting nature of aspects of our psychological experience.

Conceiving of psychological forces as bonds or fetters reminds us that 'achieving change' is as often a matter of unwinding or cutting bonds as it is of adding something new. Identifying and removing, shifting, or altering these fetters, ever so subtle and even trivial though they may seem, is the basis of personal freedom.

— The Spirits —

The Otherworld, where the spirits dwelled, are in our parlance, 'states of mind'. But for the early Europeans the premise upon which spirit worlds were conceived differed radically from our views today. They could never speak of the spirit world as being 'only' in the imagination, as we might now, for the psychological space of the Lowerworld was rather like Jung's collective unconscious – a realm for the deepest of human experiences.

Liminal points provided the boundaries between the everyday state of consciousness and the Otherworld states, in which one was open to communication from the spirit world. Fords across rivers, the ridges of mountains or high hills, the boundaries demarcating tribal lands – all these were charged with magical power and were points through which the mist of the Otherworld could seep into this world. Other liminal points serving as catalysts for psychological shifts between states of consciousness included variations in light at dawn and dusk, turning points in the periodic waxing and waning of the moon, New Year's Day, the summer and winter festivals. All were occasions when the normally unseen powers from the Otherworld were accessible.

Of course, in the process of shamanic initiation visions are not random. They are conditioned, shaped and culturally fired by the structured imagination of the tribal tradition. As the apprentice enters 'heated' body-mind realms, the images that spontaneously arise are interpreted, discussed, and empowered by the shaman. The apprentice's experiences are structured by the poetry of the shaman who sings of the visions, and narrates the action.

This elaborated and highly structured view of modified states of consciousness is rather like a dream psychology, but one which acknowledges the direct power of images to forge changes in everyday life, rather than to see images as symbolic of something other than themselves in the material world. It is an aspect of psychology little developed today, but might yield important insights into the workings of the imagination, dreams, reverie, altered states, and schizophrenia. A new 'Wyrd psychology' beckons.

— Death —

The shamans of ancient northern Europe looked upon the region of the Lowerworld not only as a realm of the dead, but as a source of great knowledge. In contemporary secular Western culture, where the emphasis is on death as separate from life, we become attached to the concept of self, the idea that we have an existence which will be lost when we die. We will go into nothingness and be no more. The early European shamanic view was different, for nothing died, everything lived on in the Lowerworld. Their image of the realm of the Lowerworld was the Earth in midwinter. It was frozen and everything looked dead, but the Earth was not really dead, for they knew that it came back to 'life' in the spring. The 'death' of the Earth in the winter was really a sham death, a hibernation.

Like the Earth, human life would be reborn, clothed in a new body. Life was a cycle, and everything returned in time, to flower again.

On a psychological level, the Lowerworld mirrored layers of consciousness, going down to the most primitive realms of intuitive knowledge, shared experience which is more than the merely internal. Indeed it is the arena in which we are connected to the organic experience of other species, where all living forms meet.

— The Cosmos and the Psyche —

Odin's visions created, represented, illustrated, reflected the structure of the cosmos. He was not 'there' at the beginning of creation, but rather discovered and articulated the structure of 'everything' as a result of the visions he achieved in his shamanic journeying. It is possible that this structure is a universal human one; that we are constructed to be able to apprehend reality in a particular way, through certain dimensions and in specified forms, and that Odin articulated this. It is also possible that Odin was attuning to something that is outside human consciousness, and was 'seeing' a structure which has a reality in the language of the spirit. However one positions oneself on this dimension, the images Odin describes were to be at the root of much of Wyrd cosmology.

During his quest for visionary experience, Odin saw the cosmos as shaped like a vast tree, which encompassed all levels of existence. Connected to and emanating from this vision is a complex and vivid system of worlds, realms, levels, each of which symbolically represents a particular kind of knowledge, power and dimension in the spiritual world.

The tree appeared in Odin's vision as a giant ash tree called Yggrasil, so vast, says Sturluson, that 'its branches spread out over the whole world and reach up over heaven.' This massive construction served as the axis of the cosmos, and everything else was constructed around it. Featured around the tree was the universe, visualised as a tricentric structure, like three gigantic discs set one above the other with a space in between each. This is a vision which shamanic cultures all over the world have seen in the accounts from the intervening centuries. The top disc is conceived of and usually called the Upperworld, the middle one is called Middle Earth or Middle World, and the bottom is the Lowerworld. Structured among these three realms were nine worlds . . . nine places or domains of knowledge, each with a particular ambience and energy. They were conceived of by the people of ancient Europe as locations, space, positions in a cosmic firmament.

The tree into which Odin climbed was visioned as the path to other worlds, other realms, other states, a way of journeying metaphorically from one realm into another. In shamanic cultures the structure of the tree provided the construct for their depiction of the realm of the sacred. And the great tree of imagination, which joined everything together, was called the World Tree.

The World Tree is a sacred image: a Western shamanic version of the meditational images of Tibetan Buddhism. All archetypes, the World Tree included, are image expressions of a deeper level of reality. They do not 'stand for something', like a logo of a company. Their meaning is within the image itself, encompassing myriad nuance and subtleties that can be apprehended by our imagination but beyond the capacity of the conscious mind to process cognitively. The people of ancient Europe thought of the tree as structured holographically, in which every place, every tree – and in fact every human being – is considered to be the essence, the centre. This belief gives rise to a cosmos with a sacred dimension from every aspect, like light shining through a complex crystal, a cosmos in which each detail represents and incorporates the whole so that everything is related to everything else.

But although we talk of Odin climbing into the World Tree, the tree transforming into a horse and carrying Odin to the worlds of wisdom, it is also important to reverse this process of imagery. It is just as true to say that the imaginal process of horse and Odin journeying to the spirit worlds created the World Tree. The World Tree was also a construction of the shaman's making.

In our contemporary discourse we would conceive of these worlds as being located in our psyche, perhaps deep in the unconscious. The imaginal structure of the World Tree, and the process of imagining journeying on the tree as it transforms into a magical horse, would be tools and techniques for entering and accessing areas of the unconscious which might otherwise be closed to us except in the most deeply symbolic dreams.

For the early Europeans, the concept of the imaginal was not physically bounded by the body, was not thought of as 'only' an internal event. For the peoples of Wyrd the everyday, logical, analytical, material world was a tiny microcosm of the magnificent, boundless imaginal world. Shamans were expected to be able to journey, and act, in the latter on behalf of the community.

Today we are expending considerable effort trying to redress the imbalance we have created of 'them and us', in which we pose as being 'separate' from the world for the purposes of scientific observation and analysis, and 'joining' ourselves back into contact, thinking ourselves back into relationship with the environment. Our human-centred, separatist view has brought us great benefits through science and engineering, but it has brought also great disadvantages, not least in our very poorly developed sense of self-understanding which is perhaps the most crucial challenge facing us. We need to understand ourselves once more in relation not only to the physical, organic environment from which we have separated ourselves, but also from the cosmos in which our imaginal powers might afford us spiritual insights which will give direction to our lives. Odin's visions are an awe-inspiring example of what we were once capable.

We need to value more highly the talents of those who are able to journey in and articulate the languages of the imaginal: actors, storytellers, artists, dancers, musicians, writers, film-makers, poets. These are crucial to our re-enchantment.

— Keeping Our Heads —

I here reprise some of the points I made earlier in the book concerning 'losing our heads'. I believe that important lessons lie here awaiting our discovery.

Giving up an eye is an intriguing pledge. Our two eyes, used together, provide perspective. Certainly in modern Western society, sight is the primary sense that we employ in maintaining our everyday reality — the waking state of consciousness. Under altered states such as meditation, hypnosis, drug-induced, other senses come into more prominence, and sight of the material world may be a minor or even absent factor. So one way of regarding Odin's sacrifice, his pledge, is that in giving up an eye on his way to initiation, Odin is making an investment in altered reality.

The beheading game was one in which the two protagonists 'surrendered their heads' to the other, gave themselves into each other's power, absolutely, in a form of bonding. To make oneself so vulnerable as to have one's head chopped off by an 'adversary', on the understanding that it can be put back on again is a truly remarkable level of trust. It must be akin to the notion of 'blood brother' which has survived into modern culture. This latter contains no hint of rebirth, but rather the notion that self-inflicted wounds can lead to a sharing of blood in a bonding ritual.

Finally, one more perspective rounds out the picture. For if the life force of a person resides in the head, then the taking of that head adduces the power of the person to the taker. It is not just a count of success, it is a taking of that power for oneself. And if the Anglo-Saxons believed in a spiritual soul-matter which pervades the whole body but is concentrated in the head, a soul-matter which maintains all life, then the taking of a head brings also the effectiveness of the soul-matter to the taker and his people. This is in effect what happens when Odin takes Mimir's head and uses its wisdom for his and the Aesirs' good.

For us, the dynamics of 'keeping our head' in times of trouble, 'sticking our necks out' to take risks, and the complexities of obligations, pacts, deals and trust, are all stirred up by Odin's ritual encounters with the wise giant Mimir.

— Sacred Love —

Odin sought the mead of inspiration, the essence of creative and poetic potency, which fired the imaginations of shamans throughout history. He carried out his quest for the mead on behalf of his community of gods, the Middle Earth community of shamans-to-be, and the cosmos as a whole. The mead symbolises that essence in Wyrd represented by the pearl in Tantric art. Life force was a subtle energy which gave access to wisdom, healing powers, and the ability to enter a radically altered state of consciousness: the spirit world. This was accomplished by journeying to the depths of the Underworld – deep heritage – and integrating the forces of life, the ice and fire, to embody the essence of dragon. And then the task was to journey up the World Tree through Middle Earth to the upper reaches, where through self-sacrifice of a sort the dragon-powered life force turned the shaman into an eagle and he could fly.

And since the achievement of the mead of knowledge, resulting in Odin transforming from a serpent into an eagle, is cast so clearly in sexual terms with his winning the love of Gunnloth, the possibility of a ritual of love seems plausible. I believe that the seat of Odin's wisdom is love. And when Gunnloth, in Odin's words, 'Sat in the golden seat, and poured me precious mead', the mead was formed from their sex together. The golden seat was the sexual position during intercourse, and the precious mead was the nectar of their subtle energies produced by their union.

Clearly the quality of nature's productivity was seen through the pulsating perspective of sexuality, especially in the presence of the goddesses Frigg and Freya, and the practice of shamanic initiation, as described in the previous chapter, between Odin and Gunnloth. This viewpoint is quite different from our contemporary models of psychological sexuality, which are mostly derived from the principles of psychodynamics developed by Freud. The Wyrd perspective was closer to those traditional disciplines of transpersonal psychology which characterise the Eastern ways of spiritual liberation, such as Tantra and Tao. These elaborated ways of action see the experience of sacred and ritualised sexual intercourse as symbolic of, and a metaphor for, the balance and forces of polarities in the cosmos. Sexual experience in this context is a transcending of opposites, a uniting of the separate into one.

Overtly sexual metaphors for the dynamics of the natural world seem alien to us. We are now much more accustomed to scientific metaphors, in which the stories of nature are recounted in a more objective fashion. In seeking to restore a consciousness in which we are once again connected to the Earth, perhaps we can rediscover love. If we equally value, and complement our objective understanding of the world with poetic metaphor, artistic vision, dramatic involvement, language modalities which are much more appropriate to aesthetic, deep psychological and sacred dimensions of the natural world than the mechanistic calibrational language of scientific discourse, then we might learn again how to apply the language of love to ourselves and the world.

— The Wisdom of the Wyrd —

In one book it is possible only to touch the surface of a subject as all-encompassing as the world view of an indigenous people. And then there is of course all that material which we simply do not know about, or have no evidence for. Research goes on, and gradually we may know more. But I think that the recognition that once we were indigenous peoples ourselves is an important step, and the acknowledgement that our ancestors may have something worthwhile for us to learn from them. At the moment recognition of this fact is hampered by our assumption of a linear view of progress: that we have left our past far behind us, and that it has no value today.

I believe that it is emphatically clear from the material reviewed in this book that our own traditions of tribal lore are rich with significance still; a thousand years is a long time, but fifty generations connect us with those times past, with the wisdom of our ancestors. Certainly there have been important gains for Western cultures since those times, but there have been important losses, too. We need to ask what it is that we once knew that we have long forgotten, and reassess how may it help us today.

What the journey of this book has shown, I hope, is that in invigorating, informing and inspiring a sacred way for today, and for all our tomorrows, a crucial step is the rediscovery of the wisdom of the Wyrd.

Notes

The following numbered notes serve as an indication to the reader of the main sources on which the relevant section of each chapter is based. The research background is now very substantial, and to keep the notes to manageable proportions I have listed only those references which contributed directly to the paragraph numbered, except in a few cases where a longer list seemed useful. I have listed books rather than journal articles for as much of the material as possible, because for most readers books are more readily obtainable through libraries.

INTRODUCTION
The Ancient Wisdom of Our Ancestors

1 The searching for 'other wisdoms' can be seen in a variety of disciplines, as in the work of physicists who are finding parallels to their work in Eastern mysticisms, e.g. F. Capra, *The Tao of Physics* (London: Wildwood House, 1982); the high level of interest in the application of Buddhist thought to contemporary issues, e.g. F. Fremantle and Chogyam Trungpa, *The Tibetan Book of the Dead* (Boston: Shambhala, 1990); Sogyal Rinpoche, *The Tibetan Book of Living and Dying* (London: Rider, 1992); the classic works on the wisdom of the African Bushmen by L. van der Post, including *The Heart of the Hunter* (London: The Hogarth Press, 1961), *The Lost World of the Kalahari* (London: Chatto and Windus, 1986); the remarkable level of interest in the application of the insights of tribal shamanism to Western settings, including books by psychiatrists and psychologists such as R. Walsh, *The Spirit of Shamanism* (Los Angeles: Tarcher, 1990); H. Kalweit, *Dreamtime and Inner Space* (Boston: Shambhala, 1988); and an excellent book on shamanic approaches to the arts: M. Tucker, *Dreaming with Open Eyes: The Shamanic Spirit in Contemporary Art and Culture* (London: Harper Collins, 1993); Australian aboriginal culture has been documented by J. Cowan, *The Mysteries of the Dreamtime* (Prism Press, 1989), and their integration of physical and sacred geography in B. Chatwin, *The Songlines* (London: Jonathan Cape, 1987). There have been numerous television documentaries, and even feature films dealing with indigenous cultures as peoples with 'lost' knowledge, including *The Emerald Forest*; *The Last of the Mohicans*; *Dances with Wolves* and even (in animation!) *Pocohontas*.

2 Bernhard Schaer (who directs the Tantra Gallery, Interlaken, Switzerland, one of Europe's leading centres for shamanic workshops, and among the first to intro-

duce Native American medicine peoples to the West), personal communication.
3   R. Metzner, *The Well of Remembrance* (Boston: Shambhala, 1994) p. 217. This invaluable book considers the relevance of Germanic mythology for, in particular, our emerging ecological awareness.
4   S.O. Glosecki considers how early Anglo-Saxon societies fulfil the main characteristics of tribal cultures in *Shamanism and Old English Poetry* (New York: Garland, 1989).
5   See for example recent and informed discussion of this point in R. Hutton, *The Pagan Religions of the Ancient British Isles* (Oxford: Blackwell, 1990) especially Chapter 7, and H.R.E. Davidson, *Myths and Symbols in Pagan Europe* (Manchester University Press, 1988). P. Berresford Ellis, *Celt and Saxon: The Struggle for Britain AD 410–937* (London: Constable, 1993) provides, as a counterbalance to this new togetherness, a full account of the warfare between Saxons and Celts over the centuries.
6   Of the many books which have considered the Celtic sacred tradition in detail, some of the best include A. Ross, *Pagan Celtic Britain* (rev. edn London: Constable, 1992), which takes a largely archaeological view; N. Tolstoy, *The Quest for Merlin* (London: Hamish Hamilton, 1985) exploring the historical and legendary material on Merlin; J. Markale, *Women of the Celts* (Rochester, Vermont: Inner Traditions, 1986) on the role of women as evidenced in lore and legend, and J. Matthews, *Taliesin* (London: Aquarian, 1991) on the Celtic poet Taliesin.
7   The first of Watts's books to make a general impact was his *The Way of Zen* (New York: Pantheon Books, 1957). His last, *Tao: the Watercourse Way* (London: Jonathan Cape, 1976) contains some of his most elegant writing. Of his many works, the ones most relevant for the present book are *Nature, Man and Woman* (New York: Pantheon, 1958), and *Psychotherapy East and West* (New York: Pantheon, 1965).
8   The British Library reference for this document is Harleian 585.
9   Critical discussion of our knowledge of ancient Druidic practice can be found in Hutton, *Pagan Religions* (especially Chapter 5); N.K. Chadwick *The Druids* (Cardiff: University of Wales Press, 1966); S. Piggott *The Druids* (London: Thames and Hudson, 1968); and a venerable text which reviews the classical sources and is still cited by scholars, T.D. Kendrick, *The Druids* (London: 1927).
10 C.G. Jung, *Alchemical Studies* (Vol 13 of *Collected Works*, New York: Pantheon Books, Bollingen Series, XX, 1967).
11 The 'original' text making a case for a historically unbroken, spiritually valid tradition of witchcraft is M. Murray, *The Witch Cult in Western Europe* (Oxford University Press, 1921); see K. Thomas, *Religion and the Decline of Magic* (London: Blackwells, 1971) for an approach to this material more in tune with modern historical research.
12 Discussions of the background to this document are included in G. Storms, *Anglo-Saxon Magic* (The Hague: Martinus Nijhoff, 1948); J.H.G. Grattan and C. Singer, *Anglo-Saxon Magic and Medicine* (Wellcome Historical Medical Museum, Oxford University Press, 1952); F. Grendon, 'The Anglo-Saxon Charms' (*Journal of American Folk-Lore*, XXII, 1909); W. Bonser, *The Medical Background of Anglo-Saxon England* (London: Wellcome Historical Medical Library, 1963); N.F.

Barley, 'Anglo-Saxon Magico-Medicine' (*Journal of the Anthropological Society of Oxford*, 3, 1972, 67–77).

13 It has sometimes been doubted by historians that shamans practised in ancient Europe; Anglo-Saxon linguistic scholar Stephen Glosecki has dispelled doubts in his comprehensive and richly documented study devoted to this precise issue: *Shamanism and Old English Poetry*. The role of shamans in the practice of Wyrd will be elucidated throughout this book. 'Shaman' is today the widely used and accepted umbrella term for practitioners of healing and the sacred in tribal societies. They are people who are believed to be especially gifted in mediating between the spirit world and the everyday world, and who perceive through a kind of dream consciousness during waking life; literally 'dreaming with open eyes' (cf Tucker, *Dreaming with Open Eyes*). H.R.E. Davidson, in her *Pagan Scandinavia* (New York: Praeger, 1967), p. 23, writing about shamans in the context of ancient Scandinavia, says that 'The shaman . . . could send out his spirit in a trance to discover what was hidden, to heal the sick, to enter the land of the Dead and return to men, to combat evil powers and to assuage the wrath of the spirits. One of the outstanding characteristics of the shaman everywhere is his close relationship with the animal world, emphasized in costume and ritual, and by the belief in animal spirits helping and hindering him in his endeavours.'

General source material on the role and activities of shamans in ancient Europe and Scandinavia can be found, for example, in Glosecki, *Shamanism and Old English Poetry*; P. Buchholz, 'Shamanism – the Testimony of Old Icelandic Literary Tradition' (*Medieval Scandinavia*, 4, 1971, 7–20); M.A. Arent, 'The Heroic Pattern: Old Germanic Helmets, *Beowulf*, and *Grettis saga*', in E.C. Polome (ed.), *Old Norse Literature and Mythology* (Austin: University of Texas Press, 1969, pp. 130–99); C. Edsman, *Studies in Shamanism: A Symposium* (Stockholm: Almqvist and Wiksell, 1967, pp. 120–65); H.E. Davidson, *Gods and Myths of Northern Europe* (Harmondsworth: Penguin, 1964, pp. 141–9); M. Eliade, *Shamanism: Archaic Techniques of Ecstasy* (London: Routledge, 1964, pp. 379–87); V. Salmon, 'The *Wanderer* and the *Seafarer* and the Old English Conception of the Soul' (*Modern Language Review*, 55, 1960, 1–10); N.K. Chadwick, *Poetry and Prophecy* (Cambridge University Press, 1952).

14 B.C. Bates, *The Way of Wyrd* (London: Century Publishing, 1983).

Chapter One
How Our Ancestors Lived

1 Hill, D. *An Atlas of Anglo-Saxon England* (Oxford: Blackwell, 1984 edition). Hill explains that the debate about the actual extent of forest cover is still going on; earlier estimates of forest cover based on geological research were later reassessed more modestly, and now place-name research is identifying new areas of woodland. Hill's conclusion from the available evidence is that 'there were then important forests in England, and that the country was more heavily wooded than in later periods.' (p.17)

2 H.P.R. Finberg, *The Formation of England 550–1042* (London: Hart-Davis MacGibbon, 1974); this book comprises a lively and interesting account. The background to the arrival and settlement of the tribal groups from mainland

Europe is described in varying detail in almost all general introductions to Anglo-Saxon England. For readers interested in the transposition of tribal groups from the continent into early England, and the nature of the early settlements, some of the books I have found useful include: J. Campbell (ed.) *The Anglo-Saxons* (London: Phaidon, 1982); D.J.V. Fisher, *The Anglo-Saxon Age* (London: Longman, 1973); N. Higham, *Rome, Britain and the Anglo-Saxons* (London: Seaby, 1992); D. Hooke (ed.) *Anglo-Saxon Settlements* (Oxford: Basil Blackwell, 1988); P. Hunter Blair, *An Introduction to Anglo-Saxon England* (2nd edn, Cambridge University Press, 1956); D.P. Kirby, *The Making of Early England* (London: Batsford, 1967); L. and J. Laing, *Anglo-Saxon England* (London: Paladin, 1982); H. Mayr-Harting, *The Germanic Invasions: The Making of Europe A.D. 400–600* (London: Paul Elek, 1975); J. Morris, *The Age of Arthur: A History of the British Isles from 350 to 650* (London: Weidenfeld and Nicolson, 1973); J.N.L. Myres, *The English Settlements* (Oxford: The Clarendon Press, 1985); M. Welch, *Anglo-Saxon England* (London: Batsford, 1992). The early cultures are reviewed in R. Hachmann (tr. J. Hogarth), *The Germanic Peoples* (London: Barrie and Jenkins, 1971) and M. Todd, *The Northern Barbarians 100 B.C.–A.D. 300* (London: Hutchinson, 1975); and the later settlements in M.L. Faull (ed.), *Studies in Late Anglo-Saxon Settlement* (Oxford University Press, 1984). Practical matters are reviewed in G.A. Lester, *The Anglo-Saxons: How They Lived and Worked* (Newton Abbott: David and Charles, 1976). A classic source which is still fascinating reading, even though some of the material has been revised by more recent research, is H.M. Chadwick, *The Origin of the English Nation* (Cambridge University Press, 1907).

3 A good discussion and diagram of the settlement and buildings is in H.E. Davidson, *The Lost Beliefs of Northern Europe* (London: Routledge, 1993) pp. 22–4.

4 King Ine was Christian, and a pioneer in detailing specific laws to structure the social relationships of his kingdom. However, many of his laws gave specificity to customs which had been in existence in Germanic tribal societies for a long time before. See F. Stenton, *Anglo-Saxon England* (3rd ed, Oxford University Press, 1971), Chapter IX 'The Structure of Early English Society', for a clear and authoritative summary of the early law-givers, including Ine.

5 B. Branston, *The Lost Gods of England* (London: Thames and Hudson, 1957) p. 52.

6 See Bonser, *Medical Background*, pp. 51–94, for a full discussion of 'pestilence' and epidemics.

CHAPTER TWO
Incantations: Attuning to the Healing Spirits

1 The arrival of Augustine and his encounter with Aethelbert is described in Chaney, *The Cult of Kingship*, pp. 156–9.

2 Bede's *History of England*, quoted by G. Owen, *Rites and Religions* p. 129.

3 J.R. Hinnells (ed.), *A Handbook of Living Religions* (Harmondsworth: Penguin, 1985) p. 407. Obviously caution needs to be exercised in extrapolating from more recent indigenous cultures to that of ancient Europe, but the parallels in

their experiences of the introduction of Christianity are striking and informative.
4   Chaney, *The Cult of Kingship*, p. 161.
5   Bonser, *Medical Background*, p. 124.
6   W.P. Ker, 'Address to the Viking Club, 1907' (*Collected Essays*, vol ii, p. 172), quoted in W. Bonser, *Medical Background*, p. 133. Of course, it could be said that the good bishop was humouring his 'native converts', and pretending to accommodate a few of their trolls in a remote part of the landscape. On the other hand . . .
7   Bonser, *Medical Background* p.121.
8   Wulfstan is quoted in M. Swanton, *Anglo-Saxon Prose* (London: Dent, 1975); the whole sermon is reported, pp. 116–25.
9   Burckhardt, *The Civilization of the Renaissance in Italy* (London: Phaidon, 1944) p. 178, quoted in Bonser, *Medical Background* p. 137.
10 Bonser, *Medical Background*, reviews similar beliefs, pp. 136–40.
11 *Laws of King Alfred 32* in Bonser, *Medical Background*, p. 129.
12 *Laws of King Cnut (secular) 5*. In Bonser, *Medical Background* p. 129. The other sources quoted in this section are all referenced and discussed in Bonser, pp. 129–36.
13 Hildegard, *Physica*, i. 56, in Bonser, *Medical Background* p. 239.
14 From the *Lacnunga*, Anglo-Saxon *Spellbook*, translated in Storms, *Anglo-Saxon Magic*.
15 Pliny The Elder, *Natural History*, introduced by Bonser, *Medical Background*, pp. 7–8.
16 Bonser, *Medical Background* for prayers to plants.
17 Storms, *Anglo-Saxon Magic* discusses plant-collecting rituals.
18 A. and B. Rees, *Celtic Heritage* (London: Thames and Hudson, 1961) includes an excellent discussion on polarities in concepts of time, seasons, light and dark, etc.
19 Snorri Sturluson *Prose Edda: Tales from The Norse Mythology.* p. 38.
20 Ibid.
21 Bonser, *Medical Background*.
22 My source for the Anglo-Saxon *Spellbook* is Storms, *Anglo-Saxon Magic*.
23 Bonser, *Medical Background*.
24 Storms, *Anglo-Saxon Magic*.
25 For a clear summary of the Pueblo perspective see Hinnells, *Handbook of Living Religions*, pp. 403–4.
26 Adomnan, *Life of St Columba*, quoted in Bonser, *Medical Background*.

CHAPTER THREE
Guardians: Learning From the Power Animals

1   D. Whitelock (ed.) *English Historical Documents* (London: Eyre and Spottiswood, 1955). Page 688 is the translator of the original account of King Edwin and the crow in the early *Life of St Gregory*, written between AD 680 and 714 by an anonymous monk of Whitby, one of the earliest pieces of literature in England.
2   Tacitus, *Germania*, Chapter 17. The Roman historian Tacitus wrote his account in AD 98. It is available in H. Mattingly (ed.), *Agricola and the Germania* (tr. S.A. Handford, rev. edn., Harmondsworth: Penguin, 1970).
3   H.P. Duerr, *Dreamtime: Concerning the Boundary Between Wilderness and*

Civilization (tr. F. Goodman, Oxford: Blackwell, 1985); see also B. Collinder, *The Lapps* (Princeton University Press, 1949) pp. 148–9 and E.O.G. Turville-Petre, *Myth and Religion of the North* (London: Weidenfeld and Nicolson, 1964) pp. 221–30. The material in this section and for the next few pages owes much to the excellent discussion in Glosecki, *Shamanism and Old English Poetry*, Chapter 6, 'Images of the Animal Guardians', pp. 181–210.
4 Salmon, 'The Wanderer'; Glosecki, *Shamanism and Old English Poetry*, p. 184.
5 Glosecki, *Shamanism and Old English Poetry* p. 96.
6 Chaney, *Cult of Kingship*, pp. 121–35, has a good discussion of animals sacred to the Anglo-Saxons. Ross, *Pagan Celtic Britain* pp. 302–446, comprehensively reviews animals sacred to the Celts.
7 Eliade, *Shamanism*, especially pp. 88–99, but very many animals feature throughout this book and are listed in the comprehensive index; see also J.E. Brown, *Animals of the Soul* (Shaftesbury: Element, 1992).
8 Glosecki, *Shamanism and Old English Poetry* p. 54. Translates and analyses animal images in *Beowulf*.

There are various renditions of *Beowulf* from the Anglo-Saxon into modern English, including the classics by E. Dobbie, *Beowulf and Judith* (The Anglo-Saxon Poetic Records, 4, New York: Columbia University Press, 1953) and R.K. Gordon (1926) republished as *Beowulf* (New York: Dover, 1992). I like M. Alexander, *Beowulf* (Harmondsworth: Penguin, 1973). Analyses and commentaries on *Beowulf* run into the hundreds; for readers wishing to explore further, some sources of relevance to this book include A. Bonjour, 'Beowulf and the Beasts of Battle' (*Proceedings of the Modern Language Association*, 72, 1957, 563–73); N.K. Chadwick, 'The Monsters and Beowulf', in P. Clemoes (ed.), *The Anglo-Saxons* (London: Bower and Bower, 1959); G.N. Garmonsway, *Beowulf and its Analogues* (London: Dent, 1968); G. Hubener, 'Beowulf and Germanic Exorcism' (*Review of English Studies*, 11, 1935, 163–81); M. Osborn, *Beowulf: A Verse Translation with Treasures of the North* (Berkeley: University of California Press, 1983); J.R.R. Tolkein, 'Beowulf: The Monsters and the Critics' (*Proceedings of the British Academy*, 22, 1936, 245–95); D. Whitelock, *The Audience of Beowulf* (Oxford: Clarendon Press, 1951).
9 Davidson, *Pagan Scandinavia*, pp. 70–1.
10 Glosecki, *Shamanism and Old English Poetry*, p. 198.
11 K. La Budde, 'Cultural Primitivism in William Faulkner's *The Bear*', in F. Utley (ed.) *Bear, Man, and God* (New York: Random House, 1964), pp. 226–339; R. Carpenter, *Folktale, Fiction, and Saga in the Homeric Epics* (Berkeley: University of California Press, 1946).
12 Carpenter, *Folk Tale, Fiction, and Saga*.
13 T.O. Rahilly, *Early Irish History and Mythology* (Dublin Institute for Advanced Studies, 1976) pp. 323–5; also the discussion in Tolstoy, *Quest for Merlin*, p. 148.
14 Davidson, *Gods and Myths*, pp. 66–70; M. Eliade, *Rites and Symbols of Initiation* (tr. W. Trask, New York: Harper and Row, 1975) p. 72.
15 Duerr, *Dreamtime*, p. 62.
16 Davidson, *Gods and Myths*, p. 68.
17 Snorri Sturluson, *Heimskringla* (tr. L.M. Hollander, Austin: University of Texas, 1964); Eliade, *Shamanism*, p. 93; J. Halifax, *Shamanic Voices* (Harmondsworth:

Penguin, 1979).
18. See Halifax, *Shamanic Voices*, for first-hand narration of experiences of 'animal presence'.
19. Lopez, B. *Crossing Open Ground* and Lopez, B. *Arctic Dreams: Imagination and Desire in a Northern Landscape* (London: Macmillan, 1986)

CHAPTER FOUR
Mother Earth: Freeing the Flow of Life Force

1. A good introduction to the peat bog finds is in Davidson, *Gods and Myths*, pp. 95–6. The primary source for Nerthus and her procession is Tacitus's *Germania*. Other interesting accounts of the wagons and Nerthus's travels are included in P. Berger, *The Goddess Obscured* (London: Robert Hale, 1988); Davidson, *Lost Beliefs*; B. Branston, *Gods of the North* (London: Thames and Hudson, 1980).
2. Discussions of Frigg which I found useful include those in Branston, *Lost Gods of England*, especially pp. 127–34; K. Morris, *Sorceress or Witch? The Image of Gender in Medieval Iceland and Northern Europe* (New York: University Press of America, 1991); K. Crossley-Holland, *The Norse Myths* (Harmondsworth: Penguin, 1980); especially interesting on the corn spirit is Berger, *Goddess Obscured*.
3. For examples of ancient European notions of life force in people see R.B. Onians, *The Origins of European Thought* (Cambridge University Press, 1954) pp. 129 and 474, on which the material in this section is based.
4. Almost all general books on Scandinavian mythology and religions have good sections on Frey, e.g. the classic by Turville-Petre, *Myth and Religion*; a review of his saga appearances in M. Magnusson, *Iceland Saga* (London: The Bodley Head, 1987); insightful perspectives on his nature and significance throughout, Davidson, *Myths and Symbols*; Sturluson's 'original' description of Frey is in *Prose Edda*. A particularly interesting account and discussion of Frey's wooing of Gerd is in Branston, *Gods of the North*.
5. Branston, *Gods of the North*, p. 160.
6. Crossley-Holland, *Norse Myths*, pp. 54–8 for lively version of this story, and discussion.
7. Magnusson, M. *Hammer of the North* (London: Orbis, 1976) pp. 74–7.
8. J. and C. Bord, *Earth Rites: Fertility Practices in Pre-Industrial Britain* (London: Granada, 1982); see Hutton, *Pagan Religions*, for a more sanguine view of these carvings.
9. An account of this research is provided by Lopez, *Arctic Dreams*.
10. Y.F. Tuan, *Topophilia* (Berkeley: University of California Press, 1968).
11. Davidson, *Gods and Myths*, pp. 111–12.
12. T. Buckley and A. Gottlieb (eds), *Blood Magic: The Anthropology of Menstruation* (Berkeley: University of California Press, 1988); M. Sjöö and B. Mor, *The Great Cosmic Mother: Rediscovering the Religion of the Earth* (San Francisco: Harper and Row, 1987).
13. Owen, *Rites and Religions*.
14. Davidson, *Gods and Myths*, p. 112.
15. M. Eliade, *Myths, Dreams and Mysteries* (London: Collins/Fontana, 1968) p. 217.
16. B.C. Bates and A. Newman-Turner, 'Imagery and Symbolism in the Birth

Practices of Traditional Cultures' (*Birth: Issues in Perinatal Care and Education*, 1985, *12* (1), 29–36).

CHAPTER FIVE
Deep Waters: Consulting the Wells of Wisdom

1 Riddle Number 2 in K. Crossley-Holland (tr.), *The Exeter Book Riddles* (rev. edn. Harmondsworth: Penguin, 1993).
2 Bord, *Earth Rites*; Hutton, *Pagan Religions*, pp. 230–1; Ross, *Pagan Celtic Britain*, pp. 46–59; for a classic collection of river names: E. Ekwell, *English River-Names* (Oxford University Press, 1928); for precious Celtic art objects found and probably dedicated to the Thames in London: C. Fox, *Pattern and Purpose: A Survey of Celtic Art in Britain* (Cardiff: University of Wales Press, 1958).
3 J.A. MacCulloch, *The Religion of the Ancient Celts* (London: Constable, 1991) p. 184.
4 For the concepts of vital power, and the intimate interrelation of people within the landscape and the gods see R.H. Wax, *Magic, Fate and History: The Changing Ethos of the Vikings* (Kansas: Colorado Press, 1969), especially Chapter IV: 'The Ideal Typical Enchanted Point of View'.
5 Bonser, *Medical Background*, p. 238.
6 Ibid, p. 239.
7 L. Watson, *Earthworks* (London: Hodder and Stoughton, 1986) pp. 115–27.
8 See for example the photographs of a thorn tree hung with strips of paper or cloth at Heian shrine, Kyoto, Japan, and also pp. 76–7 of J. Michell, *The Earth Spirit* (London: Thames and Hudson, 1975); Bord, *Earth Rites* p. 102 lists India, Sri Lanka, Iran, north and west Africa as regions where this custom survives.
9 F. Jones, *The Holy Wells of Wales* (Cardiff: University of Wales Press, 1954).
10 Ross, *Pagan Celtic Britain*, p. 56; Bord, *Earth Rites*, p. 93.
11 This is the poetic Scandinavian version of creation, which was written later than most of the material we are considering in this book. Some scholars suggested that this material is too sophisticated to be used in conjunction with the less complete but cognate sources for ancient England and Germanic Europe. But in cautioning against a literal interpolation of the later literature these scholars have gone too far and, as is shown by Brian Branston and others, there are so many strong parallels between the Anglo-Saxon and the later Scandinavian material that over-caution takes us further from, rather than closer to, the truth. See Branston, *Lost Gods of England*, especially pp. 45–55.
12 Snorri Sturluson, *Prose Edda*, p. 46.
13 Owen, *Rites and Religions*; Sjöö and Mor, *Great Cosmic Mother*.
14 Sturluson, *Prose Edda*, pp. 45–6.
15 Crossley-Holland, *Norse Myths*, p. 133.
16 T. Schwenk, *Sensitive Chaos* (New York: Schocken Books, 1976). This work is discussed in Watson, *Earthworks*, pp. 120–1.
17 Bord, *Earth Rites*, p. 98.
18 MacCulloch, *Religion of the Ancient Celts*, accounts of well customs, pp. 181–97.
19 J.M. McPherson, *Primitive Beliefs in the North-East of Scotland* (London: Longmans, Green, 1929) pp. 50–1.

Notes

20 J. Campbell, *Primitive Mythology: The Masks of God* (rev. edn, New York: Viking 1969).
21 Davidson, *Gods and Myths*, p. 195.
22 Onians, *Origins of European Thought*, p. 476.

CHAPTER SIX
Weavers of Destiny: Changing Our Life Patterns

1 J. Graham-Campbell, *The Viking World* (London: Frances Lincoln, 1989) pp. 114–21 on clothing, jewellery, cleanliness of Anglo-Saxons and Vikings, and even 'an artificial make-up for the eyes' for both men and women. J. Graham-Campbell and D. Kidd, *The Vikings* (London: British Museum Publications, 1980), includes discussion on pp. 101–18, and colour illustrations of likely clothing designs on p. 103; Branston in *Lost Gods of England*, p. 33, says: 'The womenfolk frequently adorned themselves with two and sometimes three brooches, often with festoons of glass and amber beads looped from brooch to brooch. Their waists were spanned by a girdle from which might hang characteristic T-shaped iron or bronze trinkets, ivory rings, strike-a-lights and knives.'
2 Graham-Campbell, *Viking World*, on the craft of the jeweller, pp. 102–7.
3 See Tucker, *Dreaming With Open Eyes*, for a comprehensive analysis of the presence of the sacred in art.
4 As well as the two books listed above by J. Graham-Campbell, there are many publications which feature this artwork in good reproductions, for example: R. Bruce-Mitford, *The Sutton Hoo Ship-Burial* (London: The British Museum, 1972), for the impressive range of Anglo-Saxon jewellery recovered from this site, including for example the interwoven design of the 'great gold buckle' (colour plate on p. 65); Magnusson, *Hammer of the North*, for excellent photographs of some pieces; E. Roesdale et al. (eds) *The Vikings in England* (London: The Anglo-Danish Viking Project, 1981).

The Sutton Hoo archaeological finds, displayed now in the British Museum, are reproduced in many books, including the official research publication: R.L.S. Bruce-Mitford, *The Sutton-Hoo Ship Burial* (4 volumes, London: British Museum, 1972). Discussions of the Sutton Hoo treasure and its significance may be found in Hutton, *Pagan Religions*, pp. 275–9; C. Hills, 'The Archaeology of Anglo-Saxon England in the Pagan Period: A Review', *Anglo-Saxon England*, 8 (Cambridge University Press, 1979) pp. 318–26; G. Owen, *Rites and Religions of the Anglo-Saxons* (Newton Abbott: David & Charter, 1981) pp. 67–79. A very good recent summary of the findings and their significance is in Davidson, *Lost Beliefs* pp. 17–24. Of particular interest is S.O. Glosecki, 'Wolf Dancers and Whispering Beasts: Shamanic Motifs from Sutton Hoo?' (*Mankind Quarterly*, 26, 1986, 305–19).
5 Wax, *Magic, Fate and History*, p. 39.
6 Rawson and Legeza, *Tao*, p. 9.
7 Wax, *Magic, Fate and History*, p. 40.
8 Writing about this vision in Viking cosmology, Wax, *Magic, Fate and History*, p. 50, says: 'Another intrinsic aspect of the magical world view is the idea that man, the gods, and all other phenomena are related or connected to each other by a

web of empathy.'
9   Branston, *Lost Gods*, pp. 68–71.
10 Opening stanzas of *The First Lay of Helgi*; my source is P.B. Taylor and W.H. Auden (tr.) *The Elder Edda. A Selection* (London: Faber & Faber, 1969) p. 9.
11 An interesting discussion along similar lines is in N. Pennick, *Games of the Gods* (London: Rider, 1988) pp. 27–31.
12 A. Ereira, *The Heart of the World* (London: Jonathan Cape, 1990).
13 Sjöö and Mor, *Great Cosmic Mother*, p. 51.
14 Summarised clearly with illustrations in Graham-Campbell, *Viking World*, pp. 121–2.
15 Sjöö and Mor, *Great Cosmic Mother*, p. 51.
16 Branston *Lost Gods of England*; Davidson, *Myths and Symbols*, p. 164, are two of the many sources which have discussed the significance and cross-cultural parallels of the Wyrd Sisters.
17 It is appropriate to describe this work on life patterns of fibres or threads here, but see the discussion of the webs and strings of shamanic visions in Chapter 9 for another perspective on this visionary process.

CHAPTER SEVEN
Dwarfs: Transforming With the Web of Wyrd

1   Story of Fenrir in Snorri Sturluson, *Prose Edda*, pp. 56–9.
2   Ancient stories which have retained their essence through folklore, fairy tale or mythology, are like archetypal spells, capturing perennial inner dynamics, knotting elements of individual psyche into one another in timeless formulae, and connecting the individual to the universal level of experience. See C.P. Estes, *Women Who Run with The Wolves* (London: Rider, 1992) for story analysis like this from Jungian inspiration: e.g., p. 80, 'To grasp such a tale, we understand that all its components represent a single woman's psyche. So all aspects of the story belong to a single psyche undergoing an initiatory process.' An interesting perspective on the gods as aspects of Odin is in E. Thorsson, *Runelore* (York Beach, Maine: Samuel Weiser, 1987) pp. 175–200. On the value of 'stories' in general: A.K. Coomaraswamy, in his *Christian and Oriental Philosophy of Art*, (New York: Farrar, Straus, 1956)139ff: 'What has really been preserved in folk and fairy tales and in popular peasant art is, then, by no means a body of merely childish or entertaining fables of crude decorative art, but a series of what are really esoteric doctrines and symbols . . . it is really a body of custom and belief that "stands over" from a time when its meanings were understood.'
3   On Loki, Davidson, *Myths and Symbols*, pp. 212–13; on the Trickster figure a classic text is P. Radin, *The Trickster: A Study in American Indian Mythology* (New York: Philosophical Library, 1956). See also H.R. Davidson 'Loki and Saxo's Hamlet', in P. Williams (ed.), *The Fool and the Trickster* (Ipswich: Folklore Society, 1979).
4   Snorri Sturluson, *Prose Edda*, pp. 86–90.
5   In comparing 'masculine' and 'feminine' paths to problem-solving, and identifying confrontational and analytical problem-solving as 'masculine', I am of course writing in the broadest possible mythological terms. See F. Capra, *The Turning*

Point: Science, Society and the Rising Culture (London: Wildwood House, 1982) for an analysis of the over-dominance of 'masculine' problem-solving in our scientific/technological culture; e.g. p. 29; 'our culture has consistently promoted and rewarded the yang, the masculine or self-assertive elements of human nature, and has disregarded its yin, the feminine or intuitive aspects.'

For interesting discussions of elements, or themes, in the masculine mythological psyche, see for example, R. Moore and D. Gillette *King, Warrior, Magician, Lover* (New York: Harper Collins, 1991).

6 Davidson, *Gods and Myths*, pp. 63–4. The 'binding power' of Odin has been compared with the lines and knots of the Indian Varuna; cf G Dumezil, *Gods of the Ancient Northmen* (ed. E. Haugen, Berkeley: University of California, 1973).
7 Eliade, *Shamanism*, pp. 102–3; A. Bleakley, *The Fruits of the Moon Tree* (London: Gateway, 1984) pp. 208–14.
8 Bleakley, *Fruits of the Moon Tree*.
9 See for example Storms, *Anglo-Saxon Magic* pp. 166–73, and for a translation of the spider creature spell. Other translations of this and associated spells are in Grattan and Singer, *Anglo-Saxon Magic*.
10 Cf Glosecki, *Shamanism and Old English Poetry*, for a comprehensive consideration of the shamanic bases of these texts.
11 See for example the accounts of their initiatory sicknesses given by shamans in Halifax, *Shamanic Voices*.
12 There are many accounts of the creation cosmology of ancient northern Europe, especially the later, more literary and poetic versions of the Icelandic writers. A clear and perceptive account is in Crossley-Holland, *Norse Myths*, especially the Introduction, and Myth 1, The Creation. A detailed account of the relation between the Anglo-Saxon creation myths and the later Norse versions can be found in Branston, *Lost Gods of England*, pp. 177–87.
13 Tolstoy, *Quest for Merlin*, pp. 161–70, has a good account of the Celtic 'Otherworld'.
14 Rees, *Celtic Heritage*, for excellent discussion of the phenomena of sidh and halja.
15 Storms, *Anglo-Saxon Magic*.
16 Eliade, *Shamanism*, p. 86.
17 Campbell, *Primitive Mythology*, pp. 444–51. I first learned of this remarkable ritual from Jane Mayers, whom I supervised for a thesis on Shamanism and Analytical Psychotherapy.
18 See Storms, *Anglo-Saxon Magic*.
19 Crossley-Holland, *Norse Myths*, contains an account of Freya's possible relationships with the dwarfs, as does Davidson, *Lost Beliefs*, pp. 108–9.
20 Alexander, *Beowulf*, p. 88.
21 For the use of dreams in divination in ancient northern Europe see H.E. Davidson, 'The Germanic World' in M. Loewe and C. Blacker (eds), *Divination and Oracles* (London: Allen and Unwin, 1981).

CHAPTER EIGHT
Seeress: Divining Through Deep Intuition

1. There are a number of translations of this saga; my source is G. Jones, *Eirik the Red* (Oxford University Press, 1961). The Thorbiorg episode is narrated on pp. 135–6.
2. Mattingly, *Agricola and the Germania*.
3. Davidson, 'The Germanic World'.
4. Ibid, p. 129. Other discussions of seidr include Glosecki, *Shamanism and Old English Poetry*, pp. 96–102; N.K. Chadwick, *Poetry and Prophecy*, pp. 9–10; Collinder, *The Lapps*, p. 137; Edsman, *Studies in Shamanism*, pp. 143–5; Eliade, *Shamanism*, pp. 385–7; G. Johnston (tr.) *The Saga of Gilsi The Outlaw* ((ed) P. Foote, University of Toronto Press, 1963) p. 79.
5. P.V. Glob, *The Mound People* (tr. R. Bruce-Mitford.) (London: Faber and Faber, 1969) p. 116.
6. Glosecki, *Shamanism and Old English Poetry*, p. 98.
7. There may be a similarity here with Odin's magical spear, called Gungnir, and also the totem pole of some Native American traditions.
8. Davidson, 'The Germanic World', p. 131.
9. Davidson, 'The Germanic World'.
10. See C.M. Bowra, *Primitive Song* (London: Weidenfeld and Nicolson, 1962).
11. Davidson, 'The Germanic World'.
12. Kalweit, *Dreamtime*, p. 144 quotes the Arctic explorer Rasmussen.
13. Ibid, pp. 153–5.

CHAPTER NINE
Heart of the Wolf: Transcending Warriorhood

1. B.C. Bates, *The Way of the Actor* (London: Century Hutchinson, 1986).
2. Branston, *Gods of the North*; Davidson, *Lost Beliefs*.
3. Crossley-Holland, *Norse Myths*, p. xxvi.
4. Snorri Sturluson, *Prose Edda*, pp. 26–7.
5. For a probable common identity between the Germanic Odin or Woden and the Celtic Lugh deities, see Hutton, *Pagan Religions*, p. 269; Tolstoy, *Quest for Merlin*, pp. 238–9.
6. Glosecki, *Shamanism and Old English Poetry*, p. 72; Davidson, *Gods and Myths*, p. 147.
7. Snorri Sturluson, *Prose Edda*, p. 26.
8. These ancient cave paintings, which may have had many purposes including shamanic activity, stretch back as far as 20,000 BC. See Tucker, *Dreaming With Open Eyes*, for a sustained consideration of the shamanic spirit in the production of art.
9. Eliade, *Shamanism*, for many examples of how shamanic ritual aims to recreate the 'original' stage, the primal, the beginning.
10. This source is the *Elder Edda*. Metzner in *Well of Remembrance*, pp. 91–7, give a clear exposition of the identity and character of the ancient manuscripts. He explains that there are two ancient manuscripts written in Old Norse given the

name *Edda*. The *Elder* or *Poetic Edda* consists of songs and poems about gods and heroes, as well as prophetic visions and wisdom teachings, which were sung and recited by Icelandic poets at celebrations and festivals. Although the earliest manuscript of the *Elder Edda* dates from the thirteenth century, scholars agree that the songs are much older, and some may have been composed in the fifth or sixth century AD. The *Prose Edda*, composed by the Icelandic scholar/poet Snorri Sturluson, uses songs and legends from the oral tradition, and retells some of the material from the *Elder Edda* in prose form. There is some debate about the meaning of the word 'Edda'; Metzner translate it as 'great-grandmother', and suggests that it might refer to stories told by grandmothers to their children and grandchildren.

The lines I quote are from the translation by Taylor and Auden, *The Elder Edda*, p. 245. Another widely consulted translation is by L.M. Hollander, *The Poetic Edda* (Austin: University of Texas Press, 1962).

11 'Sitting out', especially on or in the vicinity of burial mounds, was a recognised practice of seership in ancient northern Europe; this may be what Gullveig was doing. See Metzner, *Well of Remembrance*; also Markale, *Women of the Celts*, p. 194.
12 Branston, *Gods of the North*, pp. 174–5.
13 E.g. Crossley-Holland, *Norse Myths*, p. 184.
14 Davidson, *Gods and Myths*, p. 115.
15 See Metzner's translation and interesting discussion in *Well of Remembrance*, pp. 169–72.
16 'Death and rebirth' is invariably cited as a central aspect of shamanic initiation. See Eliade, *Shamanism*, for many examples, and Tolstoy for an interesting treatment in *Quest for Merlin*, pp. 161–86.
17 See, for example, M. Adler, *Drawing Down the Moon* (2nd edn, Boston: Shambhala, 1986); C. and J. Matthews, *The Western Way* (London: Arkana, 1985).
18 'Cunning men' were a well-known social presence in the Middle Ages, as attested by Thomas in *Religion and the Decline of Magic*.
19 Eliade, *Myths, Dreams and Mysteries*, pp. 88–96.
20 Kalweit, *Dreamtime*, pp. 1–55, for various perspectives on journeys beyond the physical body.
21 Eliade, *Shamanism*, has many examples of 'death-and-rebirth' rituals.
22 Metzner, *Well of Remembrance*.
23 Moore and Gillette, *King, Warrior*, pp. 75–96; J.S. Bolen, *Gods in Everyman* (San Francisco: Harper and Row, 1989); A. Stevens, *The Roots of War: A Jungian Perspective* (New York: Paragon House, 1984).
24 Moore and Gillette, *King, Warrior*, p. 75.
25 Ibid, pp. 76–7.
26 Ibid, p. 90.
27 Bleakley, *Fruits of the Moon Tree*.
28 A. Bleakley, *Earth's Embrace: Facing the Shadow of the New Age* (Bath: Gateway Books, 1989) p. 131.
29 J. Hillman, *In-Search: Psychology and Religion* (Dallas: Spring Publications, 1979).
30 Branston, *Gods of the North*, pp. 173–5.

31 Bleakley, *Fruits of the Moon Tree*, p. 147.
32 An excellent evocation of the spirit of the wolf is to be found in B. Lopez *Of Wolves and Men* (New York: Dent, 1978), from which I have taken the quotes concerning wolf behaviour.
33 Lopez, *Of Wolves and Men*.
34 H. Hesse, *Steppenwolf* (New York: Bantam, 1969).
35 Sturluson, *Heimskringla*, p. 11; Davidson, *Gods and Myths*, pp. 144–6 for an account of Odin as a shaman and knower of magic.
36 Davidson, *Gods and Myths*, p. 121.
37 H.R.E. Davidson and P. Fisher, *Saxo Grammaticus* (Ipswich: Folklore Society, 1979).
38 Taylor and Auden, *The Elder Edda*.
39 Thorsson, *Runelore*.

CHAPTER TEN
Vision Journey: Riding the Tree of Knowledge

1 There are many translations of Odin's initiation on the World Tree, including: Branston, *Gods of the North*, p. 115; Davidson, *Gods and Myths*, pp. 143–4; Crossley-Holland, *Norse Myths*, pp. 15–17; Tolstoy, *Quest for Merlin*, pp. 176–8; Metzner, *Well of Remembrance*, pp. 192–9.
2 Shamanic rituals to acquire guardian spirits are described in, for example, Eliade, *Shamanism*, pp. 110–44; Kalweit, *Dreamtime*, pp. 209–12; P. Vitebsky, *The Shaman* (London: Macmillan, 1995) pp. 59–63; Halifax, *Shamanic Voices*
   The journeys to the Lowerworld were often described in the ancient literature with a seemingly objective geography. For the relationship between sacred Wyrd landscapes and the material world see H.R.E. Davidson, 'Mythical Geography in the Edda Poems', in G.D. Flood (ed.), *Mapping Invisible Worlds* (Yearbook 9 of the Traditional Cosmology Society: Edinburgh University Press, 1993) pp. 95–106.
3 J. Swan, 'Sacred Places in Nature: One Tool in the Shaman's Medicine Bag', in G. Doore, *Shaman's Path* (Boston: Shambhala, 1988 pp. 151–60).
4 Shamanic states of consciousness are described in, for example, S. Nicholson (ed.), *Shamanism: An Expanded View of Reality* (Wheaton, Illinois: The Theosophical Publishing House, 1987).
5 Eliade, *Shamanism*.
6 C.G. Jung (ed.) *Man and His Symbols* (New York: Dell, 1964).
7 Crossley-Holland, *Norse Myths*, pp. xxii–xxiv.
8 Tolstoy, *Quest for Merlin*, p. 177; Branston, *Gods of the North*, pp. 114–15.
9 Davidson, *Gods and Myths*, pp. 142–5.
10 Eliade, *Shamanism*, p. 469, and pp. 466–70 for discussion of symbolism of the horse in shamanic societies.
11 Davidson, *Gods and Myths* pp. 142–3.
12 On the imaginal in ancient Europe, see Glosecki, *Shamanism and Old English Poetry*; for the close relationship between the literal world and the imaginal Otherworld, see Tolstoy, *Quest for Merlin*, p. 162; Markale, *Women of the Celts*, pp. 194–5.

Shamanic journeys from more recent cultures into the dangerous but wisdom-bestowing environs of the Lowerworld are recounted in, for example, H. Kalweit, *Shamans, Healers and Medicine Men* (tr. M. Kohn, Boston: Shambhala, 1992); Halifax, *Shamanic Voices*.

13 K. Rasmussen, *Intellectual Culture of the Hudson Bay Eskimos. Report of the Fifth Thule Expedition 1921–1924*. Vol VII (Copenhagen: 1930).
14 Snorri Sturluson, *Prose Edda*, p. 83.
15 Rees and Rees, *Celtic Heritage* pp. 343–4 and elsewhere for excellent discussions of mythological time.
16 Tolstoy, *Quest for Merlin*, p. 177; Eliade, *Shamanism*, pp. 274–9 for a consideration of the shamanic significance of the number nine; also A. and B. Rees comprehensively review the symbolism of 'nine' in Celtic tradition in *Celtic Heritage* pp. 192–6, on which the following section is based.
17 Tolstoy, *Quest for Merlin*.
18 Rees and Rees, *Celtic Heritage*.
19 Thorsson, *Runelore*, pp. 153–7, discusses the cosmological structure as a model of the world, but 'also the pattern of the "world within" – the macrocosm of man if you will'. He cites in support the poetic language of northern Europe in which humans are often 'paraphrased' in terms of trees as, for example, when a warrior will be called 'the oak of battle'. Thorsson says these 'kennings' are derived from the mythic fact that humans were 'shaped' from trees . . . See also Grattan and Singer, *Anglo-Saxon Magic* for a discussion of concepts of microcosm and macrocosm.
20 J. Halifax, *Shaman: The Wounded Healer* (London: Thames and Hudson, 1982) for an attempt to illustrate the various visions of shamanic states of consciousness through artwork, costume, mask and ritual.
21 Snorri Sturluson, *Prose Edda*, p. 42.
22 There is a good account of this structure in Crossley-Holland, *Norse Myths* (Introduction).
23 Cf Branston's assessment of the correspondence between the two in *Gods of the North* and *Lost Gods of England*.
24 Crossley-Holland, *Norse Myths*, again provides a clear guide to the cosmology.
25 Snorri Sturluson, *Prose Edda*, p. 40.
26 Snorri Sturluson, *Prose Edda*, p. 46

Chapter Eleven
Giants: Trusting Death and Rebirth

1 Snorri Sturluson, *Prose Edda*, pp. 32–6, describes creation, and the primeval giant called Ymir.
2 Snorri Sturluson quoted in Branston, *Gods of the North*, pp. 60–1.
3 Mimir's proposed identification as Odin's uncle is in Branston, *Gods of the North*, pp. 224–5; see also there the good discussion of the beings at the creation of the world, pp. 47–65, and that of Davidson, *Gods and Myths*, pp. 167–8.
4 Snorri Sturluson, *Prose Edda*, p. 43.
5 Snorri Sturluson, *Prose Edda*, pp. 83–4; Branston, *Gods of the North*, pp. 91–2, 272–5.

6 The story of the end of the world is in Snorri Sturluson, *Prose Edda*, pp. 86–90.
7 Branston, *Gods of the North*, pp. 273.
8 Ibid, p. 273.
9 Ibid, p. 274.
10 Eliade, *Shamanism*, pp. 247–9.
11 Branston, *Gods of the North*, pp. 98–102, and Metzner, *Well of Remembrance*, pp. 203–5, and Davidson, *Gods and Myths*, pp. 198–9 for good summaries of information about the land of the giants and their nature.
12 A very good consideration of the nature of this god in England is in Branston, *Lost Gods of England*, pp. 109–26, and in his Scandinavian identity as Thor; Davidson, *Gods and Myths*, pp. 73–91.
13 Snorri Sturluson's story of Thor and the giants is in *Prose Edda*, pp. 73–6.
14 An interesting account of the nature of Mimir's well is in Metzner, *Well of Remembrance*, pp. 219–24.
15 The main sources for the story of how Odin came to seek the mead are Snorri's poetic diction appendix of *The Prose Edda* and in a section of the famous poem from the *Havamal* (stanzas 104–10). A lively account of the 'plot' by which Odin sought the magic mead is in Branston, *Gods of the North*, pp. 219–25, and the nature of the task he has to perform to obtain it is identified in Metzner, *Well of Remembrance*, pp. 239–240.
16 Snorri Sturluson's account of this event is in *Prose Edda*, p. 43.
17 Eliade, *Shamanism*, p. 54.
18 Branston, *Gods of the North*, p. 149.
19 This story is related by Markale, *Women of the Celts*, pp. 184–5.
20 Branston, *Gods of the North*, pp. 219–21.
21 J. Loth, *Mabinogian*, Vol 1, pp. 142–49, quoted in Markale, *Women of the Celts*, p. 182.
22 Onians, *Origins of European Thought*, pp. 150–4.
23 Ibid, p. 154.
24 Branston, *Gods of the North*, p. 149.
25 Eliade, *Shamanism*, p. 246.
26 Branston, *Gods of the North*, pp. 219–21.

Chapter Twelve
Love Magic: Creating the Elixir of Life

1 This story is told by Snorri Sturluson in the manual of poetic arts following the main text of *The Prose Edda*, as part of his discussion of the origins of poetic inspiration. There are also references to the story in the *Havamal*, the section in the *Elder Edda* in which Odin is giving advice and telling some of his own experiences. The quoted passages in my narration come from Snorri Sturluson, *Prose Edda*, pp. 100–3.
2 Stanzas 13–14 of the *Havamal*, here from Branston's *Gods of the North*, p. 223.
3 Dumezil, *Gods of the Ancient Northmen*, p. 21, proposes that the name Kvasir refers to a fermented beverage: 'It is an onomastic personification of an intoxicating drink which recalls the *kvas* of the Slavs. It is natural the precious intoxication given by the mead of poetry and wisdom should have honey as an ingredient. It

is equally natural that a drink fermented from squashed vegetables should be made to ferment by spittle. This technique is frequently attested; it is at least conceivable, as we are here dealing with a ceremonial or communal drink, sanctioning the agreement between two social groups, that such fermentation should be caused by the spittle of all concerned.'
4 Stanzas 104–10 of the *Havamal*, Taylor and Auden, *The Elder Edda*.
5 Taylor and Auden, *The Elder Edda*.
6 Branston, *Gods of the North*, p. 224
7 Ibid, p. 224.
8 See Morris, *Sorceress or Witch?*
9 In fact Snorri Sturluson says in *The Prose Edda* that Odin came from Turkey.
10 Eliade, *Shamanism*, pp. 431–5.
11 P. Rawson, *Tantra: The Indian Cult of Ecstasy* (London: Thames and Hudson, 1973), p. 7.
12 Ibid, p. 23.
13 See the discussion on this point in Thorsson, *Runelore*, pp. 176–7; also Rees, *Celtic Heritage*. For an intriguing consideration of how the relation between the universal and the individual was coded in the numbers and rules of games, especially board games, see N. Pennick, *Games of the Gods* (London: Century Hutchinson, 1988).
14 All quoted material on Tantra in this chapter is from P. Rawson, *Tantra*, pp. 7–30, and Rawson and Legeza, *Tao: The Chinese Philosophy of Time and Change*, (London: Thames and Hudson, 1973) pp. 9–30.
15 Branston, *Gods of the North*, pp. 221–4.
16 Sturluson, *Prose Edda*, pp. 43–5.

Bibliography

Most of the books and articles listed below I have referred to directly in the Notes that accompany the text. However, I have added a selection of additional sources which I think will add to an understanding of *The Wisdom of the Wyrd* for those who would like to read more widely. Some of the references include substantial bibliographies which will serve as guides to further reading. Scholarship continues to add to our knowledge of this field, but some of the old sources make for more colourful and less technical reading, and I have included a selection of those not invalidated by recent research.

Achterberg, J., *Woman as Healer*, Boston: Shambhala, 1990
Adler, M., *Drawing Down the Moon* (2nd edn), Boston: Shambhala, 1986
Alexander, M., *The Earliest English Poems*, Harmondsworth: Penguin, 1966
Alexander, M., *Beowulf*, Harmondsworth: Penguin, 1973
Anderson, G.K., *The Literature of the Anglo-Saxons*, New York: Russell and Russell, 1962
Arent, M.A., 'The Heroic Pattern: Old Germanic Helmets, *Beowulf*, and *Grets saga*', in E.C. Polome (ed.), *Old Norse Literature and Mythology*, Austin: University of Texas Press, 1969, pp. 130–99
Baker, S., *Picturing the Beast: Animals, Identity and Representation*, Manchester University Press, 1993
Bancroft, A., *Origins of the Sacred: The Spiritual Journey in Western Tradition*, London: Routledge, 1987
Bannard, H.E., 'Some English Sites of Ancient Heathen Worship', *Hibbert Journal*, XLIV, 1945, 76–9
Barley, N.F., 'Anglo-Saxon Magico-Medicine', *Journal of the Anthropological Society of Oxford*, 3, 1972, 67–77
Bates, B.C., *The Way of Wyrd*, London: Century, 1983
Bates, B.C. and Newman-Turner, A., 'Imagery and symbolism in the birth practices of traditional cultures', *Birth: Issues in Perinatal Care and Education*, 1985, 12 (1), 29–36
Bates, B.C., *The Way of the Actor*, London: Century Hutchinson, 1986
Berger, P., *The Goddess Obscured*, London: Robert Hale, 1988
Berresford Ellis, P., *Celt and Saxon: The Struggle for Britain AD 410–937*, London: Constable, 1993
Blair, P.H., *An Introduction to Anglo-Saxon England* (2nd edn), Cambridge University

Press, 1956
Blair, P.H., *The World of Bede*, London: Secker, 1970
Bleakley, A., *The Fruits of the Moon Tree*, London: Gateway, 1984
Bleakley, A., *Earth's Embrace: Facing the Shadow of the New Age*, Bath: Gateway Books, 1989
Bolen, J.S., *Gods in Everyman*, San Francisco: Harper and Row, 1989
Bonjour, A., 'Beowulf and the Beasts of Battle', *Proceedings of the Modern Language Association*, 72, 1957, 563–73
Bonser, W., 'The Significance of Colour in Ancient and Medieval Magic, with some Modern Comparisons', *Man*, XXV, 1925, 194–8
Bonser, W., 'Magical Practices Against Elves', *Folk-lore*, XXXVII, 1926, 356–63
Bonser, W., 'Animal Skins in Magic and Medicine', *Folklore*, 73, 1962, 128–9
Bonser, W., *The Medical Background of Anglo-Saxon England*, London: Wellcome Historical Medical Library, 1963
Bord, J. and Bord, C., *Earth Rites: Fertility Practices in Pre-Industrial Britain*, London: Granada, 1982
Bowra, C.M. *Primitive Song*, London: Weidenfeld and Nicolson, 1962
Branston, B., *The Lost Gods of England*, London: Thames and Hudson, 1957
Branston, B., *Gods of the North*, London: Thames and Hudson, 1980
Brown, J.E., *Animals of the Soul*, Shaftesbury: Element, 1992
Bruce-Mitford, R.L.S., *The Sutton-Hoo Ship Burial* (4 volumes), London: British Museum, 1972
Buchholz, P., 'Perspectives for Historical Research in Germanic Religion', *History of Religions*, 1968, *8*, 111–38
Buchholz, P., 'Shamanism – The Testimony of Old Icelandic Literary Tradition', *Mediaeval Scandinavia*, 4, 1971, 7–20
Buckley, T. and Gottlieb, A. (eds), *Blood Magic: The Anthropology of Menstruation*, Berkeley: University of California Press, 1988
Byock, J.L., *Medieval Iceland*, Berkeley: University of California Press, 1988
Cameron, K., *English Place Names*, London: Batsford, 1961
Campbell, J., *Primitive Mythology: The Masks of God*, (rev. edn) New York: Viking, 1969
Campbell, J., *The Way of the Animal Powers* (*Historical Atlas of World Mythology*, Volume I) London: Times Books, 1984
Campbell, J., *The Way of the Seeded Earth* (*Historical Atlas of World Mythology* Volume II) New York: Harper and Row, 1988
Campbell, J. (ed.), *The Anglo-Saxons*, London: Phaidon, 1982
Capra, F., *The Tao of Physics*, London: Wildwood House, 1982
Capra, F., *The Turning Point: Science, Society and the Rising Culture*, London: Wildwood House, 1982
Carpenter, R., *Folktale, Fiction, and Saga in the Homeric Epics*, Berkeley: University of California Press, 1946
Chadwick, H.M., *The Cult of Othin*, London: Cambridge University Press, 1899
Chadwick, H.M., *The Origin of the English Nation*, Cambridge University Press, 1907
Chadwick, H.M., *The Heroic Age*, London: Cambridge University Press, 1912
Chadwick, N., *The Druids*, Cardiff, University of Wales Press, 1966
Chadwick, N.K., *Poetry and Prophecy*, Cambridge University Press, 1952

Bibliography

Chadwick, N.K. 'The Monsters and Beowulf', in P. Clemoes (ed.), *The Anglo-Saxons*, London: Bower and Bower, 1959
Chadwick, N.K., 'Dreams in Early European Literature', in J. Carney, and D. Green (eds), *Celtic Studies: Essays in Memory of Angus Matheson*, London: 1968, pp. 33–50
Chaney, W.A., 'Paganism to Christianity in Anglo-Saxon England', *Harvard Theological Review*, LIII, 1960
Chaney, W.A., *The Cult of Kingship in Anglo-Saxon England*, Manchester University Press, 1970
Chatwin, B., *The Songlines*, London: Jonathan Cape, 1987
Chetan, A. and Brueton, D., *The Sacred Yew*, London: Arkana, 1984
Clemoes, P. (ed.), *The Anglo-Saxons*, London: Bower and Bower, 1959
Clemoes, P. (ed.), *Anglo-Saxon England*, London: Cambridge University Press (an annual collection of essays, beginning 1971)
Cockayne, T.O., *Leechdoms, Wortcunning and Starcraft of Early England* (three volumes), Rolls Series 1964–6, reissued London: Holland Press, 1961
Collinder, B., *The Lapps*, Princeton University Press, 1949
Condren, M., *The Serpent and the Goddess: Women, Religion and Power in Celtic Ireland*, San Francisco: Harper-Collins, 1989
Cook, R., *The Tree of Life: Image for the Cosmos*, London: Thames and Hudson, 1988
Coomaraswamy, A.K., *Christian and Oriental Philosophy of Art*, New York: 1956
Cowan, J., *The Mysteries of the Dreamtime*, London: Prism Press, 1989
Crawford, J., 'Evidences for Witchcraft in Anglo-Saxon England', *Medium Aevum*, 32, 1963, 99–116
Crossley-Holland, K., *The Norse Myths*, Harmondsworth: Penguin, 1980
Crossley-Holland, K. (tr.), *The Exeter Book Riddles* (rev. edn) Harmondsworth: Penguin, 1993
Damico, H., *Beowulf's Wealhtheow and the Valkyrie Tradition*, Madison: University of Wisconsin Press, 1984
Danielli, M., 'Initiation Ceremonial from Norse Literature', *Folklore*, 56, 1945, 229–45
Davidson, H.E. (ed.), *The Seer: In Celtic and Other Traditions*, Edinburgh: John Donald, 1989
Davidson, H.R.E., 'The Hill of the Dragon: Anglo-Saxon Burial Mounds in Literature and Archaeology', *Folk-lore*, LXI, 1950, 169–84
Davidson, H.R.E., *Gods and Myths of Northern Europe*, Harmondsworth: Penguin, 1964
Davidson, H.R.E., *Pagan Scandinavia*, New York: Praeger, 1967
Davidson, H.R.E., 'Loki and Saxo's Hamlet', in P. Williams (ed.), *The Fool and the Trickster*, Ipswich: Folklore Society, 1979
Davidson, H.R.E., 'The Germanic World', in M. Loewe and C. Blacker (eds), *Divination and Oracles*, London: Allen and Unwin, 1981
Davidson, H.R.E., *Myths and Symbols in Pagan Europe*, Manchester University Press, 1988
Davidson, H.R.E., *The Lost Beliefs of Northern Europe*, London: Routledge, 1993, pp. 22–4
Davidson, H.R.E., 'Mythical Geography in the Edda Poems', in G.D. Flood (ed.) *Mapping Invisible Worlds*, Yearbook 9 of the Traditional Cosmology Society:

Edinburgh University Press, 1993

Davidson, H.R.E. and Fisher, P., *Saxo Grammaticus*, Ipswich: Folklore Society, 1979

Devereux, P., *Earth Memory*, Slough: Quantum, 1991

Dickins, B. (ed.), *Runic and Heroic Poems of the Old Teutonic Peoples*, London: Cambridge University Press, 1915

Dickins, B., 'English Names and Old English Heathenism', *Essays and Studies* (of the English Association), XXIX, 1934

Dobbie, E.V.K. (ed.), *The Anglo-Saxon Minor Poems*, The Anglo-Saxon Poetic Records, 6, New York: Columbia University Press, 1942

Dobbie, E., *Beowulf and Judith*, The Anglo-Saxon Poetic Records, 4, New York: Columbia University Press, 1953

Doore, G., *Shaman's Path*, Boston: Shambhala, 1988

Dossey, L., *Space, Time and Medicine*, Boulder: Shambhala, 1982

Duerr, H.P., *Dreamtime: Concerning the Boundary Between Wilderness and Civilization* (tr. F. Goodman), Oxford: Blackwell, 1985

Dumezil, G., *Gods of the Ancient Northmen*, E. Haugen (ed.), Berkeley: University of California Press, 1977

Edsman, C., *Studies in Shamanism: A Symposium*, Stockholm: Almqvist and Wiksell, 1967

Ekwell, E., *English River-Names*, Oxford University Press, 1928

Eliade, M., *Shamanism: Archaic Techniques of Ecstasy*, London: Routledge, 1964

Eliade, M., *From Primitives to Zen: A Thematic Sourcebook of the History of Religions*, London: Collins, 1967

Eliade, M., *Rites and Symbols of Initiation* (tr. W. Trask), New York: Harper and Row, 1975

Eliade, M., *A History of Religious Ideas*, Volume 2, University of Chicago Press, 1982

Ereira, A., *The Heart of the World*, London: Jonathan Cape, 1990

Estes, C.P., *Women Who Run with The Wolves*, London: Rider, 1992

Faull, M.L. (ed.), *Studies in Late Anglo-Saxon Settlement*, Oxford University Press, 1984

Fell, C., *Women in Anglo-Saxon England*, Bloomington: Indiana University Press, 1984

Fox, C., *Pattern and Purpose: A Survey of Celtic Art in Britain*, Cardiff: University of Wales Press, 1958

von Franz, M-L., 'The Transformed Berserk: Unification of Psychic Opposites', in S. Grof (ed.) *Human Survival and Consciousness Evolution*, Albany: State University of New York Press, 1988

Fremantle, F. and Chogyam Trungpa, *The Tibetan Book of the Dead*, Boston: Shambhala, 1990

Finberg, H.P.R., *The Formation of England 550–1042*, London: Hart-Davis MacGibbon, 1974

Fisher, D.J.V., *The Anglo-Saxon Age*, London: Longman, 1973

Garmonsway, G.N., *Beowulf and its Analogues*, London: Dent, 1968

Gelling, M., 'Place-names and Anglo-Saxon Paganism', *University of Birmingham Historical Journal*, 8, 1961–62, 7–24

Gimbutas, M., *The Gods and Goddesses of Old Europe*, London: Thames and Hudson, 1982

Ginzburg, C., *Ecstasies: Deciphering the Witches' Sabbath*, London: Hutchinson, 1990
Glob, P.V., *The Mound People* (tr. R. Bruce-Mitford), London: Faber and Faber, 1969
Glosecki, S.O., 'Wolf Dancers and Whispering Beasts: Shamanic Motifs from Sutton Hoo?', *Mankind Quarterly*, 26, 1986, 305–19
Glosecki, S.O., 'Wolf of the Bees: Germanic Shamanism and the Bear Hero', *Journal of Ritual Studies*, 2, 1988, 31–53
Glosecki, S.O., *Shamanism and Old English Poetry*, New York: Garland, 1989
Godden, M.R., 'Anglo-Saxons on the Mind', M. Lapidge and H. Gneuss (eds), *Learning and Literature in Anglo-Saxon England*, Cambridge University Press, 1985, 271–98
Gordon, R.K., *Anglo-Saxon Poetry* (rev. edn) London: Dent, 1954
Gordon, R.K., *Beowulf*, New York: Dover, 1992 (first pub 1926)
Graham-Campbell, J. and Kidd, D., *The Vikings*, London: British Museum Publications, 1980
Graham-Campbell, J., *The Viking World*, London: Frances Lincoln, 1989
Grattan, J., 'Three Anglo-Saxon Charms from the Lacnunga', *Modern Language Review*, XXII, 1927, 1–6
Grattan, J.H.G. and Singer, C., *Anglo-Saxon Magic and Medicine*, Wellcome Historical Medical Museum, Oxford University Press, 1952
Green, M., 'Women's Medical Practice and Health Care in Medieval Europe', *Signs*, 14, 1989, 55–73
Gardner, J., *Grendel*, London: Deutsch, 1972
Grendon, F., 'The Anglo-Saxon Charms', *Journal of American Folk-Lore*, XXII, 1909
Grimm, J., *Teutonic Mythology* (tr. J.S. Stallybrass) (4th edn, 4 volumes), New York: Dover, 1966
Hachmann, R., *The Germanic Peoples* (tr. J. Hogarth) London: Barrie and Jenkins, 1971
Hagen, A., *A Handbook of Anglo-Saxon Food Processing and Consumption*, Pinner, Middlesex: Anglo-Saxon Books, 1992
Halifax, J., *Shamanic Voices: The Shaman as Seer, Poet and Healer*, Harmondsworth: Penguin, 1979
Halifax, J., *Shaman: The Wounded Healer*, London: Thames and Hudson, 1982
Halsall, M., *The Old English Rune Poem*, University of Toronto Press, 1981
Hargrove, E. (ed.), *Religion and the Environmental Crisis*, Athens: University of Georgia Press, 1986
Harner, M., *The Way of the Shaman*, San Francisco: Harper and Row, 1980
Hesse, H., *Steppenwolf*, New York: Bantam, 1969
Higham, N., *Rome, Britain and Anglo-Saxon England*, London: Seaby, 1992
Hill, D., *An Atlas of Anglo-Saxon England*, Oxford: Blackwell, 1984
Hill, T.D., 'The Aecerbot Charm and its Christian User', in P. Clemoes (ed.) *Anglo-Saxon England*, 6, Cambridge University Press, 1977
Hillman, J., *In-Search: Psychology and Religion*, Dallas: Spring Publications, 1979
Hills, C., 'The Archaeology of Anglo-Saxon England in the Pagan Period: A Review', *Anglo-Saxon England*, 8, Cambridge University Press, 1979, 318–26
Hinnells, J.R. (ed.), *A Handbook of Living Religions*, Harmondsworth: Penguin, 1985
Hollander, L.M., *The Poetic Edda*, Austin: University of Texas Press, 1962
Hooke, D. (ed.), *Anglo-Saxon Settlements*, Oxford: Blackwell, 1988

Hoult, J., *Dragons: Their History and Symbolism*, Glastonbury: Gothic Image, 1987
Hubener, G., 'Beowulf and Germanic Exorcism', *Review of English Studies*, 11, 1935, 163–81
Hunter, M., 'Germanic and Roman Antiquity and the Sense of the Past in Anglo-Saxon England', in P. Clemoes (ed.) *Anglo-Saxon England*, 3, Cambridge University Press, 1974
Hutton, R., *The Pagan Religions of the Ancient British Isles*, Oxford: Blackwell, 1991
Huxley, F., *The Dragon*, London: Thames and Hudson, 1979
Huxley, F., *The Way of the Sacred*, London: Bloomsbury Books, 1989
Jackson, K.H., *A Celtic Miscellany: Translations from the Celtic Literatures* (rev. edn) Harmondsworth: Penguin, 1971
Johnston, G. (tr.) *The Saga of Gilsi The Outlaw* (ed. P. Foote), University of Toronto Press, 1963
Jones, F., *The Holy Wells of Wales*, Cardiff: University of Wales Press, 1954
Jones, G., *Eirik the Red and Other Icelandic Sagas*, Oxford University Press, 1961
Jung, C.G., *Alchemical Studies*, Vol 13 of *Collected Works*, New York: Pantheon Books, Bollingen Series, XX, 1967
Kalweit, H., *Dreamtime and Inner Space*, Boston: Shambhala, 1988
Kalweit, H., *Shamans, Healers and Medicine Men* (tr. M. Kohn), Boston: Shambhala, 1992
Kendrick, T.D., *The Druids*, London, 1927
Kirby, D.P., *The Making of Early England*, London: Batsford, 1967
Kliman, B., 'Women in Early English Literature', *Nottingham Medieval Studies*, 21, 1977, 39–50
Krapp, G.P. and Dobbie, E. (eds), *The Anglo-Saxon Poetic Records* (6 volumes), including Vol III, *The Exeter Book*, New York and London: 1931–53
La Budde, K., 'Cultural Primitivism in William Faulkner's *The Bear*', in F. Utley (ed.) *Bear, Man, and God*, New York: Random House, 1964
Laing, L. and J., *Anglo-Saxon England*, London: Paladin, 1982
Lancaster, B., *Mind, Brain and Human Potential*, Shaftesbury: Element, 1991
Larsen, S., *The Shaman's Doorway* (2nd edn), New York: Station Hill Press, 1988
Larson, G.J., *Myth in Indo-European Antiquity*, Berkeley: University of California Press, 1974
Lester, G.A., *The Anglo-Saxons: How They Lived and Worked*, Newton Abbott: David and Charles, 1976
Linsell, T., *Anglo-Saxon Runes* (illus. B. Partridge) Pinner, Middlesex: Anglo-Saxon Books, 1992
Lopez, B., *Of Wolves and Men*, New York: Dent, 1978
Lopez, B., *Arctic Dreams: Imagination and Desire in a Northern Landscape*, London: Macmillan, 1986
Lopez, B., *Crossing Open Ground*, London: Macmillan, 1988
Lyle, E., *Archaic Cosmos: Polarity Space and Time*, Edinburgh: Traditional Cosmology Society, 1990
MacCulloch, J.A., *The Mythology of All Races* (vols 2 and 3, Eddic/Celtic), Boston: 1918/1930
MacCulloch, J.A., *The Religion of the Ancient Celts*, London: Constable, 1991 (first published 1911)

Bibliography

Magnusson, M., *Hammer of the North*, London: Orbis, 1976
Magnusson, M., *Iceland Saga*, London: The Bodley Head, 1987
Magoun, F.P., 'On Some Survivals of Pagan Belief in Anglo-Saxon England', *Harvard Theological Review*, XI, 1947, 85
Mallory, J.P., *In Search of the Indo-Europeans*, London: Thames and Hudson, 1989
Mander, J., *In the Absence of the Sacred: The Failure of Technology and the Survival of the Indian Nations*, San Francisco: Sierra Club Books, 1991
Maringer, J., 'Priests and Priestesses in Prehistoric Europe', *History of Religions*, 17, 1977, 101–20
Markale, J., *Women of the Celts*, Rochester, Vermont: Inner Traditions, 1986
Mathews, C.M., *Place Names of the English-Speaking World*, London: Weidenfeld and Nicolson, 1972
Matthews, C. and Matthews, J., *The Western Way*, London: Arkana, 1985
Matthews, J., *Gawain: Knight of the Goddess*, London: Aquarian, 1990
Matthews, J., *Taliesin*, London: Aquarian, 1991
Mattingly, H. (ed.), *Agricola and the Germania* (tr. S.A. Handford, revised), Harmondsworth: Penguin, 1970
Mayr-Harting, H., *The Coming of Christianity to Anglo-Saxon England*, London: B.T. Batsford, 1972
Mayr-Harting, H., *The Germanic Invasions: The Making of Europe AD 400–600*, London: Paul Elek, 1975
McCaskill, D. (ed.) *Amerindian Cosmology*, Edinburgh: Traditional Cosmology Society, 1988
McKenna, T., *Food of the Gods: the Search for the Original Tree of Knowledge*, London: Rider, 1992
McPherson, J.M., *Primitive Beliefs in the North-East of Scotland*, London: Longmans, Green, 1929
Meroney, H., 'Irish in the Old English Charms', *Speculum*, XX, 1972, 182
Metzner, R., *The Well of Remembrance*, Boston: Shambhala, 1994
Michell, J., *The Earth Spirit*, London: Thames and Hudson, 1975
Moore, R. and Gillette, D., *King, Warrior, Magician, Lover*, New York: Harper Collins, 1991
Morris, J., *The Age of Arthur: A History of the British Isles from 350 to 650*, London: Weidenfeld and Nicolson, 1973
Morris, K., *Sorceress or Witch? The Image of Gender in Medieval Iceland and Northern Europe*, New York: University Press of America, 1991
Murray, M., *The Witch Cult in Western Europe*, Oxford University Press, 1921
Myres, J.N.L., *The English Settlements*, Oxford: The Clarendon Press, 1985
Nelson, M., 'An Old English Charm Against Nightmare', *Germanic Notes*, 13, 1982, 17–18
Nicholson, S. (ed.), *Shamanism: An Expanded View of Reality*, Wheaton, Illinois: The Theosophical Publishing House, 1987
Niles, J.D., *Beowulf: the Poem and its Tradition*, Harvard University Press, 1983
Onians, R.B., *The Origins of European Thought*, Cambridge University Press, 1954
Opland, J., *Anglo-Saxon Oral Poetry*, Yale University Press, 1980
O'Rahilly, T.F., *Early Irish History and Mythology*, Dublin Institute for Advanced Studies, 1976

Owen, G., *Rites and Religions of the Anglo-Saxons*, Newton Abbott: David & Charles, 1981

Osborn, M., *Beowulf: A Verse Translation with Treasures of the North*, Berkeley: University of California Press, 1983

Palsson, G., 'The Idea of Fish: Land and Sea in the Icelandic World-View', in R. Willis, (ed.), *Signifying Animals: Human Meaning in the Natural World*, London: Routledge, 1994, pp. 119–33

Payne, J.F., *English Medicine in Anglo-Saxon Times*, Oxford: Clarendon Press, 1904

Pennick, N., *The Ancient Science of Geomancy*, London: Thames and Hudson, 1979

Pennick, N., *Earth Harmony*, London: Century, 1987

Pennick, N., *Games of the Gods*, London: Rider, 1988

Piggott, S., *The Druids*, London: Thames and Hudson, 1968

Polome, E.C. (ed.), *Old Norse Literature and Mythology*, Austin: University of Texas Press, 1969

Polome, E., 'Germanic Religion', in C. Long, *Spirituality: Ancient Europe*, New Jersey: Crossroads Press, 1985

Post, van der, L., *The Lost World of the Kalahari*, London: The Hogarth Press, 1958

Post, van der, L., *The Heart of the Hunter*, London: The Hogarth Press, 1961

Post, van der, L., *A Walk With a White Bushman*, London: Chatto and Windus, 1986

Radin, P., *The Trickster: A Study in American Indian Mythology*, New York: Philosophical Library, 1956

Rasmussen, K., *Intellectual Culture of the Hudson Bay Eskimos. Report of the Fifth Thule Expedition 1921–1924*, Vol Vii, Copenhagen: 1930

Rawson, P., *Tantra: The Indian Cult of Ecstasy*, London: Thames and Hudson, 1973

Rawson, P. and Legeza, L., *Tao: The Chinese Philosophy of Time and Change*, London: Thames and Hudson, 1973

Reaney, P.H., *The Origin of English Place-Names*, London: Routledge, 1960

Rees, A. and Rees, B., *Celtic Heritage*, London: Thames and Hudson, 1961

Richards, J.D., *Viking Age England*, London: Batsford, 1991

Robertson, D., 'Magical Medicine in Viking Scandinavia', *Medical History*, 20, 1976, 317–22

Rodrigues, L.J., *Anglo-Saxon Verse Charms, Maxims and Heroic Legends*, Pinner, Middlesex: Anglo-Saxon Books, 1993

Roesdale, E. et al. (eds), *The Vikings in England*, London: The Anglo-Danish Viking Project, 1981

Ross, A., *Celtic Britain*, London: Routledge, 1985

Ross, A., *Pagan Celtic Britain* (rev. edn) London: Constable, 1992

Roszak, T., *The Voice of the Earth: An Exploration of Ecopsychology*, New York: Touchstone, 1992

Rothenberg, J. (ed.), *Technicians of the Sacred: A Range of Poetries from Africa, America, Asia, Europe and Oceania* (2nd edn), Berkeley: University of California Press, 1985

Runeberg, A., *Witches, Demons and Fertility Magic*, Helsingfors: Societas Scientiarum Fennica, 1947

Ryan, J.S., 'Othin in England: Evidence from the Poetry for a Cult of Woden in Anglo-Saxon England', *Folk-Lore*, 1963, 460–80

Salmon, V., 'The *Wanderer* and the *Seafarer* and the Old English Conception of the Soul', *Modern Language Review*, 55, 1960, 1–10

Seed, J., Macy, J., Fleming, P. and Naess, A., *Thinking Like a Mountain: Toward a Council of All Beings*, Philadelphia: New Society Publishers, 1988

Schwenk, T., *Sensitive Chaos*, New York: Schocken Books, 1976

Shook, L.K., 'Notes on the Old English Charms', *Modern Language Notes*, 55, 1940, 139–40

Simpson, J., 'Otherworld Adventures in an Icelandic Saga', *Folklore*, 77, 1966, 1–20

Singer, C., *From Magic to Science*, New York: Dover, 1958 (originally published 1928)

Sjöö, M. and Mor. B., *The Great Cosmic Mother: Rediscovering the Religion of the Earth*, San Francisco: Harper and Row, 1987

Skemp, A.R., 'The Old English Charms', *Modern Language Review*, 6, 1911, 289–301

Smith, A.W., 'The Luck in the Head: Some Further Observations', *Folklore*, LXXIX, 1963, 396–8

Sogyal Rinpoche, *The Tibetan Book of Living and Dying*, London: Rider, 1992

Snorri Sturluson, *The Prose Edda: Tales from the Norse Mythology* (tr. J.I. Young), Berkeley: University of California Press, 1954

Snorri Sturluson, *Heimskringla* (tr. L.M. Hollander) Austin: University of Texas Press, 1964

Speake, G., *Anglo-Saxon Animal Art and its Germanic Background*, Oxford: Clarendon Press, 1980

Stenton, F., *Anglo-Saxon England* (3rd edn), Oxford University Press, 1971

Stevens, A., *The Roots of War: A Jungian Perspective*, New York: Paragon House, 1984

Storms, G., *Anglo-Saxon Magic*, The Hague: Martinus Nijhoff, 1948

Strutynski, U., 'Germanic Divinities in Weekday Names', *Journal of Indo-European Studies*, 3, 1975, 363–84

Swan, J., 'Sacred Places in Nature: One Tool in the Shaman's Medicine Bag', in G. Doore, *Shaman's Path*, Boston: Shambhala, 1988

Swanton, M., *Anglo-Saxon Prose*, London: Dent, 1975

Taylor, P.B. and Auden, W.H. (tr.), *The Elder Edda. A Selection*, London: Faber and Faber, 1969

Thomas, K., *Religion and the Decline in Magic*, London: Blackwells, 1971

Thorsson, E., *Runelore*, York Beach, Maine: Samuel Weiser, 1987

Thun, N., 'The Malignant Elves', *Studia Neophilologica*, 41, 1969, 378–96

Todd, M., *The Northern Barbarians 100BC–AD 300*, London: Hutchinson, 1975

Tolkein, J.R.R., 'Beowulf: The Monsters and the Critics', *Proceedings of the British Academy*, 22, 1936, 245–95

Tolstoy, N., *The Quest for Merlin*, London: Hamish Hamilton, 1985

Toulson, S., *The Winter Solstice*, London: Norman and Hobhouse, 1981

Tuan, Y.F., *Topophilia*, Berkeley: University of California Press, 1968

Tucker, M., 'Not the Land, But an Idea of a Land', in J. Freeman, (ed.), *Landscapes From a High Latitude: Icelandic Art 1909–1989*, London: Lund Humphries, 1989

Tucker, M., *Dreaming with Open Eyes: The Shamanic Spirit in Contemporary Art and Culture*, London: Harper Collins, 1993

Turville-Petre, E.O.G., *Myth and Religion of the North*, London: Weidenfeld and Nicolson, 1964

Vitebsky, P., *The Shaman*, London: Macmillan, 1995

Walsh, R., *The Spirit of Shamanism*, Los Angeles: Tarcher, 1990

Watson, L., *Earthworks*, London: Hodder and Stoughton, 1986

Watts, A., *The Way of Zen*, New York: Pantheon Books, 1957
Watts, A., *Nature, Man and Woman*, New York: Pantheon, 1958
Watts, A., *Psychotherapy East and West*, New York: Pantheon, 1965
Watts, A., *Tao: the Watercourse Way*, London: Jonathan Cape, 1976
Wax, R.H., *Magic, Fate and History: The Changing Ethos of the Vikings*, Kansas: Colorado Press, 1969
Welch, M., *Anglo-Saxon England*, London: Batsford, 1992
Whitelock, D., *The Audience of Beowulf*, Oxford: Clarendon Press, 1951
Whitelock, D. (ed.), *English Historical Documents*, London: Eyre and Spottiswood, 1955
Whitelock, D. (ed.), *Anglo-Saxon Chronicle*, London: Eyre and Spottiswood, 1961
Whitman, C.H., 'The Old English Animal Names', *Anglia*, XXX, 1907, 389–90
Wood, J., 'The Fairy Bridge Legend in Wales', *Folklore*, *103*, 1992, 56–72

Index

Aberdeen 105
Adam of Bremen 81
Adomnan, *Life of St Columba* 53
Aegir (god of the sea) 89
Aesir 181, 209, 234-5, 239, 265
Aethelbert, King 26-28
Aethelburga 54
Alaska 84
Alfred, King, the laws of 34
All Hallow's Eve 47
Allfather 48, 209
Alvis (dwarf) 141
Amazon rainforest 44, 194
Angli and other tribes 73
Anglo-Saxon Chronicle 24
Anglo-Saxon Herbal 45
Anglo-Saxons 23, 50, 228, 265
  churches 31
  medical manual 93
  riddles 89
  saints wells 98
  Spellbook 36-9, 41, 45, 49-50, 132, 135-6, 157
  tribes 58-9
  words 59, 112, 131, 138-9
Angrboda (giantess) 125
Angrbotha 186
animals 60-8

guardian 58-61, 67
spirits 57-8, 69
Aran Island, Ireland 103
Arason, Icelandic Bishop Gudmund 30
Araucanian shamans 224
Asgard 211, 215, 239
Astri 140
Augustine 31
Aurinaia 152
Australia, shaman of Yaralde tribe 137

Bagri Mare 197
Balder 217
Baleworker 237-8, 241
Baltic, west coast 73
Barrey 82
Baugi 237-8
bears 60-1
Bede 27
beheading game 224-9
Beowulf 58-9, 139, 227
Biarki, Bothvar 62
Bifrost (Trembling Way) 210, 246
Big Bang 212
Black Beauty 67
Bleakley, Alan 184, 186
Bleakley, Sue 96
Bolthor (father of Bestla) 212-13, 234
Bon Po 243
Bonser reports 49
Borghild 111

Bothn 236, 238, 247
Bralund 111
Bran the Blessed 226-7, 229
Branwen 226
Bricriu 206
The Bride's Well, Corgarff, Grampian 105
Brisings, necklace 139-40
Britain
  games 205
  Roman inscriptions 86
Brocolitia, Roman fort 97
Bronze Age 97, 141, 155
Brown, Joseph Epes 29
Bructeri tribe 152-3
Buddhism 203, 263
Burchard, Bishop of Worms 86
Burckhardt (historian) 33
Buri (father of Bor) 213
Buryat shamans 197

Campbell, Joseph 105
Carpenter, Rhys 61
Cartesian dualism 66
Catholic Church 98
celandine (plant) 40
Celtic
  artwork 108
  literature 202, 226

Merlin 153
  peoples 19-20, 134
  settlements 20
  tribes 21, 42, 135, 225
  wells 97-8
chaos and spontaneity
  125-6
Chatti tribe 153
Cheddar, Somerset 22
Cheyenne shaman 188
childbirth 84-8, 105-6,
  257-8
  Mother Earth 88
Christianity 26-32, 35-
  36, 40-41, 43, 55-
  56, 98, 133, 159
  censorship 242
  Church 55
  cosmology 76
  observance 254-5
  substitution 247
  writers 140
  Wyrd 32
Christians 29
  Church-dominated
    Europe 164
  God 32, 35, 43, 98
  missionaries 26, 33, 56
Christmas 31
Church festivals 31
Cnut, King 34
computers 117, 247
Conall 225
concealment, the world
  of 132-5
concrete jungle, lessons
  for 25
consciousness, altered
  states 141-4
corn, symbolism of 78
Cornwall 21, 95-6
cosmology 76, 81, 210-
  11, *see also* Wyrd,
  cosmology
Cosmos 244-5, 262-4
Coventia, well dedicated
  to 97

Crossley-Holland, Kevin
  89
Crows, heeding 54-7,
  69-71
Crucibles, the three 246-
  7
Cu Chulainn 206, 225
Cybele (Syrian goddess
  of fruitfulness) 74

Dainn 140
Dark Ages 30, 53, 107
Daughters of the Night
  100, 115
Davidson, Hilda Ellis 59,
  140-1, 160, 197
Day (son of Night and
  Shining One) 46,
  48
death 48, 261-2
  and rebirth 171-5,
  212-33
Denmark 20, 72-3, 86-7
  Bronze Age 141, 155
destiny and free will
  116-17
divination 159-60, 162-7
dominion 32-4
Dromi (chain) 122-3,
  125
Duerr, Hans Peter 57
Duradrorr 140
Dureyrr 140
Dvalinn 140
dwarfs 121-48, 235

Earth 43-4, 262, 267
  fertility 256, 261-2
  and sky 25, 51, 116
  see also Mother Earth
Earth Goddess 72-4, *see
  also* Frigg
Earth Mother *see* Mother
  Earth
East Anglia
  cremation urns 129
  Redwald, King of 29

Eastern traditions 243
Echoing Bridge 216
Echoing space 216
Edda poems 85, 141
Edgar 35
Edwin, King of
  Northumbria 54-6,
  58
Eir 77
Elder Edda 171, 190,
  192, 213
Eliade, Mircea 197, 204,
  214, 217, 224
elixir of life, creating
  234-68
Elves, Arrows 37-41
enchantment, plants of
  36-7
English Channel 20, 27
Erik the Red 149-50, 153
Eskimo shamans 63
Europe
  ancestors 112
  ancient 112-3, 135,
    258, 261-3
  cosmology 210-11
  cultures 115
  Wyrd people 204, 257
  mythology 139, 242,
    244
  northern 26
  pre-Christian god
    Woden 55, 170-1,
    205, 259
  rituals of ancient 72
  shamans 78, 149, 211,
    245-6
  south-east 73-4
  tribespeople 117, 207,
    252, 255, 259-60
  warriors 62
  west 26
Europe cultures 79, 143
Europeans, early 264
'eve of the first day of
  summer' 39-40
eye sacrifice 223-4, 265

Index

facts of life 85
Fairhair, Harald 189
Feast of Bricriu 225
females 74-5, 256-7
  intuition 258-9
  and male 180-2, 184-5
  three powers 111
Fenrir (wolf) story 121-6, 128-30, 181
Fentress, John 187
fertility
  gods 141
  rituals 105
fields, fertility 49
fire giants 219, 222
Fjalar 235, 239-40
Food and Drink 22-4
forbidden wyrd 34
forces, psychological 259-60
forest people 19-21
free will and destiny 116-17
Freki 187
Freud, Sigmund 77, 266
Frey (Frigg in male disguise) 81-2, 139
  Uppsala, Sweden, wooden image 81
Freya 77, 80, 139-40, 158, 180-5, 187-91, 196, 242, 258
  comes back to life 177-80
  dwarfs 140-1
  the presence of 175
  volva 154, 158, 162
  wisdom 127
  women in labour 85, 154
Frigg (Mother Earth goddess) 77, 80, 84-5, 88, 154, 162, 258
Frija 85
Frosty-Mane 48
Fulla 77

Galar 235
Ganna (priestess of the Semnones) 153
Gefjun 77
Gerd 81-2
Geri 187
Germania 73
Germany 20, 73
  ancient customs 152-3
  idioms 78
  Roman inscriptions 86
  tribes 153
giants 141, 210, 212-33, 218-21, 236-7
Gillette, Douglas 183
Ginnangagap 214
Ginnungagap 212
Glast tribe 21
Glastingii (Glastonbury) 21
Gleipnir 123
Glob, P.V. 155
Glosecki, Stephen 59, 157
Gna 77
God of Christianity 32, 35, 43, 98
gods, three 121-5, 128
Gods and Myths of Northern Europe 140-1
Gonds, India 197
Great Mystery 104
Great Spider 114
Greenland 149, 151
Grimm brothers 106
Grimnismal 212-213, 222
Gudrid 151
Guillinbursti (Gold Bristled) 139
Gullveig 178, 180, 185-186, 189
Gunmar 58
Gunnloth 236, 238-49, 247, 249, 266

Hall of Hel 217
Halls of Chieftains 22
Hamlet 115
Havamal 192-3, 203, 239, 247
heads
  beheading game 224-9
  how it spoke 230
  keep out 265
  healing spirits 26-53
  water 93-5
Heidr 159, 178, 185, 189
Hel 215-16
Helgate 217
Helgi, a future king 111
Helway 217
Herbarium of Apuleius Platonicus 36
Hermigisel, King of the Warni 56
Hermothr 215
Hess, Hermann 188
Hethdraupnir, skull 230
High One, door of the hall 264
Hildisvin (Battle Pig) 139
Hillman, James 185
Himalaya 245
Hlin 77
Hoddrofnir, horn 230
Hoddrofnir (Treasurer-Opener) 230
Holland 20
  Roman inscriptions 86
Holle, Frau 106
Hood, Robin 19
Hopi 51
Hrolf, King of Denmark 62
Hughes, Kirsten 165-6
Huginn and Muninn (two ravens) 55
human-centred viewpoint 253

Hvergelmir, Spring of 211
Hwicce Wood 21

Ice Age glaciers 213
Iceland 151
  historian *see* Sturluson, Snorri
  myths 115
  poem 111
  sage of Njal 58
  writer 82
Idunn 77
Igjugarjuk 179
Iglulik Eskimo of Hudson Bay 200
Illerup 60
illnesses 39–40
imagery, power of 251–3
Imma, Mercia king's warrior 129
incantations 41
India, calendar 47
Indigenous peoples 28–32
Indo-European root 'sed' 153
Ine, King 23
Inspiration, the mead of 247–9
inter-tribal warfare 79
interlace 107–10
intuition 163
  divining through deep 149–69
Irish, literature 61, 205–206

jewellery 107–8, 113, 131, 139
Jochelson 217
Jones, Francis 97
Jotunheim (home of the giants) 81, 210–1, 218, 236
Jung, C.G. 142, 186, 195, 260

Kalweit, Holger 160, 179
Kent, King of 54
Kerberos 215
Kingdom of Shadows 218
kings, conversion of 29
Knit Mountain 236–43
Knowledge 192–211, 198, 245–6
Kogi tribes of Colombia 112
Kundalini 246–7
Kvasir 235, 239, 244
Kveldulfr 62

LaBudde, Kenneth 60
Landnamabok 154
Lapp shamans 63
Lay of the Nine Herbs 38
life, pattern of 259–60
life and death 25
life forces 79, 98
  binding 78–80
  cosmological imagery 81
  freeing the flow 72–88
life patterns 107–20
Loding (chain) 122, 125
Loegaire (Irish warrior) 225
Loegaire, King 206
Lofn 77
Loki 125–6, 186
Lopez, Barry 66
Lourdes, France 98
love
  magin 234–68
  sacred 266–7
Lowerworld 60, 156, 199, 211–12, 214–6, 240, 245, 247, 260–262
  dwarfs (blacksmiths) 123–4, 126, 131
  Europ. shamans 211

Queen 125
Lug 205
lust and fertility 80–3

Mabinogion 226
mac Cairill, Tuan 61
McPherson, J.M. 105
Magical Quality of Night 141
Magnusson, Magnus 82
Malekulan culture 137–8
Markale, Jean 226
masculine principle 259
May, first day 47
May Eve 48
mead
  inspiration 247–9, 266
  love ritual 242–5
  the magic 234–6
Meadwolf 222
meals, ritual 157
Medb 206
medicine, taking 39
Mellitus 31
Melshach well, Kennethmont, Grampian 105
menstruation 85, 87
Mercia, Imma, king's warrior 129
Mexico, nagual 57
Middle Earth 60, 100, 156, 209–11, 236, 246, 263, 266
  community of shamans-to-be 266
  serpent 125
Middle World 210, 245, 263
Midgardh-Serpent 140
Midsummer festival 38
Mighty Giant 221
Mimir 185, 193, 213–5, 224, 237, 265
  head 224–30, 229–233, 231
  significance of 231

Index

spring of 211, 214
well 211
what Odin wanted
  from 221-3
missionaries 26-8, 30
Mist of Creation 214
Moirai (Greek) 100, 111
moments, liminal 254-5
monks 40, 53, 135
  rain dance 53
moon
  cycle of power 254
  influence 46
moon glow dew 50
Moore, Robert 183
Mother Earth 43, 72-8,
  104, 106, 139
  childbirth 84-8
  motherhood 86, 88,
  257-8
Mothers, dance of the
  86-8
The Mothers, inscriptions
  86
Mothguthr 216
The Mound People 155
mugwort 38
Muspellheim 212

Nanna 77
Native Americans 46,
  51, 228
  tribes 29
natural connection 247
nature, living in 24-5
Navajo peoples, North
  America 114
nectar, supernatural 247-
  9
Nerthus 73-4, 77, 80-1
New Hebrides 137
New Year's Day 134,
  261
Nidavellier (Dark
  Home) 210
Nidhogg 211
Niflheim 133, 210, 212

night 253-4
Night Mare 142
Night (woman) 46, 48
Nine Spells of Power
  212, 236
Njal 58
Njal's Saga 115-16
Nordhri 140
Norman
  churches 31
  Crusaders 24
Nornir 100, 121
Norse Realm of Death
  227
Norsemen 227
North America 84, 114,
  130
Northumbria 24, 54-5,
  129
Norway 149
November Eve 48

obstetrics, male-
  domination 87
Ocean sea 73
Oddrunargratr 85
Odhr 190
Odin (god of the
  shamans) 101, 55,
  62-3, 168-78, 180-
  1, 184-7, 189-92,
  196, 205, 259, 262
  Baleworker 237
  family tree 213
  High Seat 81
  mentor 212-33
  pledges an eye 223-4,
    265
  wolf 121-5, 129
Odrerir 236, 238, 242,
  247
Okolnir 222
Old Age 221
omens, value of 70
Oriental traditions 62
Otherworlds 44, 101,
  132-5, 143, 202-3,

207-11, 236, 240,
  260-1
  riding Sleipnir to the
    214-18
Ox dance 87

Parcae 86, 100, 106, 111
Paris, King of 27-8
Paulinus 54-6
Pin Well, Brayton near
  Selby 104
plants 36-7, 42-5
Plateau Groups 130-1
Pliny, Roman writer 42
poetry 192-3
power animals, learning
  from 54-70
pre-Christian culture
  255
pregnancy 85
Prose Edda 219
Psyche 262-4
psychic world 78
Pueblo Indians 51, 186

rain dances, monks 53
Rainbow Bridge 200
Rasmussen, Knud 161,
  200
Rati 238
Rawson, Philip 109,
  243, 245, 247
Realm of Shadows 216
Redwald, King of East
  Anglia 29
Rees, Alsyn and Brinley
  202, 205-206
reflections 250
Regent's Park Zoo,
  London 69
river names 90
rock giants 219
Roman Empire 33, 57,
  152
Romans 19-20, 86, 97,
  265
  fort Brocolitia 97

inscriptions 86
writers 73, 76-7, 153
Rome 30-1, 72
  Pope Gregory 27-8, 31
Royal Academy of Dramatic Art, London 165

sacred
  plants 42
  practices 31
sacres, attunements to 34-6
Sagas 77
Sagas 209
St Columba 53
St Eaney's Well 103
St Eligius 35, 40
St Helen's Well 104
St Hildegard 40
St John's Eve 38
St Martin 74
St Patrick 206
St Paul 83
Samhain (Hallowe'en) 134
Sancreed Well 96, 104
Saviour Jesus Christ 41
Saxon seaman 30
Scandinavia 169, 209
  giants 219
  medicine pouch 155
  mythology 126
Schleswig, secret ceremonies 86-7
Schwenk, Theodor 101-2
Scotland 160, 205
seeresses 149-69, 153-4, 159
seership 163
seidr 154, 159
Sequana (goddess of source of the Siene) 90
sexuality 83-5, 249

shamans 39, 43, 49, 51, 56, 60, 63-4, 143, 258, 260-1, 264
  cultures 59, 130-2, 143
  journeys 131, 134, 159-60
  rituals 57-8, 137, 204
  songs 160
shapeshifting, the practice of 66-9, 138
Shining One (god) 46
Shining-Mane 48
Short Voluspa 186
Siberia 197, 264
  shamans 57, 194
  Sibo 204
  tribes 57
Siene (river), source 90
Sif 77
singing 159-62
Sjofn 77
Sjöö, Monica 113
Skuld 115
slavery 79
Sleep's Soothing 141
Sleipnir 196, 198, 200, 202, 214-18
Snotra 77
society, contemporary 253
Son 236, 247
Sonnenfeld, Joseph 84
South America, traditions 57
spells 129, 135-8, 141, 212
spiders
  goddess 132-3, 136, 139
  spell 135-6, 141
spinning
  into the sacred 114-16
  and weaving 113-14
spirits 260-1
  helpers 136

liberation Eastern ways 266
trance 159-62
springs 97-8, 211, 214
Steady-State Universe 212
Steppenwolf 188
Stone-Age 97
tribal society 137
Sturluson, Snorri 63, 81, 99, 121, 140, 154, 168-70, 176, 189, 208, 210, 212-14, 223, 234-5, 239, 242, 263
  Heimskringla 189
  Prose Edda 236
Stuttung 234-5, 237
Sudhri 140
sun and moon 48-53
supernatural power 47-8
Surt 222
Suttung (giant) 236, 238-9
Svartalfheim (Land of the Dark Elves) 210
Svipdaqsmal 106
Svithrir and Svithurr 222
Swiss Alps 198
Sybil's Vision 223
Syn 77
Syrd Sisters 116

Tacitus 57, 73-5, 152
Tain Bo Cuailnge 206
'talking heads' ritual 232-3
Tantra 77, 242-8, 266
Tantrikas 243
Tao 247, 266
Teutonic myth 219
Third World 73
Thor (god) 121-5, 218-20
Thorbiorg 149-54, 157-62, 189
  high seat 158-9

pouch 154-7, 156
Thorgerda 139-40
Thorkel, Master 150
Thorssen, Edred 190
Thought and Memory (Odin's ravens) 55
Three Norns 111
Three Sisters (Parcae) 86, 100, 106, 111, 115, 137
Thunderer 219-20
Tibet, Buddhism 263
time, cycles of 255-6
Tolstoy, Count Leo 213
Toyon, Ai 204
Tree of Knowledge 192-211
Tree of Life
  journey on 198-202
  rebirthing 88
tribal
  cultures 26, 121, 179, 194
  groups 20, 73-4, 90
  heritage 89
  people 64, 157
  settlements 21-2, 86
tribespeople
  Angli and others 73
  Anglo-Saxons 58-9
  Bructeri 152-3
  Celtic 21, 42, 135, 225
  Chatti 153
  Europe 117, 133, 144, 207, 247, 252, 255, 259-60
  German 153
  Glast 21
  Hwicce 21
  Kogi of Colombia 112
  Native American 29
  Plateau Groups 130-1
  seers 264
  Siberia 57
  Wyrd 78, 259, 261-2
  Yaralde 137

Tuan, Yi-Fu 84
Tungus shamans 63
Tyr (sky god) 121-5

Uath Mac Immonain (the Terrible Son of Great Fear) 225
Ulf 262
Underworld 106, 210
Upperworld 156, 209-11, 215, 245, 263
Uppsala, Sweden 81
Urdr 115
Uvavnum, song 161-2

Var 77
Veleda 152-3, 155
Verdandi 115
Verse Edda 224
Vervain 37-8, 41
Vespasian, Emperor 152
Vestri 140
Vicarello, thermal springs 97
Viking Age 80
Vikings 32, 108, 223
vision journey 192-211
Visions of the Seeress 172, 176
Volsungakvitha 175
volvas 154, 158, 160, 162
Vor 77

Wagner, Richard, *Ring* cycle 168
Wales 21, 205
war gods 141
warrior kings 30
warriorhood 168-91, 182-4
water 89-93, 101-3
  fountains 91
  healing 93-5
  women, wells 103-6
waterways 89, 91
Watson, Lyall 94-5, 102

waves 254
Wax, Rosalie 109-10
Weaver of Dreams 141
weavers of destiny 107-20
Web of life 144-8
Web of Wyrd 121-48, 144, 164
Well of Mimir 214, 221
Well of Our Lady 104
Well of Wisdom 212, 217
Well of Wyrd 98-101, 106, 211
wells 89-106
  Anglo-Saxon saints 98
  Celtic 97-8
  Coventia 97
West Saxons 20
Western world 72-3, 79, 116, 162
  cultures 254, 267
  shamans 263
  society 72, 223, 259
White Hill, London 227
Whittlesford church, Cambridge 83
witch-burning of the Middle Ages 32
Woden (European pre-Christian god) 55, 170-1, 205, 259
wolves 168-91
women
  diviners 152-4
  in labour 85, 154
  water, wells 103-6
wooden wagons 72-3, 75
The Words of the High One 240
World of Dark Elves 141
World Tree 99-100, 106, 156-7, 214-16, 221, 231, 234, 236, 243-5, 247, 263-4, 266

nourishing 50
Odin's nine nights on 206-7
roots 100
of Wyrd 248
worlds, etymology of 57
Wotan (German) 170-1, 205, 259
Wulfstan, Archbishop of York 32-3, 35
Wychwood, Oxfordshire 21
Wyrd 24, 41, 56-7, 192, 222, 243-4, 247, 251, 256, 266
  birth 88, 257
  cosmology 99, 158, 247, 257, 262
  culture 49, 61, 76, 79, 108, 114, 152, 257
  mysteries 232
  mythology 99
  peoples 32, 42, 45-6, 52, 57, 206-7, 213, 254-5, 257
  perspective 266
  practices 29, 34, 43
  psychology 261
  revivals 34
  spellcasting 129
  Sun and Moon 45-8
  threads of 121-5, 216
  traditions 32, 193, 247
  tribespeople 78, 259, 261-2
  view of 84, 108-9
  web of 121-48
  wisdom of 25-6, 73, 191, 267-8
Wyrd Sisters 38, 50, 100, 106, 108, 111-12, 115, 133, 135-6, 139, 162, 211, 257
Wyrdtime, people of 91, 99

Yaralde tribe 137
Yeavering, Northumbria 22
Yggdrasil 109, 193-7, 208, 211, 244, 263, 266
yin and yang 46
Ymir 212
Ynglinga Saga 62-3
Yukagir method of divination 230